50 YEARS
of the
HISTORIC SPORTS CAR CLUB

1966 – 2016

Historic racing at its best: Sam Mitchell and Benn Simms,
2016 Oulton Park Gold Cup in Historic Formula Ford

Paul Lawrence

Foreword by Sir Stirling Moss OBE, Club Patron-in-Chief

www.tfmpublishing.com

tfm Publishing Limited
Castle Hill Barns
Harley
Shrewsbury
Shropshire
SY5 6LX

Tel: +44 (0)1952 510382; Fax: +44 (0)1952 510192

E-mail: paul@tfmpublishing.com
Web site: www.tfmpublishing.com

Design and layout: Nicki Averill

First Edition: November 2016

ISBN: 978 1 910079 54 6

Printed by Cambrian Printers, Aberystwyth

Contents

Acknowledgements

Many people have given freely of their time to help take this book from the germ of an idea to reality in little more than 12 months and I am very grateful to all of them for their time and assistance.

Grahame White and the team at Silverstone have been central to the project, of course, and I thank them for their help, patience and good humour. Marcus Pye was a tremendous source of information and knowledge.

My particular thanks go to Nicki Averill for the design and layout, to David Addison for proof-reading and to Cambrian Printers for the production. All of them worked to laughably tight deadlines to ensure printed copies of the book were available just 33 days after the end of the racing season.

PHOTOGRAPHS
We are indebted to the following photographers:
Action 35, Harold Barker, Jeff Bloxham, Phil Broster, Steve Clarke, Ferret Fotographics, John Gaisford, Guy Griffiths, Chris Harvey, Gary Hawkins, Peter Hird, Jim Houlgrave, Phil Jones, Steve Jones, Paul Lawrence, Tony Quinlan, Brian Roberts, Fred Scatley, Ray Stewart, Charlie Wooding

Paul Lawrence
Shropshire
October 2016

Charlie Wooding

Gary Hawkins

Jeff Bloxham

Cover photographs:
Front cover (top): *Neil Corner's Jaguar D-type in the Castle Combe paddock, May 1966.* (photo: Ferret Fotographics)

Front cover (bottom): *Formula 5000s in the Derek Bell Trophy at Brands Hatch in July 2015* (photo: Paul Lawrence).

Back cover: *Bernard Worth leads the 50th anniversary parade at Castle Combe in April 2016* (photo: Charlie Wooding).

Foreword

I was very pleased to be asked to write the foreword for this book telling the story of 50 years of the Historic Sports Car Club.

Without the organising clubs we would have no motor racing. Some of the last races of my career were at events organised by the HSCC and, like so many racers, I appreciate the work of all the people involved behind the scenes of the sport we all love.

Having been patron-in-chief of the HSCC for more than a decade, I hope that everyone has enjoyed the 50th anniversary season.

Here's hoping the club is around for another 50 years, delivering pure historic racing for its members!

Sir Stirling Moss O.B.E.
London
October 2016

Club Patron-in-Chief Sir Stirling Moss OBE

One of his final races in his OSCA

Introduction

It is my great pleasure to welcome you to this celebration and record of 50 years of the Historic Sports Car Club.

Back in 1966, Guy Griffiths and Betty Haig could never have imagined what they were starting with the inaugural Griffiths Formula race at Castle Combe.

Over the following half-century, that movement has grown and developed out of all recognition to the point where, in 2016, we have been celebrating 50 years of the Historic Sports Car Club. I have been very fortunate to hold the office of Chairman for the 50th anniversary season.

So many people have played key roles in the evolution of the HSCC and, sadly, some of them are no longer with us. However, I would like to pay tribute to all those people who gave up their time and energy to serve on committees and promote the Club and its racing. Without the work of these dedicated volunteers the Club could never have grown to where it is today: the UK's leading provider of racing for the cars from the 1960s, 1970s and 1980s.

Bringing the story up to date, I am very grateful to all those who play a role in the modern HSCC. From Grahame White and the office team of Alan Jones, Donna Skipworth-Mitchell, Carrie Bedford and Emma Jemmett, to the championship chairmen and registrars, we have a very strong team in place to uphold everything that is good about historic racing.

I look forward to the HSCC success story continuing for many, many years!

Frank Lyons
Chairman
Felstead Essex, November 2016

Frank Lyons, Club Chairman

Jonathan Palmer, Michael Lyons and Frank Lyons at the awards evening in 2011

Racing his Formula 5000 Eagle FA74 at Silverstone in 2016

Welcome

Welcome to this book that tells the story of the first 50 years of the Historic Sports Car Club.

This is a result of many hours of work and completes the story of the Club so far and what it has achieved: the ups and downs, the highs and lows, the members' successes and, most importantly, it records many years of providing historic motor racing and enabling its members to use and enjoy their racing cars to the full.

Grahame White, Chief Executive Officer

When the talk of a book to celebrate the 50th anniversary of the HSCC first started it was not long before Paul Lawrence took up the challenge when approached to put it all together. It was a huge task and a massive responsibility with an immense amount of research required because up until this time the Club's archive was far from complete, almost non-existent in fact. Paul has worked with the Club over many years as he edits the Club magazine, produces all its press releases and now runs the Club's social media. He is also a respected freelance motor racing journalist. We must thank him for all his hard work.

It was while I was helping with some of the book's research I realised that I have been involved with running the Club for nearly half of its race organising years. It was almost 20 years ago when I was first approached and asked if I would have time and, if so, would I be prepared to get involved to try and put the Club on a more professional and financially sound footing. I said no four times, I think, but was finally persuaded to say yes and really I'm so glad I did.

With Sir Stirling Moss at Oulton Park

We now have a very successful Club. As a highly-respected race organisation, we are financially very sound, and have a very strong membership and are leaders in our field. To help build the Club to its present position has been quite challenging at times but extremely enjoyable and satisfying.

There are too many people to thank personally but because I have always had the full support of the main Board and Committees it has made my work a lot easier. If I have helped make our members feel proud of the Club, enjoy the race meetings we put on and very importantly have fun racing their cars, marshalling or just spectating then that's fine: thank you for allowing me to do this for you. It has been a privilege and very great pleasure.

I hope you enjoy the book.

Grahame White
Chief Executive Officer
Silverstone
October 2016

With Graham Hill in the late 1960s

1

1966 to 1968

In the beginning

The Castle Combe paddock scene in May 1966

Contemporary action: future HSCC patron Derek Bell
(Lotus 41) in the F3 race at the 1966 International Trophy
meeting at Silverstone

The inaugural Griffiths Formula race at Castle Combe in 1966 was the catalyst for the formation of the HSCC.

Manfred Mann was at number one in the popular music charts with 'Pretty Flamingo', the England football team was in training ahead of winning the World Cup and the cost of a pint had risen to 1/8d (about 8p). It was 1966 and life was a lot different back then!

1966 was a landmark year for historic motor racing in Britain. Although not yet known by its full name, the creation of the Historic Sports Car Club sparked from an idea of celebrated motor racing photographer Guy Griffiths. Concerned that sports cars from the 1950s were being heavily modified in order to try and

Colin Crabbe drove Corner's D-type in other races in May 1966

keep them competitive in the 1960s, he saw the need to offer them a place to race alongside other cars in genuine period trim.

Initial discussions involved the Vintage Sports-Car Club, but the club decided not to take on the extra commitment and move beyond its Pre-War focus. So the idea grew within the Frazer Nash section of

the VSCC and was led by Griffiths and race and rally driver Betty Haig. She was a formidable force and was unhappy about the number of period sports cars being sold to America. Her support for the project was a way of trying to keep these cars in Britain.

Suitably inspired by a strong initial response from car owners, Griffiths and Haig decided to organise a

BETTY HAIG

Founding force of the HSCC

Elizabeth 'Betty' Haig was born in 1906, the great-niece of Field Marshal Haig. She owned her first car at the age of 16 and her early cars included a Salmson and a Singer Le Mans. At 29, she entered her first event, the Paris-St. Raphaël Rally in 1935.

She drove a Singer, with some factory backing, competed at Brooklands and won the 1936 Olympic Rally which was centred on Berlin to link-in with that year's Olympic Games. In 1938, she competed in the Paris-St Raphael again in an MG and finished second, reportedly after being held up on a stage by another competitor.

Betty Haig's Frazer Nash in the paddock

After the Second World War Betty took up motor sport again as soon as events started to run and she entered rallies, trials and hillclimbs. In 1946, in an AC, she won the 2-litre class on the Rallye des Alpes as well as winning the Coupe des Dames. In 1949 she drove a Morris Minor on the Monte Carlo Rally, sharing the driving with Elsie Wisdom and Barbara Marshall. In the same year she won the 1500cc class on the Rallye des Alpes and the Coupe des Dames with Barbara Marshall in an MG TC.

In 1950 she continued rallying and also competed in some races and speed events in a Cooper, racing at Brands Hatch and hillclimbing at Prescott. Betty partnered Yvonne Simon to 15th place in the 1951 Le Mans 24-Hours in Yvonne's Ferrari 166 MM. They were third in the 2-litre class, having challenged for the class lead throughout the race.

Despite her obvious talent behind the wheel, she rarely competed in major meetings, although she was a regular on the club scene and enjoyed a considerable hillclimb career. She held the ladies' record at Prescott for six years

Haig in action at Castle Combe in May 1966

and competed in an HRG, a pre-war Frazer Nash and various MGs and ACs.

In 1953, she raced an MG Magnette at Goodwood and two years later she competed in a Goodwood Ladies' Whitsun race in an AC Ace. She continued to race and rally various cars until 1967 and was a major force for the establishment of the HSCC after the inaugural Griffiths Formula race at Castle Combe in 1966. Betty Haig died in 1987.

Instigator of the Griffiths Formula

Guy Griffiths was the man who started it all. His initial idea to create a place for historic sports and sport-racing cars of the 1950s to race ultimately led to the formation of the Historic Sports Car Club.

Griffiths was a renowned racing photographer and competed in the 1930s as

THE GRIFFITHS FORMULA FOR HISTORIC SPORTS CARS

(Under the auspices of The Frazer-Nash Car Club)

Presidents: Guy Griffiths and Miss Betty Haig

Secretary: Miss Penny Griffiths,
11 Newlands Avenue,
Thames Ditton,
Surrey, (01-398. 4092 Emberbrook)

Competition Jeremy Broad,
Secretary: 74 Willow Road,
Solihull,
Warwickshire, (Solihull 7280)

Promotions Committee: Peter Skidmore (*Jaguar Owners*); Clive Aston (*Aston Martin Owners*); Brian Dermott (*Healey Owners*); Bernard Worth (*Ferrari Owners*); Stuart Young (*H.R.G. Owners*); Betty Haig (*Frazer-Nash Owners*); Bill Goodman (*Porsche Owners*); Gerry Belton (*Allard Owners*)

The letterhead for the Griffiths Formula

a young man as he started buying and selling old cars. Bill Boddy, the respected editor of Motor Sport magazine, described Griffiths as the best racing photographer of his era.

Born in the small Cotswold town of Chipping Campden in 1916 to wealthy parents, Griffiths gained his passion for racing from reading about the sport in magazines but didn't see his first race until he was 16-years old. By then he had bought his first motor bike, when he paid seven shillings for an ex-war department Douglas.

He went to Stowe school and developed an interest in photography. He taught himself and became the official photographer at school events, earning money by selling prints to fellow pupils.

At 16 he left school and started work as a film cameraman for 20th Century Fox, but turned down a chance to take his skills to Hollywood. Instead, he decided to try and make a living buying and selling sports and racing cars. In the early days of trading he bought an Alvis for £10 and sold it for £16 and sold a Grand Prix Bugatti for £48. The business did well and he started to compete in sprints and hillclimbs in cars that included an ex-Henry Segrave Grand Prix Sunbeam.

In the 1930s Griffiths started taking photographs at race meetings but the outbreak of the Second World War changed everything. Griffiths said he was fortunate to be asked to work for Napier on the development of aircraft engines. Through that work he met journalist Denis Jenkinson and they became lifetime friends.

After the war Griffiths returned to racing photography as soon as the sport was re-established and worked at tracks like Silverstone, Castle Combe and Goodwood. However, photographic equipment was in short supply and he often used cine film, cut to size and loaded into cassettes. At a typical race meeting he would 20 cassettes of 36 images at a time when many photographers were still using glass plates and would have only 24 plates for a complete race meeting.

As well as capturing action images from the very edge of the track, with little or no protection, Griffiths also took superb off-track images of the drivers and got to know many of them very well. Stirling Moss once described him as the 'outstanding motoring photographer of his day'.

After the War he owned retail premises in London and sold menswear and lingerie, but the passion for cars continued and in the early 1960s he competed in a C-type Jaguar.

In 1965 Griffiths came up with the idea of a race series for pre '55 sports cars. "By the mid-1960s, many of the sports-racing cars of the early 1950s were being lost. They had no value and nowhere to race and many of them were being scrapped, destroyed, unsuitably modified or exported. So to stop this, I started the Griffiths Formula," he later said.

Griffiths was diagnosed with cancer in 1964 and was not expected to survive but developed the Griffiths Formula while under-going treatment. However he did survive and was still taking photographs at events until well into his eighties. He died in 2003 aged 87 and left behind a remarkable legacy, including a collection of more than half a million images.

PORSCHE

PATRON: W. H. ALDINGTON   PRESIDENT: A. H. SHEFFIELD
CHAIRMAN: H. M. GOODMAN

JMB/GAB

400 London Road,
Isleworth,
Middlesex.

3rd March, 1966

reply 17/3/66

S. C. Blyther Esq.,
Jupiter Owners Auto Club,
14 Pyrland Road,
Highbury,
London, N.5.

Dear Mr. Blyther,

On May 14th 1966, the Porsche Club of Great Britain will combine with the Frazer Nash Car Club to promote a race meeting at Castle Combe in Wiltshire. Apart from races for Frazer Nash and Porsche cars, the "Griffiths" formula for interesting sports cars manufactured between 1945 and 1955 will be launched. In this connection the word "interesting" may be loosely defined as "similar to type of Sports Car which competed in such International Events as the Alpine Trial or Le Mans", but the final classification will rest with the organising committee.

There will be a ten lap race for these cars. They will also be eligible for a sprint-one standing, one flying lap, a half hour speed trial and several all comers handicap races.

The raison d'etre for this race meeting is to provide competition for those cars and drivers who are seldom catered for elsewhere. There will be no Minis and no Lotuses. The results will not be regarded by the organisers as of prime importance.

Your Club is invited to participate. A whole day's practice is laid on for March 26th, details attached.

Yours sincerely,

Michael Bum

Secretary of the Meeting

PORSCHE   CLUB   GREAT   BRITAIN

race for post-war competition sports cars in original specification. It was called the 'Griffiths Formula' and the race was run at Castle Combe on 14 May 1966 during a race meeting organised by the Frazer Nash and Porsche Clubs. By running under the umbrella of the Frazer Nash club, administration overheads and paperwork were kept to a minimum.

Penny Woodley, the daughter of Guy Griffiths, had the honour of dropping the union jack to start the race. "In the 1960s my father had started collecting post war sports cars including a C-type Jaguar and a couple of Healey Silverstones," recalled Penny. "He had become increasingly frustrated by the fact that, while there were opportunities to race historic single-seaters, no organisation catered for obsolete Post-War sports cars.

Many of these cars were going to the USA and some were being modified to make them more competitive.

"It was because of this that the Griffiths Formula was born," said Woodley. "It was intended to encourage the preservation and use of competition sports cars of the 1945 to 1955 era. The later date was designed to be movable to bring in later cars as they became obsolete, and the whole thing was not meant to be taken too seriously."

The initial response was excellent, with 25 entries for the race divided into three classes in a field split at 1500cc and 2500cc. Notable entries included three Jaguar D-types for Neil Corner, Peter Skidmore and Guy Griffiths, although Griffiths sadly missed the race that he had created due to illness. Also running in the over 2500cc class were an Austin Healey 100S, an Aston Martin DB3S and a pair of Allard J2s.

Fred Damodaran

The Allard J2X of Fred Damodaran was one of only eight such cars sold in the UK. The remaining 75 examples all went to the US, usually with a 5.4-litre V8 Cadillac engine delivering a remarkable 400bhp. Damodaran paid £320 for 'ORL 320' in 1961 and owned it for nearly 30 years. Its current value is nudging up towards half a million pounds.

Damodaran recalled the 1966 race with great affection. "It was a very interesting race and there were three Allards including Brian Croot in his Jaguar-engined J2R. I did a huge number of miles in ORL 320 and we used it for everything. I drove it to work every day in London and my work involved a lot of travelling. I did everything from racing to hillclimbs and long-distance trials. We used to compete on an absolute shoe-string.

"ORL 320 was running a Chrysler engine at that time which had been put in by a previous owner," said Damodaran. "The Allard Motor Company supplied cars with three different engines; the original Cadillac, the Chrysler V8 and an Ardun overhead valve conversion of the Ford V8, which was designed by Zora Arkus-Duntov who went on to design the

Event 5	4.15 p.m.	10 Lap Race for Griffiths Formula
		(Internationally famous types of car made or raced between 1945 and 1955)

Class 3 Over 2500 cc		
2.	P. K. Skidmore	Jaguar D Type
3.	Guy Griffiths	Jaguar D Type
4.	E. N. Corner	Jaguar D Type
5.	W. B. Croot	Allard/Jaguar
6.	A. M. Greig	H.W.M./Jaguar
7.	J. Le Sage	Aston Martin DB 3S
19.	Mr. Damodaran	Allard J Z X
23.	M. Ward	Aston Martin D B 2
29.	R. Welling	Austin Healey 100S
55.	L. Richards	Allard J Z R X

Class 2 1501 cc - 2500 cc		
8.	C. Drake	Lotus Bristol
9.	M. H. Morris	Frazer Nash
10.	S. G. Curtis	Cooper Bristol
11.	C. J. S. Drewett	Frazer Nash
16.	Miss B. Haig	Frazer Nash
22.	B. R. Worth	Ferrari
25.	B. Sykes	Healey Silverstone
26.	D. L. Rickard	Healey Silverstone
27.	G. Walker	Healey Silverstone
28.	B. A. R. Dermott	Healey Silverstone

Class 4 UP to 1500 cc		
33.	G. B. Thomas	Porsche 1500
39.	I. Sharrock	H.R.G. 1500
40.	P. E. Martino	H.R.G. 1500
41.	I. Dussek	H.R.G. 1500
42.	F. J. Mockridge	Jowett Jupiter

The entry list for the 1966 race at Castle Combe

Ian Dussek's HRG in the 1960s at Castle Combe

Chevrolet Corvette. The Chrysler engine was the one used by all the American dragsters of the time and it was fabulously good in a straight-line but in the corners the engine suffered oil surge and it used to run bearings from time to time."

Meanwhile, the Aston Martin DB3S was typical of the type of car that Griffiths was eager to preserve.

JOHN LE SAGE

Aston Martin racer in the first Griffiths Formula race

John Le Sage raced in the inaugural Griffiths Formula race at Castle Combe in a very rare Aston Martin DB3S, now one of the most valuable cars of its type.

Only 30 DB3S models were ever built, of which 10 were works cars. DB3S/4 was the third works-entered Le Mans car of 1953 although it failed to finish. Later that year it won the Tourist Trophy at Dundrod in Northern Ireland driven by Peter Collins.

It continued to be raced extensively and contested the Mille Miglia before the factory sold the car to Graham Whitehead. John Le Sage bought it for £500 in good running order in June 1965, and raced it in the UK for a couple of years before selling it to Cameron Millar. It was later exported to New Zealand, where it remains.

"I originally became involved in racing through my love of vintage cars. My first race was at Silverstone in April 1964 in a 1930 supercharged 1750 Alfa. In June 1965 I bought my first 'real' racing car, the famous 1953 TT winning DB3S, UXC 999. I raced this in club events 10 times over the next 18 months, including the first Griffiths Formula race at Castle Combe.

"In June 1965 I bought the ex-Graham Hill Lotus 16 Grand Prix car. I had to fit the correct 2-litre Coventry Climax engine to the car and did race it with some success in 1966/67. I held the historic lap record on the Silverstone short circuit in July '67. I sold the car to my friend Tom Wheatcroft and it went into the Donington Grand Prix Collection.

"In November 1966 I bought the ex-John Coundley Lotus 19. I raced this with little success in 1967/68 although I did gain the 2- to 3-litre sports car lap record at Silverstone. The Brabham BT8s were always quicker. I also raced a Merlyn Mk4 at this time.

"My last racing car was a Crossle sports racer into which I fitted the 2.5-litre Climax engine and the Colloti gearbox from the Lotus 19. I raced this here and had seven races in Europe in 1968, including the famous road race, 40 miles per lap, at Mugello in Tuscany which was won by Arturo Merzario in a 2-litre Abarth. My professional life is of little interest; I worked as a dentist in the NHS for 43 years!"

Chassis DB3S/4 was one of the works team cars at Le Mans in 1953 and later won the Tourist Trophy at Dundrod with Peter Collins and Pat Griffiths, scoring Aston Martin's first victory in a World Championship event. Over a decade later it was simply an out of date racing car and was owned and raced by John Le Sage. Within a year of the Castle Combe race it had been sold to New Zealand, where it remains.

Four Healey Silverstones topped the 2500cc class, along with Bernard Worth's splendid Ferrari Type 166 Mille Miglia, a Lotus Bristol for Chris Warwick-Drake and one of three Frazer Nashes for Betty Haig. This was an ex-John Gott Le Mans Replica, while Martin Morris was in a similar car. Morris bought MPX 100 for £950 in the autumn of 1957 and would go on to cover 150,000 miles in it. In 1960, he and his new wife Sue took the car on a tour of Europe for their honeymoon.

In the 1500cc class, three HRGs, a Porsche and a Jowett Jupiter completed the entry, although the Jowett Jupiter of Frank Mockridge was a non-starter after being dramatically rolled at Old Paddock in a previous race.

"I decided I wanted to speed it up a bit and I was going really nicely," said Mockridge. "It was sliding nicely but then it went over and I was so, so lucky. The car was a bit damaged but I'm still here. My father was around at the event and he was car mad, but all of a sudden he said: 'he won't be using that car anymore!' It was a wonderful time of life.

Frank Mockridge

BERNARD WORTH

Raced a Ferarri in the first Griffiths Formula race

Bernard Worth

"I'm fortunate to still own the car I raced in 1966, a Ferrari Type 166 Mille Miglia. It was just a second-hand car when I bought it from a small advert in Autocar in 1960. I went to see it up in Cheshire where it was owned by the chief designer at Rolls Royce at Crewe.

"I had an accident racing and couldn't go back for three weeks until I could walk again. But he hadn't had anyone coming up with the money, so I got a bit off the price and bought it on the last day of our honeymoon. It was bought with the proceeds of a bachelor uncle's estate, who left some money to six of us.

"I had a letter from Betty Haig inviting me to take part in the Griffiths Formula race at Castle Combe in 1966. I was then on the early committee of the HSCC with people like Betty and Rupert Glydon.

"I raced the Ferrari until 1982 and I did a lot of races with it. I did a couple of JCB Championships and the Lloyds and Scottish Championship. I had three engines at one stage. My wife used to wind the winch and I'd change the engine. I ran it at one stage with a 3-litre motor, which made it very quick and very exciting in the wet.

"I did a historic race at Le Mans in 1973 to mark the event's 50 years and I did the Mille Miglia in 1982 and 1986. I still use it on the road; I'm very fortunate!"

"Mike Surridge had to get the car back home after I crashed it. The wheels were more or less pointing in the same direction and they towed it back with Mike steering it and he was absolutely freezing cold the whole way home. It would have taken several hours to get home."

Not surprisingly, Neil Corner dominated the 10-lap race in his D-type, the ex-Ecurie Ecosse Le Mans car registered RSF 302, with Drake chasing and Le Sage's Aston Martin DB3S in third. The Jaguar-engined Allard of Brian Croot chased Corner valiantly in the early laps until a core plug blew out and ended Croot's race.

Neil Corner's D-type en route to victory

GEOFF THOMAS

Competitor in the first Griffiths Formula race

The man who went on to become an authority on tuning and developing cars from the VW range was on the grid in May 1966 for the first Griffiths Formula race at the wheel of a Porsche 356.

"It started with a Jaguar D-type for sale in the early 1960s at £1500; which was my dream car only 10 years earlier. Okay, a decent house was about that much then, so perhaps it was not as cheap as it appears today, but I could have most likely begged, borrowed and flogged off stuff to get the money. But what put me off was an acquaintance who had a C-type and had just spent £150 on a new clutch for it.

"That was about six weeks' salary. I'd never keep up with that. Anyway, it was just an old racing car, uncompetitive and with nowhere really to race it. The historic movement hadn't got off the ground by then so I talked myself out of that one.

"However, in late 1965 I saw a piece in Autosport about a racing series for pre-1955 cars of a type that had raced at Le Mans, for which my 356 complied. My racing career was on again and the first race was at Castle Combe in May 1966. I'd done some sprints and hillclimbs but I'd not done any racing.

"At that time I was on chatting terms with Denis Jenkinson, as he was a near neighbour of mine. He was a charming and modest man - none of the old: 'Oh when I won the Mille Miglia with Stirling' or 'I was only talking to Jimmy Clark the other day' from him. We always seemed to meet in the local ironmongers.

"He told me about a four-into-one exhaust he'd made for his famous 356, which I could have if I collected it from him. His house, I discovered, actually doubled up as his workshop, being filled with all sorts of car and bike bits and projects on the go. It was rather surreally set off by a rather nice red left-hooker E-type sitting outside, having moved on from his 356.

"Now Jenks clearly wasn't a committed gardener and the exhaust was somewhere in the elephant grass along with just about every discarded mechanical thing he'd ever owned. Eventually we found it, rusty but usable, and it sounded the part.

"So I rolled up at Castle Combe on 14 May 1966 for my first race. It wasn't hard winning the 1500 class and I finished eighth overall, in front of Bernard Worth's 2-litre Ferrari, but lapped once by the winning D-type of Neil Corner. I overheated the engine in that race. I had the wrong section fan belt and the temperature went way up. I carried on and the following weekend I did a sprint at Brands and it ran a big end there. But the damage was done at Castle Combe.

"I was looking for an engine for the 356 and ended up putting a Beetle engine in it. They were hard to get and I went to a place where a guy had 30 for sale. I only wanted one but he said he only wanted to sell the whole lot. So I bought all of them and set to rebuilding them and that's what got me into business. It's amazing really. I was a humble draughtsman and ended up with a VW tuning business."

Later Thomas competed in autocross and rallycross and then raced in the Modsaloons category in a VW Golf. Later still, a period in a Lola T300 Formula 5000 was his swansong and he raced the Lola up until about 2001.

"I sold the car but you never think you are retired and I still nurture the idea of a comeback one day. My son Mark has a Formula 3 March 793 in the garage and I'd like to get that out. We're rebuilding it, but it's been sat in the garage since 1985. He was Formula Vee champion in 1986 and bought this March with a cracked engine block. Maybe one day we'll bring it out!"

Thomas in his Porsche 356 at Castle Combe

Brian Dermott's Healey Silverstone

PHILIP MARTINO

had his ony race in the first Griffiths Formula race

Back in 1966, the 20-year old Philip Martino was an impoverished engineering student and the Griffiths Formula race proved to be the one and only race he ever contested.

"My HRG 1500 had raced at Silverstone in about 1949 in a sports car race and had done fairly well. I was instrumental in the college motor club at the old Woolwich Polytechnic and there was a call from the HRG association for anyone who wanted to have a bash. There was a certain amount of arm twisting to do the race. That was the only time I ever raced.

"The licence cost me about £5 and that was it. Have you got a driving licence? Are you reasonably fit? Okay, off you go. I think I borrowed a crash helmet for the race. I had a crash helmet from the days when I had a Lambretta, but it was deemed unsuitable which is perhaps not surprising as it was probably 30 years old by then.

"I just about managed to race with seven out of eight cams still on the camshaft. It was good fun and someone had to come last. But I only had three and a half cylinders working so I probably only had about 50 horse power. The D-type rather disappeared into the middle distance and lapped me."

After 10 laps and 13 minutes of racing, Corner was over 40 seconds clear and duly collected the Griffiths Cup. Behind Drake and Le Sage, fourth-placed Martin Morris was the only other driver to complete 10 laps as 14 cars finished the race. Drake also won the 1500cc to 2500cc class while Geoff Thomas won the up to 1500cc class with eighth overall in his Porsche 356.

One of two Healey Silverstones on the grid was driven by Graham Walker, who had contested a few sprints and hillclimbs at the time. "The Silverstone fitted the Griffiths Formula and a friend of mine called Brian Dermott had a Healey as well. It wasn't very fast and didn't have any brakes! It had drum brakes all round and on some tracks the brakes would only last for about two laps. You got a smell of burning, but very little else, so it was quite exciting. I remember passing Bernard Worth in his Ferrari just before I spun off into the bushes!

"We had a lot of fun for very little expense and we'd drive to the race and hopefully drive home afterwards," said Walker. "If only we'd all known what would happen to car values. I eventually sold my Silverstone for £450 and the same car changed hands for £220,000 in 2015."

Reporting the race for Autosport magazine, John Stanley commented on an "impressive line-up of history making machines". He concluded his report with a wish that "others will follow the lead of Betty Haig, Guy Griffiths and (event secretary) Michael Burn and help retain some of the outstanding sports-racers in this country."

Destined not to finish the race during his first race meeting was Chris Drewett who entered his Targa Florio Frazer Nash. "It had started life as a Le Mans replica and then when Le Mans banned cycle wings it got sensibly re-bodied as a Targa Florio. I know I competed in the Frazer Nash race at the same meeting. I had it for three years and it was a very quick car. I had a big battle with Martin Morris in his Le Mans Replica and he was quicker than me.

"In practice I remember arriving much too fast at Quarry and thinking 'oh crikey'. Luckily I got away with it. I had Betty Haig in front of me in her Le Mans Replica and I got past her and had a big battle with

Martin Morris in another Frazer Nash in period

Martin Morris in his Frazer Nash

Martin. I loved it! I sold it two years later to Robert Mansfield who had still got it 50 years later."

Watching the race from behind his camera was a youthful Ted Walker. "There was a lot of excitement about it. The 1950s sports cars had really been forgotten and this was something that appealed to me." Having driven his Austin Healey 100M to the circuit, Walker thinks that Corner may well have driven the D-type on the road from his hotel that morning. "It was a fantastic day and was really the start of it all. In those days a C-type was probably worth £500 and Corner likely only paid about £3000 for the D-type!"

Another car driven to the circuit that day was the Aston Martin DB2 of Michael Ward. "I found a DB2 advertised in the Nottingham Evening Post for £400. It was near Worksop and I went to look at it in a barn. Being an Aston enthusiast, I saw it had Perspex side windows and thin body panels and I knew it was a works team car.

"So I bought it and stripped the engine and then heard about the Griffiths Formula and entered the race at Castle Combe," said Ward. "I drove down early in the morning from Newark. I had breakfast in Burford, competed in the race and drove back home.

IVAN SHARROCK

HRG driver in the first Griffiths Formula race

At the wheel of an HRG 1500 for the 1966 race was Ivan Sharrock whom, half a century later, still owned the car. He served on the early HSCC committee, representing the interests of HRG owners.

"The car was first built in 1948 and delivered to a test pilot who subsequently crashed and was killed and so the car went to a character called Richard Green, a farmer from Gloucestershire. He raced it a lot in the 1950s and

then, after a couple of other owners, it came to me. I bought it in 1963.

"I raced it in the 1960s, but not that successfully. The Griffiths Formula race of 1966 was interesting with the types of cars that were there. Some of them were hugely fast and I was in a one-and-a-half litre car. On the straights they went zooming past, but I had a wonderful dice with the Ferrari of Bernard Worth. I could claw it back on the corners because the HRG has amazing road-holding.

"The very first meeting for the HSCC was at Betty Haig's house and at the time I had the HRG and an AC Ace Bristol, and my wife was driving the AC Ace. Back then, one could just about afford to go racing."

Event 5   10 Lap Race for Griffiths Formula

Car No.	Driver	Car	Time	Class Placing	Final Order
4.	E.N. Comer	Jaguar D Type	13.13	Griffith Cup	1
8.	C. Drake	Lotus Bristol	13.56.6	1 1500-2500	2
7.	J. Le Sage	Aston Martin DB3S	14.07.2	1 over 2500	3
9.	M.H. Morris	Frazer Nash	14.24.8	2 1500-2500	4
9 Laps					
10.	S.G. Curtis	Cooper Bristol	13.20	3 1500-2500	5
16.	Miss B. Haig	Frazer Nash	14.15.2	4 1500-2500	6
23.	M. Ward	Aston Martin DB2	14.17.2	2 over 2500	7
33.	G.B. Thomas	Porsche 1500	14.24.4	1 up to 1500	8
28.	B.A.R. Dermott	Healey Silverstone	14.30.8	5 1500-2500	9
8 Laps					
39.	I Sharrock	H.R.G. 1500	13.45.6	2 up to 1500	10
22.	B.R. Worth	Ferrari	13.46	6 1500-2500	11
41.	I Dussek	H.R.G. 1500	13.46.4	3 up to 1500	12
27.	G. Walker	Healey Silverstone	14.00.8	7 1500-2500	13
7 Laps					
40.	P.E. Martino	H.R.G. 1500	13.16.8	4 up to 1500	14

I was still running the engine in so I was keeping the revs down in the race."

The race had been a resounding success and a committee was quickly formed to promote more events, with Griffiths and Haig as Presidents, supported by Penny Griffiths as secretary and Jeremy Broad as competitions secretary. Other committee members represented the interests of each of the major marques. They were Gerry Belton (Allard), Clive Aston (Aston Martin), Brian Dermott (Healey), Bernard Worth (Ferrari), Betty Haig (Frazer Nash), Stuart Young (HRG), Bill Goodman (Porsche) and Peter Skidmore (Jaguar). Other marques were also welcomed and in celebration of Haig's early involvement, the HSCC badge continues to show a Frazer Nash.

Dermott, who later emigrated to Australia but maintained his passion for Healeys, recalled the debate over the logo for the new club. "I remember the meeting where the design for the club logo was approved. Betty Haig was very firm in what she wanted, as she was in all matters relating to the goal. As a young bloke, I found her very inspiring."

Stephen Curtis, another driver from the first race, recalled the membership application process at the time. "When Betty was forming the club Michael Burn, who was a sales manager at Frazer Nash at one time, chaired the first meeting and he said: 'there are no eligibility rules for this club. The only thing that goes is that they are cars that Betty, Guy and I like driven by people that Betty, Guy and I like! If you comply with that, you are in. So I crept in.'

"I was in a Cooper Bristol, which had been a Formula 2 car and was converted into a sports car. I'd been racing for three or four years by then but I hadn't had the car long and I was delighted that Betty was doing these races as it was the right thing for the cars.

Stephen Curtis

"They were very happy times and very informal," said Curtis. "Racing was very different back then. I'd have been wearing a sweater and gardening gloves. We did have helmets and I used to borrow a helmet from my girlfriend; it was one she used for her scooter."

Two Griffiths Formula races were run in 1967, including a support race to the RAC Tourist Trophy at

Oulton Park; thought to be 1967

Peter Skidmore and Mike McGrath on the grid at Castle Combe in 1967

A scene from Castle Combe in May 1968

Oulton Park on Bank Holiday Monday 29 May. The feature race was a round of the European Saloon Car Championship run over a distance of 110 miles and which was won by Italian Andrea de Adamich in an Alfa Romeo Giulia GTA. Seven months later, De Adamich made his Grand Prix debut with Ferrari in the South African Grand Prix.

The Griffiths Formula race ran over five laps but earlier in the afternoon over 30 cars complying with the formula took part in a two-lap parade. There was a remarkable

line-up of cars including four Jaguar D-types and two C-types, a pair of DB3S Aston Martins, a Ferrari 250GT and a gaggle of cars with Le Mans and Mille Miglia history. Ninian Sanderson drove his Ecurie Ecosse 1956 Le Mans-winning D-type MWS 301, while other notable cars were the HWM Alta Jaguar of hillclimber Phil Scragg and a pair of Lister Jaguars to show that Betty Haig's attitude to these cars was softening.

Penny Woodley has good reason to remember that day at Oulton Park, as it was her first race in her father's D-type and one of the earliest races she ever contested. "I just remember the noise on the grid and being totally intimidated by Betty Haig, who drove her Frazer Nash like a 10-ton lorry!"

An excellent field of 24 cars lined-up for the race and Corner won again after five laps of the full track at the Cheshire venue, with Rupert Glydon (Aston Martin DB3S) second and a youthful John Harper third in his Cooper Jaguar.

However, Harper was out of luck when a second race for 1967 was held at the Frazer Nash/Porsche Club meeting at Castle Combe in August, when a major accident befell the Cooper Jaguar. With Corner absent, Peter Skidmore won in his D-type, a result he repeated a year later. In 1967, Skidmore lapped everyone bar Richard Pilkington in a 1950 Talbot S6, thought to be an ex-Louis Rosier car.

2 1969 to 1973
The early days of the club

The cover of the first edition of the club magazine in 1969

After the success of the early races for the Griffiths Formula, the fledgling Historic Sports Car Club was officially formed in March 1969 with RAC recognition and continued to develop as the 1960s gave way to the 1970s. The move to encourage preservation and use of post-war competition sports cars was gathering momentum.

However, the Griffiths father and daughter duo realised that the concept was growing fast and that it was rapidly getting too big for them. "We'd done what we set out to do and people were taking notice," said Woodley.

Clive Aston continued as chairman and Betty Haig remained as secretary into the new decade. But before that, the first issue of the club's magazine called 'Recent History' was published in September 1969. At the end of the 1969 the Club had 136 members and the committee members were Peter Skidmore (Jaguar), Leslie Cato (Healey), Ian Mahany (HRG), Bernard Worth (Ferrari), John Lucas (Porsche) and Barry Bird (AC). As chairman and treasurer, Aston represented the Aston Martin marque and Haig represented Frazer Nash. The club's office address was at Haig's home of Shellingford House near Faringdon in Oxfordshire.

Earlier in 1969, a race was arranged at very short notice at a meeting at Crystal Palace on Whitsun Bank Holiday Monday in late May. With just two

DAVID BECKETT

Racer with the club for 40 years

David Beckett, pictured in 2016

David Beckett raced with the HSCC for 40 years, starting in 1967. He talked about his memories of the club from the early days through to 2007.

"Betty Haig didn't want Listers in the HSCC. She called them 'cut and shut'," recalls Beckett of the very earliest days of the club. That was at the beginning in 1966, and his 1959 Costin Lister was considered rather too new for the fledgling club. But a year later, the Listers were admitted and Beckett started an association with the HSCC that spanned four decades. "After 18 months, someone relented and let us in and I started racing with the HSCC as soon as I could get in."

David started competing in 1957, sprinting a Triumph TR2 and a Frazer Nash Le Mans. Then, his work as a dairy engineer took him to Kenya for four years, where he competed with support from Standard Triumph. He raced a TR3 and even had a Cooper 500 single-seater that he bought for £40. But it was at the wheel of a Mercedes that he scored one of his biggest successes when he won the 1961 East African Safari Rally.

"That was a 3500-mile rally that started on Thursday and ran until Monday over the Easter weekend. There was only one break of eight hours, but if you were running late you barely had time to stop! The motor sport scene out there was fantastic."

When he returned to the UK in 1962, David bought the 1959 Lister, although plans to collect it and drive it home on the road were seriously delayed by the very bad winter of 1962/63. He raced the Lister right through the 1960s, and the chance to race with the HSCC came in 1967. "From 1963 onwards we were up against the Lotus 23Bs and the Brabham BT8, so we didn't have a chance in modern events," he recalls. "Racing with the HSCC was a great alternative."

Rivals back then included Neil Corner, and a photo on the wall of David's office forty years later showed Corner's D-type and the Lister racing just inches apart. "Peter Skidmore was a good friend and always went well in his D-type, particularly at Castle Combe, then there was David Ham's Aston DBR1 and Clive Aston's DB3S. It was a good era and the club ran enough races to keep us impecunious chaps racing."

The Lister was sold in 1970 and replaced with the ex-Bluebell Gibbs Lola Mk1. Although sometimes unreliable, David won the 2-litre sports car race at the final Crystal Palace meeting in late 1972 before taking a sabbatical from racing.

He returned to racing with the HSCC in the early 1980s, racing a rare Costin Nathan in the Atlantic Computers Historic GT Championship. "I finally demolished it completely at Surtees at Brands Hatch. It had a wooden chassis and it was as though an elephant had sat on it!" At the same time, he saw the even rarer Nerus Silhouette for sale and that was a logical replacement for the Costin Nathan.

In the meantime, championship success came in 1991 with a Lister Chevrolet in the HSCC's Pre '60 sportscar championship. Yet, early in the new millennium, he was still racing the Nerus. "It was an excellent car. I raced it in the RJB Mining Championship and that was a lovely series and I really enjoyed it," he says. Unfortunately, when the RJB series ended, there was no obvious place for the Nerus, so Beckett was delighted when the Classic Sports Car Championship was re-worked for 2006.

"Out of the blue, David Methley rang me up about the new regulations. The Classic series was very good and I could have the odd battle with a Chevron B8," said David who celebrated his 70th birthday in 2007.

Supported by his wife Sylvia, David also raced a 1958 Manx Norton in classic motorbike races, even though he made his bike racing debut some time after starting racing on four wheels.

weeks to put the race together, a decent grid was assembled and it was David Beckett who won the Brian Lister Trophy in his Lister Jaguar. Beckett won again in the Holland Trophy race for historic sports cars at the Aston Martin Owners' Club race meeting at Silverstone on 12 July. In the wake of the flying Lister, the D-types of Mike Bradley and Martin Morris battled for second with Wolf Zeuner's Ferrari 860 Monza.

In June, six cars from the club competed in a dedicated class at Shelsley Walsh during a round of the British Hillclimb Championship. Peter Skidmore was the master of the 1000-yard rush up the side of the Teme Valley and set a best run of 40.38s. David Muirhead (Lister Bristol) and Mike Jefferson (Jaguar) were second and third and stopped the clocks within a second of Skidmore's best, although the class record set by George Tatham in a Lister Corvette of 37.66s was never under threat. Jefferson had broken the 40s mark in practice, but had an off at the Esses on his first timed run and damaged a front wing.

A planned race at the annual Bentley Drivers' Club meeting at Silverstone on 16 August was cancelled due to lack of entries, although most of the HSCC entrants transferred to an allcomers' handicap race. On 13 September 1969 an HSCC race was run within an MG Car Club meeting at Castle Combe. Bradley's D-type won from Betty Haig's AC Ace, but only seven cars started the race. The club also entered a team in the Birkett Six Hour Relay Race at Silverstone in August, comprising Mike McGrath (Jaguar D-type), David Muirhead (Frazer Nash Targa Florio), Don Imrie (Tojeiro Bristol), Eric Hall (Healey Elliott) and Chris Warwick-Drake and Ken Roger in Lotus Xs. In at times very wet conditions, the team ended the race five laps down on the winning Viva Drivers' Club team. However, the HSCC team still won two trophies and £10 from STP, to be split between six drivers.

Hall, an early HSCC member, recalls a wonderful era of cheap motor racing. "I joined the club in about 1968 and in those days I had the Healey Elliott saloon, which I used to race," he said. "The car cost me £40 and I had a lot of fun at very little expense. Its number plate was ETR 775 and when I started racing it everybody said that ETR stood for Eric's toy racer. They

Maserati versus Lotus; Brands Hatch in 1970

were very happy times. It was very low key because I was recently married and didn't have much money to spend. The entry fees were around £5 to £7."

The club's award winners for the 1969 season included Peter Woodley (Austin Healey), David Beckett (Jaguar) and David Muirhead (Frazer Nash). When reporting on the 1969 season, club secretary Betty Haig identified growing pressure from circuits and organising clubs to have fuller grids, a theme that runs just as true nearly 50 years later.

For 1970, the annual subscription was £2 10s and the club now had 118 members, with an annual turnover of £290. New on the competition front was a hillclimb section, set up under the guidance of Dr Sandy Gibb, who competed in an AC Ace.

At a lively AGM, the major discussion raged over whether roll bars should be banned. Ultimately, no ban was put in place, but the committee felt that it was wiser not to fit them.

The 1970 season offered races at Castle Combe (twice), Silverstone (twice), Lydden Hill, won by Skidmore's D-type, Crystal Palace and the Birkett Relay at Silverstone. In early May at the AMOC St John Horsfall Silverstone meeting a much stronger grid of 17 cars included four Jaguar D-types and the Maserati T61 Birdcage of Bob Owen. Neil Corner won again, while 'Willie Eckerslyke' was third in his D-type. 'Eckerslyke' was the racing pseudonym used by Nigel Moores of the Littlewoods Pools family from Liverpool who had a habit of buying potentially valuable cars at a point when their value was at its lowest. He also raced in the name of his mechanic, Paul Kelly, as the Moores family disapproved of his racing. Sadly, Moores died in a road accident in France in 1977.

In June 1970, eight club members returned to Shelsley Walsh and Muirhead won the class again, shaving three-hundredths of a second off his winning time from 12 months earlier. Dr Lionel Stretton was second fastest in his Frazer Nash Le Mans Replica and Ron Footit was third in his Frazer Nash Le Mans.

The summer hillclimb date at Shelsley Walsh switched to the August event at the Worcestershire venue but drew only five entries for the HSCC class. Journalist and photographer Michael Bowler won the class in his Frazer Nash. Six weeks earlier, three cars contested

An award from the concours d'elegance in 1971

the HSCC class at an AMOC sprint at Curborough near Lichfield and Neil Corner was a clear winner in his D-type.

In October, Corner won again at Crystal Palace while Willie James spun his Lister Jaguar into the rhododendron bushes. J Bamford was second in another D-type while Martin Morris was third in his D-type after a race that left several cars damaged and one or two others with mechanical problems. Bob Owen suggested that the club would not return to the South London circuit, which finally closed for racing two years later.

By 1971, the club calendar had grown to eight races and the subject of crack testing was discussed for the first time. A new class structure was set-up, with cars divided into road-sports and sports-racing divisions, each split at 2-litres. When announcing the changes, newly-appointed racing secretary Bob Owen urged members to support the racing programme. "This year it is make or break for us as a competing club," he told members the January issue of 'Recent History'.

Communication with members was largely by post and that was severely hampered by a six-week postal strike in the late winter when postal workers demanded a 15% pay rise and walked out when it was not forthcoming. The strike coincided with the introduction of decimal currency into the UK.

The 1971 Annual General Meeting was held on 25 April at the Silverstone Club and Clive Aston, reporting as treasurer, recorded an annual surplus of £120 to give the club a balance of £403. While retaining the role of chairman, he then handed over the finances to new treasurer Leslie Cato.

The 1971 calendar took in races at Silverstone in March (Jaguar Drivers' Club), Oulton Park in April (Lancs and Cheshire Car Club), Silverstone in May (750 MC), Thruxton in June (Jaguar Drivers' Club), Snetterton in June for the Archie Scott Brown Trophy (West Essex Car Club), Castle Combe in June (750 MC), Silverstone in July (Aston Martin Owners' Club) and the 750 MC Birkett Relay in August at Thruxton.

New members for 1971 included The Honourable Patrick Lindsay with a Jaguar D-type recently re-imported from America and Dick Ceasar in a 1955 Bristol 405, the first car to qualify for the new road-sports section. Neil Corner planned to race an Aston Martin DBR1 and Colin Crabbe was expected to race a 3-litre Ferrari Testa Rossa.

Also new for 1971 was the formation of a touring committee to promote touring and other non-competitive events and Richard Bostock stood as the first secretary of this committee. Among the first activities for the touring committee was the organisation of a concours d'elegance and picnic in the grounds of Milton Manor near Newbury on Sunday 18 July. This event replaced the annual event held at Shellingford House under the auspices of the Frazer Nash Club.

A watershed for historic racing in Britain came in early 1971 with the announcement of the JCB Championship for historic sports and historic racing cars. It was the first time any significant sponsorship had been raised for historic racing in the UK.

The new championship was created by Nigel Moores and his personal legal advisor Bill Allen, who raced extensively in the late 1950s and early 1960s. With backing from Anthony Bamford at JCB, it was the

first significant UK championship for historic cars and catered for both single-seaters and sports cars and offered prize money at each event as well as at the end of the season. It was managed by Speed Merchants Ltd, a company created by Moores and Allen, and evolved into the Lloyds and Scottish Historic Championship later in the 1970s.

Back in the HSCC, Maserati Birdcage racer Bob Owen had taken over as racing secretary during the second half of 1970. "Much of the club's guidance and development came from Bob Owen over the next few years," said racer David Pratley, writing in 1996.

In July, under the organisation of Bill Allen from Speed Merchants, some HSCC members took part in a three-lap parade before the Woolmark British Grand Prix at Silverstone. Before the parade, the cars were lined up on the old Club Straight between Becketts and Woodcote and among those to take a look were Jackie and Helen Stewart. Jackie later won the race in his Tyrrell 003 on his way to a second World Drivers' Championship.

The Woolmark Parade of Historic Cars included single-seaters, topped by Colin Crabbe's Mercedes W125 and Tony Brooks in a Vanwall. Regular HSCC racers taking part included Bob Owen (Maserati Tipo 60), Peter van Rossem (Maserati 200S), Betty Haig (Frazer Nash Le Mans), Eric Studer (Porsche Carrera), Barrie Bird (AC Ace) and Michael Bowler (Frazer Nash Sebring).

The club was now thriving, with a 24-strong entry for a race with the AMOC at the St John Horsfall meeting at Silverstone. Amongst those racing with the club was Martin Grant-Peterkin in an Aston Martin. However, this race amply demonstrated how the club's racing had moved on in the space of five years. The grid was dominated by sports-racing cars like the Jaguar D-type, Lister-Jaguar, Maserati 450S and various Lotuses. Few of the road-going cars from 1966 were in the race and many of the front-running cars were back on the grid later in the afternoon for a round of the JCB Championship.

The links between the HSCC and the JCB Championship were clear as a number of races in 1971 had been rounds of both the JCB and the new HSCC Racing Championship. The 1971 HSCC champion was AC Le Mans racer Barry Bird who contested each of the 12 races and won the

THE 1971 HSCC RACING CHAMPION

HSCC Racing Championship
Barry Bird (AC Le Mans)

Goodwood Trophy for his efforts. Over 40 drivers scored points and second and third in overall terms were Owen and Peter van Rossem. Dr Sandy Gibb won the Hill Climb Challenge Cup in his AC Ace Bristol.

For sale in an issue of the club magazine of 1971 was a 1950 Healey Silverstone, complete with three spare engines and gearboxes and another complete car less body – all for the sum of £1500. Less than a year later, there was much grumbling when the competition licence fee was raised to £3 for a restricted licence and £4 for a national licence.

At the Bentley Drivers' Club meeting at Silverstone over the 1971 August Bank Holiday weekend, a modest road sports field was split away from the main historic race which was a round of the JCB and HSCC championships. The road sports shared a grid with the allcomers entry and top of the road sports cars was Nigel Clarkson's Aston Martin DB3S. This was the first time the road sports car had their own contest and it was the start of a movement that would prosper over the following years.

By the autumn of 1971, racing secretary Bob Owen was talking about regularly splitting the club's cars into two grids at some races; one for the faster sports-racing cars and one for road sports.

A magazine editorial in September reported that many of the most interesting road sports cars had disappeared from the grid as more potent sports-racing cars set the pace. The grids during 1971 were largely devoid of the Healeys, HRGs and Frazer Nashes that had helped populate the inaugural Castle Combe grid just five years earlier.

In response to this situation, at the HSCC's 1972 AGM, held on 26 March at Hopcrofts Holt Hotel on the Oxford to Banbury road, a new post-historic register was created for cars from 1959 to 1964. However, some felt this was just too modern and a big debate ensued. Membership was now up to 178 as the club's cut-off date rolled forward to 1964 and would soon hit 300, vindicating the AGM decision to move the club's dates forward by nine years.

In May 1972, the editorial in 'Recent History' detailed the committee's thinking about the whole issue of cut-off dates. It was written by Betty Haig.

THE 1972 HSCC RACING CHAMPION

HSCC Racing Championship
John Lucas (Porsche 356 Coupe)

"It seems that with the acceptance at the recent Annual General Meeting of the formation of a Register for Post Historic Sports Cars built after the end of 1959 and before the end of 1964, another milestone in the Club history has been reached.

"As stated, these will include certain listed cars which are likely to be of historic interest in the years ahead and they will form a separate Register from that of the Historic Sports Cars, have their own races and Secretary, who will at present be drawn from our existing Committee, but later on may be elected from one of their own members.

"At the end of 1965 this Club was formed with the urgent objective of salvaging and preserving the historic sports cars built during the late 1940s up until the end of 1955. This date was later extended to the end of 1959. Now, in including those up to the end of 1964, there are some who may think that we have gone too 'modern' but as the Club has no plans for further extensions, we feel that this is a reasonable date for acceptance.

"The main thing for a Club of this nature is not to lose sight of its original objectives of selectivity and originality, which have proved so successful through the years in giving it the high standing which it now holds."

Perhaps an even more pressing issue was the state of the Club's finances as reported at the AGM in March 1972. Escalating postal costs and two expensive and ultimately unsuccessful adverts in Autosport magazine had drained resources dramatically and the Club had just £31.87 in the bank in January 1972. The annual turn-over for the year ending 31 December 1971 was £630.

The 1972 racing schedule included six races for the HSCC Championship and six for the JCB Championship, with only the AMOC St John Horsfall Trophy meeting at Silverstone on 15 July featuring both championships.

The club's first Annual Dinner Dance was held on the Sunday following the AMOC Silverstone meeting at

Pattishall just north of Towcester. It was part of a club weekend that started on Friday with a club practice day at Silverstone and included a parade of non-competing cars on Saturday, evening social events and a concours d'elegance sportive on Sunday. Winner of the concours was the 1948 Frazer Nash High Speed Model of Donald Hill, which was back in the UK after being discovered in Prague.

Elsewhere, regular monthly meetings for like-minded Club members were being held at the Phoenix, Hartley Wintney and at the George Hotel, Knutsford.

At the time the officers of the club were Clive Aston, Betty Haig and Leslie Cato. The committee members were Bob Owen (his wife Pat now ran the club office), Sandy Gibb, Ian Mahany, John Lucas, Richard Bostock, Bernard Worth, the newly-elected John Harper and Barry Bird.

Full grids featured at the Silverstone and Oulton Park races in 1972 and, reporting in the September edition of 'Recent History' Bob Owen commented that a reduced programme of racing seemed to have paid off, resulting in strong grids. The Holland Trophy race at the AMOC Silverstone meeting even had reserves and Owen was hopeful that the growing group of road sports cars would soon be large enough to sustain separate races.

Meanwhile, the first race for post-historic sports cars was held at Silverstone in late August at the Bentley Drivers' Club meeting and led to the creation of the Cussons Classic GT Championship. The first race winner was James Mehew in his Bizzarini Le Mans.

The club's hillclimb section was not doing as well as the racing element and several events in 1971 featured less than four cars, while just one car arrived at Shelsley Walsh in August. Six dates were planned for 1972, three at Shelsley Walsh and three at Gurston Down, while several northern-based members were competing regularly at Harewood and if more support was forthcoming there was a possibility of a dedicated class.

At the end of the 1972 season, John Lucas (Porsche Coupe) was announced as the club's racing champion and winner of the Goodwood Trophy. Lucas narrowly beat John Harper's Lister Jaguar to the title, while Robert Mansfield (Frazer Nash) won the Alan Brownlee Trophy, presented by the Lotus 11 racer, for the most

points scored by a driver who had not competed in races or hillclimbs for the previous three years. Sandy Gibb again won the Hillclimb Cup but would stand down from his role in co-ordinating hillclimb activity due to ill health during 1973.

There was a change in the club management for 1973 when Clive Aston resigned as chairman due to pressure of business. Bob Owen took over the role, with David Muirhead as vice-chairman, while Jon Dooley was appointed to the role of Alfa Romeo representative. Meanwhile, Haig would soon retire as secretary due to the increasing volume of work involved in running the club.

Despite an upturn in activity and membership, the Club's finances were still fragile and the accounts for the year to 31 December 1972 showed a profit of just £78 to give the club a balance of £95. Without a donation of £100 from Alan Brownlee, the situation would have been even more tricky and it is clear that Club officials like Bob Owen were supporting the club by not claiming out of pocket expenses.

Nevertheless, in 1973 the club's expansion continued with classes to cover sports-racing cars, road sports, post-historic and touring cars. The class structure was updated and amended to show five major groups. One class was for touring cars of all engine sizes, the road sports were split into three classes at 1600cc and 2600cc and the sports-racing cars were divided at the 2-litre mark. The post-historic cars were split into front-engined GT cars and sports-racing cars, with rear-engined Porsches admitted with the front-engined cars, which were sub-divided at 2000cc.

The racing schedule for the 1973 season featured eight dates for the HSCC and seven for the JCB Championship with no overlap. The Cussons Classic GT Championship made its debut at the Jaguar Drivers' Club meeting at Silverstone in March and victory went to Mike Salmon in Aston Martin Project 212. Leading the chase of the

THE 1973 HSCC RACING CHAMPION

HSCC Racing Championship
Eric Studer (Porsche Carrera Speedster)

famous Aston was the lightweight E-type of Peter Walker and Mehew's Bizzarini.

Veteran racer Bill Nicholson won the 2-litre class in his MGB and provided the Club with some remarkable statistics for 286 FAC. From its race debut on Easter Monday 1963 to the end of the 1972, the MGB had covered nearly 38,000 racing miles and scooped 170 class and overall wins.

The Historic Sports Car race on the same programme dominated by Listers as Nick Faure headed Antony Hutton and Robert Cooper in the podium places.

In August, mercurial former F3 racer Charles Lucas won at Oulton Park in a Maserati Birdcage from the stable of Lord Hesketh as a 23-car field encompassed all the Club's classes. The touring car class contained a solitary Bristol 405 for Alan Bennett, while Simon Phillips topped the road sports cars in his Frazer Nash. Behind Lucas at the head of the sports-racing cars was John Harper's Lister Jaguar and Richard Bond's HWM Jaguar, while Terry Harrison headed the 2-litre sports-racing cars in a Lotus XI.

Also on the bill at the Lancs and Cheshire Car Club meeting at Oulton Park was a round of the Cussons Classic GT Championship, with a very impressive entry including two Project Aston Martins and three Ford GT40s. The race also marked the debut of the mighty and very rare Maserati Tipo 151/65 that Bob Owen had been rebuilding. It suffered teething troubles but the 5-litre car showed considerable promise.

Anthony Hutton's 'Mirage' GT40 won from John Cooper's GT40 and Brian Classick's Porsche 906. Mike Salmon was fourth in Project 212 and Nick Cussons was also there in Project 214 along with four Aston Martin Zagatos and the Ferrari 250GT 'Breadvan' in the hands of local single-seater ace Kim Mather. Two weeks later, at the Bentley Drivers' Club meeting at Silverstone, Harper won from the similar Lister Jaguar of David Ham.

The Club's racing championship, for the Goodwood Cup, went to Porsche racer Eric Studer, while Simon Phillips (Frazer Nash) won the Alan Brownlee Trophy and Mike Smailes won the Hillclimb Cup.

However, everything was turned on its head in early 1974 when the fuel crisis struck and the possibility seemed slim of any competitive motor sport being organised.

3 1974 to 1979

The unpredictable 1970s

Silverstone 1975: Hon. Amschel Rothschild's Lotus X

The fuel crisis of 1973/74 sparked from US involvement in the Yom Kippur War after Egypt and Syria launched a surprise military campaign against Israel to try and regain ground lost in the 1967 Six-Day War. The US quickly supplied Israel with arms and OPEC, the Organisation of Petroleum Exporting Countries, responded in October 1973 with an oil embargo on the US, Canada, Japan, the UK and the Netherlands.

After intense diplomatic activity, led by Henry Kissinger, the embargo was finally lifted in March 1974 by which time the cost of oil had risen from $3 per barrel to $12. The impact in the UK was to make fuel scarce and when motor sport restarted, there was a voluntary 20% cut in race distances as a gesture towards saving fuel.

In the first 1974 edition of 'Recent History', Betty Haig detailed her reasons for standing down as secretary of the Club. "I would like to thank all members both past and present for their kindness and helpfulness, which I have experienced during the ups and downs of eight years in this job, developing it from the grass roots upwards as we went. I shall not be abandoning ship completely as I have been asked on the committee as

Historic Registrar. The Club has now reached the stage of development when the early concept of a voluntary part-time secretary has become a thing of the past."

The role was taken over by Graham and Enid Boston from Leicester, with the Club committee planning to pay a modest retainer for the role. However, their tenure was brief and ended when Graham Boston was offered the chance to study at his employer's expense. By the summer of 1974 the role has been taken over by Pat Owen, albeit on a temporary basis. In the same January editorial, Haig reminded members that the post of chairman was vacant as Bob Owen had only agreed to take the position for 12 months and his work as racing secretary was taking up a great deal of time. Owen duly suggested that vice-chairman David Muirhead take over as chairman.

The fuel crisis was clearly having a big impact and committee meetings had been suspended and the Annual General Meeting was postponed until later in the year in the hope that the situation would improve.

In January 1974, as out-going chairman, Bob Owen reported that the preceding 12 months had been a good period for the club. A proper set of eligibility rules with clear cut-off dates had been established, membership had grown to over 260 and the Club had £600 in the bank. That represented the club's best financial position since it was first formed.

The 1974 AGM was held in late March and was reported in a new-look 'Recent History' magazine published in June in a more professional looking A5-size format. Race secretary Bob Owen reported that the cost of buying a race slot with organising clubs had risen and was now working out at between £200 and £250 with a club like the Aston Martin Owners' Club. David Muirhead was elected as chairman with Roger St John Hart elected as vice-chairman.

The AGM included a land-mark resolution when the members approved a proposal to admit single-seaters for the first time. Both Formula 1 and Formula 2 cars

up to the end of 1960 would be welcomed into the HSCC fold.

During the 1974 season the Club's hillclimb activity gathered momentum with Philip Rambaut now co-ordinating the competition. At Prescott in late June a bigger entry included John Harper who won the over 3-litre class in his Lister Jaguar.

In February, Bob Owen unveiled the Club's 1975 racing programme across 18 race meetings at six circuits and with eight different organising clubs. It was the club's most extensive schedule to date and included eight rounds of the Classic Car Championship and six rounds of the JCB Historic Championship. The JCB series continued under the wing of Speed Merchants, while the contact for the Classic Car Championship was Martin Ryan in Skelmersdale in Lancashire.

The 1975 Annual General Meeting was reported as pleasant and peaceful, with the business swiftly dealt with to allow plenty of time for socialising at the Paddocks Inn near Silverstone. All of the club's key officials were routinely re-elected and it was agreed that fuller clarification on the originality of engines should be drawn up.

Present at the meeting was Colin Myles, chairman of the 500 Owners' Association, and the question of the two clubs joining forces was again discussed as they shared similar aims and objectives. After discussion, it was agreed that the there should be a full liaison between the two clubs but not a merger. Other reports showed that the club's programme of touring and social events was steadily growing, while a small band of owners were busy competing in hillclimbs.

In his chairman's report, David Muirhead reported on a very successful year in 1974. Membership had broken through the 300-mark, finances were improved and the move to formalise eligibility rules had gone well. Changes to the committee included the co-option of Robert Mansfield to the role of Touring Secretary.

Newly presented for the 1975 season was the Bill Phillips Trophy, in memory of WD Phillips who raced in the 1920s and 1930s and was later a judge at the British Grand Prix for many years. His son Simon was a regular HSCC racer in his Frazer Nash and the award would be presented annually to the best performance in a road-going sports car.

THE 1974 HSCC RACING CHAMPION

Classic Sports Car Championship
Mike Salmon (Aston Martin DP212)
HSCC Racing Champion
Simon Phillips (Frazer Nash)

Ian Hilton's AC Cobra at Thruxton

THE 1975 HSCC RACING CHAMPIONS

HSCC Racing Championship
John Beasley (Lister Chevrolet)
Classic Sports Car Championship
Richard Thwaites (Elva Mk7S)

Meanwhile, the Opposite Lock Trophy was presented by Porsche 908 racer Martin Hone and was named after his motor racing-oriented club in Gas Street in Birmingham. The trophy was to be presented to the member who competed regularly and put up the best performance, regardless of his or her position in the results.

Club treasurer Leslie Cato reported on the finances for the year to 31 December 1974, which included the time of the three-day week and inflation running at 20%. Those factors had forced the club to raise the membership fee by £1 from £3, where it had been for several years and the resultant increase in revenue helped the club to increase its general fund by £89 to £434. In addition, the life membership fund sat at £195 despite the purchase of a much-needed duplicator. Heading into 1975, the club had cash reserves of £662.

From the early days of the HSCC, the subject of eligibility had been one of great debate. In the Club's early years, it was very much a matter of the committee of the time being satisfied that a potential member and their vehicle would be satisfactory.

However, by the middle 1970s, car values were starting to climb and cars began to emerge from barns, sometimes with questionable claims to their provenance. In 1976, in response to growing concerns, the club was the first organisation to introduce specific expert registrars and a formal vehicle documentation process followed in 1978. It was a ground-breaking move and helped protect the Club against a growing number of cars appearing with dubious specification and heritage.

On the committee, Philip Edbrook took over the role of secretary although he was happy to admit that his main interest was in old cars generally rather than competition cars.

In the February edition of 'Recent History', treasurer Leslie Cato warned members that the membership fee was going to increase again. After much debate within the committee, the price was pushed up to £6. Cato acknowledged that the British government was trying to get inflation back into single figures and, if this happened, he hoped that the fee would stabilise.

At the Annual General Meeting in March 1976, a small surplus was recorded for the year to 31 December 1975. However, rampant inflation was giving great cause for concern and membership numbers dipped as people tightened their belts in the challenging economic conditions.

Under 'any other business', member Hugh Clifford proposed that the club should accept Formula Juniors in original specification from up to 31 December 1960 and that the cars should be welcomed into the Club's single-seater category. The proposal was seconded by Bob Owen and carried unanimously.

In 1976, racing activities centred on the Classic Championship, now sponsored by Rochas, with reigning champion Richard Thwaites (Brabham BT8) and Mike Wood (Elva Mk7S) to the fore among the sports-racers and Martin Johnson (Ferrari Breadvan) and Brian Classick (Iso Griffo) among the leading GT cars. A pair of very smart Lotus Elans for John Webb and Ken Eady ran in the colours of the championship sponsor.

Elsewhere, John Beasley was having a mighty season in his Lister Chevrolet and bagged another win at Oulton Park in July over the similar car of Roger

Brierley-Jones. North Wales-based Brierley-Jones had taken on the role of Vice-Chairman when Roger St John Hart stood down at the AGM earlier in 1976.

Beasley was again one the club's most successful racer in his Lister Chevrolet, taking the club's championship for the second time running by winning the Goodwood Trophy in 1976. Meanwhile the 1100cc Lolas of Rupert Glydon and Michael Ostroumoff also had excellent seasons.

In March 1977, the Annual General Meeting reported a loss of £315 and the treasurer warned of the need to carefully monitor expenditure over the coming year. A significant new expense was the £265 honorarium paid to the club secretary and the club went into 1977 with reserves of £660.

Notably, absent from the AGM were chairman, David Muirhead, and vice-chairman, Roger Brierley-Jones. Nevertheless, the entire committee was re-elected en bloc. A watershed in club officials came during 1977 when Betty Haig stood down from the role of newsletter editor and effectively ended a decade at the centre of the club's activities. Her outstanding contribution had been critical to the establishment of the HSCC and her drive and energy had been a prime force behind the club's creation and development. Paul Howarth took over the job of editing 'Recent History'.

Club treasurer Leslie Cato wrote about Haig in the November 1977 issue of 'Recent History'. "Certainly I do not know anyone in the Club who has contributed so much to it as Betty has done and I am sure you would all like to express our thanks." Haig was made an honorary life member of the club in recognition of her work.

Writing in 1988, Peter Dixon recognised Haig's contribution to the development of historic racing. "Eventually, of course, the HSCC, as a result of her efforts, became too big and successful for her continued direct involvement but all historic racing in this country owes her a huge debt. She kept out the specials, the replicas, cars of no account and cars that had been unsuitably modified. She was appalled at what was happening in the mid-'60s to cars of class and had the foresight to see that racing them in original condition would up their status and value and encourage their preservation in original condition. She was right."

THE 1976 HSCC RACING CHAMPIONS

HSCC Racing Championship
John Beasley (Lister Chevrolet)
Classic Sports Car Championship
Richard Thwaites (Brabham BT8)

HSCC races continued to run within meetings organised by other clubs and in 1977 drivers like Bobby Bell (Lister Jaguar), Sid Hoole (Cooper Monaco), Richard Thwaites (Brabham BT8), Jem Marsh (Marcos Fastback) and Cyril Baxter (Marcos GT) were all leading runners.

Bobby Bell was victorious in an HSCC scratch race at the Bentley Drivers' Club Bank Holiday Saturday meeting at Silverstone in August with Hoole just beating Brewster Righter (AC Cobra) for second place. Also in the race were more AC Cobras for Lord Cross and Martin Colvill as well as Bill Wykeham in a Morgan and racing journalist Robin Rew in his well-used Reliant Sabre Six.

The following day, the AFN-backed Classic Sports Car Championship had a round at Mallory Park, with Thwaites and Wood continuing their battles and David Dawson taking his Lotus 23 to third on his way to winning the championship.

Two weeks later, Dawson won overall at Thruxton against the Lotus 23s of Brian Cocks and Jeffray Johnstone from a grid that included the Hon Amschel Rothschild (AC Cobra Daytona), Jem Marsh (Marcos GT) and former Grand Prix driver Mike Wilds having a race in Alan Hall's Lotus Elite.

In September, a planned HSCC race within a Nottingham Sports Car Club race meeting at the newly re-opened Donington Park was cancelled due to lack of entries, but the BRSCC was to organise a race for HSCC single-seaters as a support race to the European Formula 2 Championship race there at the end of October.

The Classic championship concluded with a good grid at Brands Hatch in early October and an emphatic overall win for Dawson sealed the title over his major rival Roger Friend (Lotus Elite). Dawson's Lotus had been

THE 1977 HSCC RACING CHAMPIONS

HSCC Racing Championship
Bobby Bell (Lister Jaguar)
Classic Sports Car Championship
David Dawson (Lotus 23)
Group 4 Historic GT Championship
Willie Green (Ford GT40)

originally built for the Peter Sellers Racing Team and driven by Barrie Hart. It was later crashed at Solitude in the US and rebuilt by Lotus. Dawson found it in a lock-up garage in Haringey fitted with a 1300 Triumph engine for use in the short-lived Formula F100.

The 1977 season concluded with news that the FIA would be running a new Historic Championship in 1978 for all pre-1961 cars including single-seaters and sports-racing cars. The seven-event calendar included an AMOC Brands Hatch date in May and a BRDC date at Silverstone in September. Other rounds were planned for Le Mans, Montlhery, Zandvoort, Zolder and the Nurburgring.

The winter of 1977/78 was a turbulent time for the club. In the case of chairman David Muirhead, the news was not good and his increasing ill health prompted him to step down from the role. Sadly, he died on 2 December 1977. His death would leave a vacancy at the head of the club that would be the catalyst for major change. Roger Brierley-Jones had assumed some of the work of the chairman but made it known that he did not wish to stand as the new chairman. He was, however, prepared to remain as vice-chairman to support the new chairman through a transition period.

At much the same time, Leslie Cato resigned as treasurer and Philip Rambaut stood down as hillclimb secretary and was replaced, on a temporary basis at least, by Robin Rew. Cato's resignation seems to have been linked to on-going differences of opinion about whether advertising should be permitted on cars. Racing Secretary Bob Owen argued strongly that at least some advertising should be allowed.

A tribute to David Muirhead was carried in the January 1978 edition of 'Recent History'. "David and his wife Sue were stalwart supporters in the early years in the formation of the club. During latter years, when for health reasons he had to curtail his own racing activities, he took great pleasure from seeing his car appear in the capable hands of David Childs.

"David continued his support of the club until his death, and under his leadership as Chairman great advances were made during the last two years. His experience in the racing field and his obvious managerial talent enabled him to take a very balanced view of club affairs and we have always received very sound advice, even latterly when he was unable to attend committee meetings.

"It is not perhaps widely known that he was Head Boy at Gordonstoun School, had a distinguished university career and was a considerable sportsman, which was evident from the spirited driving of his 2-litre Lister Bristol. It is, I think, fair to say that when driving in the wet, David had no peer. His death is a very great loss to us all, both in his capacity as chairman and indeed as an old and valued friend."

Heading into the 1978 season the range of classes run by the club had grown steadily and with single-seaters added, the club was moving ever closer to the critical mass needed to run its own race meetings.

The club's portfolio now covered what was referred to as Groups 1 to 4 plus single-seaters. Group 1 was for Pre-1961 single-seaters and sports-racing cars; Group 2 was for Classic Sports Cars, Group 3 for Road Sports and Group 4 for the faster and more powerful sports-racing cars.

As 1978 opened, the racing secretaries were busy trying to find sponsorship to help defray the cost of organising the racing side of the club. For the Classic Championship, David Dawson, Brian Cocks, Mike Gue and Bob Linwood were busy looking for backers, while the Group 4 Championship had secured support from Mike Harrison's Wild Rose Caravan Park. The Classic Championship calendar took in 14 rounds, starting early with a Jaguar Drivers' Club date at Silverstone on 11 March. Plans for a Pre-1961 championship faltered due to lack of a sponsor, but six races would still be run for the older cars.

The 1978 programme was ambitious, with the club's five categories involved in a total of 21 races meetings with a range of organising clubs. However, with the roles of chairman and treasurer vacant, this was also a time of inner turmoil and the Annual General Meeting of spring 1978 promised to be a major turning point in the development of the HSCC.

With acting chairman Roger Brierley-Jones absent from the AGM, Peter Dixon chaired the meeting. He explained that both Leslie Cato and Philip Rambaut had resigned during the year and that Bob Owen had not offered himself for re-election. Acting treasurer Paul Howarth reported that the club's assets had grown to around £1100.

There were four nominations for the role of chairman; Brian Cocks, John Harper, Brewster Righter and Bert Young and it was clear that this was a divided club with differing factions. When the voting was complete, Cocks was elected as chairman with Young elected as vice-chairman. Philip Edbrook agreed to stay on as secretary for another year but was later replaced by Tina Gue and Paul Howarth continued as treasurer, at least until a new treasurer was found.

When announcing his decision to stand down, Bob Owen recommended that the role of racing secretary should evolve into a competitions sub-committee and a five-man team was duly elected comprising Bert Young, Tony Standen, Pat Dawson, Paul Howard, Hugh Clifford and new hillclimb secretary Nick Atkins.

The dramatic AGM of 1978 had resulted in the biggest ever shake-up in club officials and one of Cocks' election pledges was that, if he was elected, the HSCC would run its own race meetings. However, his first task had been to re-work the club's administration as he detailed in his article 'from the chair' in the March/April issue of 'Recent History'.

"Following the AGM I find myself with the honour of chairmanship of the HSCC. For a comparative newcomer to the club this is indeed showing great trust and I sincerely hope my experience in the other areas of club motor sport can be translated successfully to the HSCC.

"My first moves have been to assess the existing administrative position and to try to spread the workload. This is always a problem in any voluntary organisation where the willing horses eventually become ridiculously over-loaded. We have re-distributed responsibility for competitions through a committee instead of, as before, a Competition Secretary. The Competitions Committee's chairman is David Dawson, who is a member of the main committee.

"Similarly, the registrars are re-organised into a sub-committee under the experienced chairmanship of Peter Dixon, who is also a member of the main committee.

"The communications aspect of the club has been a problem, mainly due to financial restrictions. I have enlisted the help of new editors for both the newsletter and 'Recent History' which will both revert to their previous style and function. The monthly

Classic Championship contender Len Bridge (Lotus Elan) in 1978

newsletter will be edited by Mike Gue, who will take over from a grossly overworked Paul Howarth in May. Its function will be to inform the membership of current events and to comment on the club in its own style."

"'Recent History' will return to its previous glossy concept with interesting articles and longer period reviews. It will be edited by brothers Jack and George Rance and the first issue will appear in July. David Capstick, our Advertising Manager, has further plans for the new 'Recent History' and will be helping set up the important advertising revenue from our magazine.

"As I undertook at the AGM, 1979 will see the first HSCC race meetings, of which more anon as the details are finalised. Already we have some exciting news, so don't plan your 1979 holidays in July.

"It is my intention to ensure that each section of the club, from social to racing is properly covered. Our main objective must be to increase membership and

Dave Preece (McLaren M1B) at Brands Hatch in June 1978

club activity, thus giving us a firm financial footing from which to work."

At the same time, new members included Richard Dodkins, Robin Longdon, Ian Giles, Steven O'Rourke and Tim Burrett who was going to race a Lancia Aurelia. By now, the club's cut-off date had been advanced to 1968 and series production sports cars were included in the club's portfolio.

On the track, the racing season started the day before the watershed AGM with a full grid for the opening round of the Classic Sports Car Championship. Carrying on where he left off in 1977, Richard Thwaites won clearly in his Brabham BT8 while racing newcomer Roger Ealand was reported to have totally demolished his ex-David Pratley Marcos.

The 1978 season didn't start so well for the HSCC single-seaters and only six of 11 entered made it to the grid at the JDC Silverstone meeting in early March. The winner was the unique, and non-HSCC registered, Monzanapolis Lister Jaguar of Martin Chapman from Gerry Walton (Connaught) and Amschel Rothschild (Maserati 250F). The trend for small grids continued over the next two races, prompting a plea for more support from Hugh Clifford. "May I appeal to all single-seater owning members to give us more support. We currently have 27 cars registered with the club and seldom produce more than six or seven entries." Clifford also reminded owners of front-engined Formula Juniors manufactured before 1960 that their cars were eligible.

In contrast, the Classic Sports Car Championship got off to a flying start with so many entries for the season opener with the 750MC at Mallory Park that the field was split across two races. After five rounds, Jeffray Johnstone (Lotus 23) had a slender points lead from the Marcos' of marque founder Jem Marsh and Cyril Baxter and Martin Colvill (AC Cobra).

In the Group 4 Championship, Rodney Bloor's Chevron B8 took the early lead in the table although the more powerful cars starred at the AMOC Brands Hatch meeting in May as Richard Pilkington's stunning Alfa Romeo T33/3 fended off Richard Bond in the Marsh Plant Lola T70. The Alfa Romeo from the Totnes Motor Museum was the car that had won the BOAC 500 at Brands just seven years earlier in the hands of Andrea de Adamich and Henri Pescarolo.

In July 1978, the first revamped edition of 'Recent History' was distributed to members. The magazine ran to 34 pages and production qualities marked a major step forward. On the cover was a superb period photo of Pedro Rodriguez in a Ferrari 312P in the Brands Hatch paddock during the 1969 BOAC 500 meeting.

In that same edition, Cocks announced the appointment of Marcos racer David Pratley as the club's new public relations officer and also gave a clear indication that work was already underway for club to run its first race meeting in 1979. A few months later it was confirmed that the club would mark the start of a new chapter by running two race meetings in 1979, both at Donington Park.

In September the club had a stand at the Classic Car Show at London's Alexandra Palace, organised by Pratley and manned by club members. On show were a Lotus 23, a Diva and a Healey Silverstone.

In December 1978, Brian Cocks reflected on a busy first year as chairman. He set a bold target to double the membership to 1000 by 1980 and confirmed plans to create the Post Historic Road Sports category for 1979, catering for cars produced between 1961 and 1968. Meanwhile, Philip and Barbara Edbrook stood down from the secretarial post and were replaced by Tina Gue.

The review of the 1978 racing season started with a disappointing year for the pre-1960 Road Sports, with just four races and all of them shared with other classes. Only 25 cars appeared across the four races and the nominal best performer was Tony Standen in his Porsche Roadster.

The Historic Car Championship enjoyed far better support across a six-race schedule, which concluded at the Brands Hatch meeting for the visiting USAC cars from America. It was the event that gave the club circuit its new 'Indy' tag. Roddy MacPherson was the most consistent performer in his hard-driven Cooper Bristol and scooped the overall title from a mixed field of sports-racing cars and single-seaters. The quality of the series was emphasised by grids that included Willie Green, Gerry Marshall, Bobby Bell, David Ham and Sid Hoole.

A total of 50 registered contenders made it a good season for the Classic Sports Car Championship, with grids regularly in the 20s. Among the big-engined cars

Jem Marsh at Castle Combe in 1978 in his Marcos GT

was the stunning Daytona Cobra Coupe of Amschel Rothschild, a Jaguar E-type for John Pearson and the rare Ginetta G10 of Chris Stewart. However, it was the pace and consistency of Jem Marsh in his diminutive Marcos GT that clinched the overall title.

The Historic GT Championship promised much as the glorious sports-racing cars of the late 1960s looked and sounded superb. However, getting them all out together regularly proved difficult and the season review in 'Recent History' predicted that 1979 would be a make or break season. A better quality of race meetings seemed to be the main objective for stepping the series forward. Rodney Bloor took the championship crown in his Chevron B8, with Bob Linwood coming through as a key challenger in his B8 as the season developed.

The big news for 1979 was that the club would organise race meetings for the first time. Two dates

THE 1978 HSCC RACING CHAMPIONS

Classic Sports Car Championship
Jem Marsh (Marcos GT)
Group 4 Historic GT Championship
Rodney Bloor (Chevron B8)

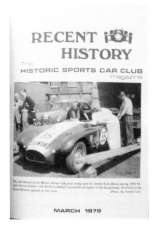

were confirmed, both at Donington Park with a one-day meeting on April 22 and a two-day weekend on July 21/22. As Brian Cocks revealed, the events would be run in partnership with the British Motor Racing Marshals' Club and would have an HSCC team in race control. The organising team included Cocks, John Felix, Mike Eyre, Val Adaway and Dallas Smith.

In his chairman's annual review, published in May 1979, Brian Cocks reported on a major year in the club's history. The balance sheet at 31 December 1978 showed a modest improvement and membership was heading for 400. He reported that the club's administration was now in good order and that the new competitions committee was working well. "I feel that the club is currently running efficiently, is properly controlled and running efficiently," said Cocks. The club's first race meeting was organised in April as Cocks delivered on one of his key election pledges.

With Mike and Tina Gue heading for a new career in Long Island, USA, they were to be replaced by David and Anne Womack.

The very first HSCC-organised race, at the April meeting was for Classic Sports, was won by John Brindley's Lotus 23, chased by the similar car of Jeffray Johnstone. The meeting included the inaugural race for the new Post-Historic Road Sports category and over 100 competitors contested seven races.

Brindley, at the wheel of the Bell and Colvill-entered Lotus, headed a one-two-three in qualifying as similar 23s for Johnstone and Michael Evans, while the second row of the three-two-three grid contained the AC Cobras of Amschel Rothschild and Martin Colvill. Also on the grid were Robin Longdon (Lotus Elite) and Jim Gathercole (Lotus Elan).

The second race was for historic sports-racing cars and single-seaters but the field was hit by the non-starting Maserati 250Fs of Bobby Bell and Amschel Rothschild. South African Formula Ford racer Kenny Gray raced Gerry Hann's Formula 2 Cooper Climax and was leading the chase of race winner John Harper (Lister Jaguar) when sidelined by a broken driveshaft. Martin Chapman brought the Monzaapolis Lister Jaguar through to second from the back of the grid.

The Historic Special GT Championship, again backed by the Wild Rose Caravan Park, had a good and varied

grid with some of the cars from the opening race back out. Mike Wheatley (Lola T70 Mk3B) won a race that included John Lepp (Chevron B8), Mike Salmon (Ford GT40) and Anthony Taylor (Willment BRM).

A guest championship marked the fourth race with a round of the Chandler Hargreaves Formula Junior Championship and a grid headed by Alan Baillie (Lotus 20) and Mike Harrison (Brabham). More Lotuses followed for Alf Skeels, Sid Hoole and Roger Baker. In the race, Harrison narrowly beat Baillie after an entertaining race-long battle.

A mixed bag of single-seaters and sports-racing cars contested the non-championship Bell and Colvill Trophy race which started in drizzle as the weather deteriorated. Bobby Bell led from the off in the Yardley-liveried BRM P153 Grand Prix car and coped well with the tricky conditions to win. John Jordan's later BRM P201 started at the back after an all-nighter to get it ready. Unfortunately, it snapped into a first-lap spin at Redgate and the racing flour miller ended his race against the wall.

The historic and post-historic road sports shared a grid, with the classes divided at 1960. David Wilding won in the famous ex-Dick Protheroe Jaguar E-Type CUT 7 from Francois Duret in his Aston Martin DB4 and Jem Marsh in his Marcos GT. The day's final race was planned to include the fastest 26 cars, but mechanical problems and the worsening weather decimated the field and just five cars started the race, which was shortened to five laps. Jeremy Lord (Coldwell C14B) beat Jeffray Johnstone, in his third race of the day, and Mike Wheatley.

Although the weather ensured that the meeting tailed off a little, the HSCC's first race meeting had been an undoubted success and had run smoothly from all perspectives. It had been a landmark day in the club's development and set the HSCC on a course to become a leading organiser of historic racing in the UK.

The country's leading historic championship, a re-incarnation of the former JCB series, was to be sponsored by the Lloyds and Scottish Finance Group for 1979 and had a high-profile six-round schedule including support races to the British Grand Prix and the Tourist Trophy meetings at Silverstone. Roddy MacPherson would race as car number 1 as reigning champion, while Stirling Moss was also expected to contest the season in a Maserati 250F, inevitably carrying number 7. Even before the season started, an impressive 55 cars were registered including 10 Lister Jaguars.

The Grand Prix support race on Saturday 14 July was massively over-subscribed and priority was given to those who had supported the earlier rounds of the championship. The pressure on grid space was compounded by the fact that the sports cars and single-seaters were merged into one race given the constraints of the F1 timetable. In a thrilling race, Willie Green just took victory in the JCB-entered Ferrari Dino but Bruce Halford (Lotus 16) and Robs Lamplough (BRM P25) were close behind. Only a last-lap spin at Club for Alain de Cadenet dropped his Aston Martin out of what had been a fantastic four-way lead contest. Both Lamplough and Patrick Lindsay arrived at Silverstone in wartime Harvard training aeroplanes.

On 21/22 July, a more ambitious two-day meeting was held at Donington, backed by Thoroughbred and Classic Car magazine. The HSCC ran Saturday's programme while the BARC took over for the international event on Sunday.

First race was a round of the AMOC's championship for road sports won by the Aston Martin DB4 of Dave Preece from the Triumph TR3 of prolific period racer Reg Woodcock. John Brindley won the Classic Sports Car race after a big battle with the similar Lotus 23 of Michael Evans while a startline accident eliminated the TVR of Bob Linwood and the Lotus 23 of Steve Mitchell.

Fresh from winning the Lloyds and Scottish race supporting the British GP at Silverstone a week earlier, Willie Green won again in the Ferrari Dino, while John Harper (Lister Jaguar) headed a combined historic sports and single-seater race. Glyn Giusti won an MG 'T' Type race and Mike Harrison repeated his April victory in a Formula Junior race that included a class for 500cc F3 cars.

Michael Wheatley added another Historic GT Championship win in his Lola T70 Mk3B over the similar car of Richard Bond while David Piper took his glorious Ferrari 330P to third place. Bobby Bell also repeated his April win in his BRM P153 in the race for 'historically interesting' cars from a field that included the sensational Porsche 908 of Siegfried Brunn.

Dave Reade won the post-historic road sports race in his Aston Martin DB4 against opposition that included

Nigel Mansell in a Jaguar E-type. The Saturday programme concluded with another attempt to draw the day's fastest 26 cars to the grid. However, only half of them appeared but the battle between Bobby Bell's F1 BRM and Brunn's Porsche 908 more than made up for the thin grid. After trading the lead with the Porsche in the early laps, Bell was able to pull clear.

Sunday's racing included some international races, but the grids were generally thinner with only a smattering of foreign drivers making the trip to Donington. A star attraction on Sunday was a demonstration by Hans Hermann at the wheel of a Mercedes-Benz 300SLR, similar to the car that he raced in the 1955 Mille Miglia.

However, the overall weekend was a great success and can perhaps be considered as Britain's first historic racing festival. Much of the credit for the event went to Michael Bowler, a racer from the early years of the club and editor of Thoroughbred and Classic Cars magazine.

Green went on to win the Lloyds and Scottish title in 1979 as a landmark season for the club came to a close. Meanwhile John Corfield won the Grand Prix Models Classic Sports title by a handy margin in his Diva 10F. Corfield had paid just £200 for the Diva four years earlier and rescued it from a front garden when it had been left for five years. Class champions

RECENT HISTORY
The HISTORIC SPORTS CAR CLUB magazine

Brian Cocks presents John Harper (Lister Jaguar) with his winner's garland after winning the Historic Race at the Donington Weekend meeting, the event being recorded on film. (Photo: Classic Cars)

OCTOBER 1979

THE 1979 HSCC RACING CHAMPIONS

Classic Sports Car Championship
John Corfield (Diva GT)
Group 4 Historic GT Championship
Mike Wheatley (Lola T70 Mk3B)
Historic Car Championship
Willie Green (Ferrari Dino)

included Amschel Rothschild (Daytona Cobra Coupe), Tony Goodwin (Diva GT), Jack Batson (Alexander Sprite) and John Brindley (Lotus 23).

In the Wild Rose Caravan Park-supported Special GT Championship, Mike Wheatley was a convincing champion in his Lola T70 Mk3B, but it took a tie-break to decide the 2-litre class in favour of John Lepp (Chevron B8) over Brindley's Lotus 23. Others to appear in the championship included Mike Salmon (Ford GT40), Richard Dodkins (Ginetta G12), Reg

Skeels (Mercury GT), Rodney Bloor (Chevron B8) and Chris Stewart (Gulf Mirage).

From a modest first race in 1966, the club had grown and evolved over 13 years to the point where it was able to run its first race meeting. There had been plenty of growing pains and few, if any, of the original forces behind the formation of the club remained involved. However, as the turbulent 1970s came to a close, the future looked bright for the HSCC.

ROBERT MANSFIELD

1970s committee member

Through the 1970s, Robert Mansfield was involved with the club as a racer and as a committee member with a particular responsibility for touring events.

"I bought my Frazer Nash Targa Florio from Chris Drewett in March 1969. It raced at Le Mans in 1952 and 1954 and it did the Dundrod TT in 1954 and raced at Goodwood many times.

"I then went straight out to Thailand with a job and left the car with a garage near Bedford. The garage then went bust and the day I came back from Thailand the car was

about to go for auction on behalf of the garage. So I got the keys back just in time.

"I've had the car ever since and have thoroughly enjoyed it. I raced it quite hard in the earlier days of the HSCC with people like Bob Owen, Brian Joscelyn, Simon Phillips and Roddy MacPherson. There was always a gang of Nashes and John Lucas with the Porsche, which was always very quick. There were some small grids, but we had good fun.

"Then I stopped racing in about 1977 and the Nash has been a good road car ever since. I was the touring secretary for a couple of years when Betty Haig was trying to reduce her involvement. David Muirhead was then the chairman before Bob Owen took it over as a club. The club went into a lull in the late 1970s but it has now been revived extraordinarily well."

4
1980 to 1984
Brian Cocks takes the helm

Important news for the 1980 historic racing season was the continuation of sponsorship from Lloyds and Scottish for the club's Historic Car Championship. The calendar took in seven high-profile race meetings including the British Grand Prix meeting at Brands Hatch and the Tourist Trophy at Silverstone, but the identity of the eventual champion went un-recorded.

In the middle of 1980 the club suffered another loss when Jack Rance succumbed to cancer the day before his 51st birthday. Alongside his brother George, he has been editor of the club's 'Recent History' magazine at the invitation of Brian Cocks and his contribution would be greatly missed.

In racing terms, John Brindley remained one of the club's most successful racers and won the 1980 Classic Sports Car title in his beloved Lotus 23. The two-day Donington weekend was repeated on 19/20 July, with the club organising both days of racing. The meeting marked the first overall race win for Amschel Rothschild in the rare Daytona Cobra Coupe in a race for pre-1964 GT cars.

The sponsorship from Lloyds and Scottish for the club's Historic Car Championship was extended into the 1981 season with a five-round calendar again capped by a race at the British Grand Prix which was at Silverstone that year.

RECENT HISTORY
The HISTORIC SPORTS CAR CLUB magazine

Sid Hoole in his Cooper Monaco on the grid during one of last years races at Silverstone. Sid is joined this year by John Harper in a similar car, both scoring good results in the opening rounds of the 1980 Lloyds and Scottish Championship. (Photo: Jack Rance)

JUNE 1980

THE 1980 HSCC RACING CHAMPIONS
Classic Sports Car Championship
John Brindley (Lotus 23B)
Group 4 Historic GT Championship
Reg Skeels (Mercury GT)

After a rather quiet season in 1980, the impetus generated by Brian Cocks was clear in 1981 with four championships headed by the Group 4 Historic GT Championship. Relatively new on the racing scene was computer expert John Foulston and he won the title in his McLaren M1B to start an association with the HSCC that would have a major impact over the next six seasons.

Steve Hitchins in his AC Cobra at Brands Hatch in May 1981

Roger Ealand took his Marcos GT to the Classic Sports Car title and racing newcomer Michael Schryver claimed the Post-Historic Road Sports Championship title in his debut season of racing in his Lotus Elan. Michael Bowler won the Historic Car Championship in his Lister Jaguar.

In 1981 the club played a part in the history of the Croft circuit in North Yorkshire. On Sunday 25 October was the final meeting before the circuit closed for racing and the organising club, the BRSCC, closed the meeting with a race form Historic Open Cars, aimed largely at HSCC members but also including local character Keith Schellenberg in his 1930s Bentley. It was a handicap race and the Bentley had three laps and 70 seconds head start over the scratch man, Tony Steele in his Formula Junior Lola Mk2. However, Mike Harrison's Brabham BT2 bounced back from a troubled qualifying session to win the race from the Bentley.

Moving into the 1980s, Brian Cocks had been clear on the direction needed for the club and set about

THE 1981 HSCC RACING CHAMPIONS
Classic Sports Car Championship
Roger Ealand (Marcos 1800GT)
Group 4 Historic GT Championship
John Foulston (McLaren M1B)
Post-Historic Road Sports Championship
Michael Schryver (Lotus Elan)
Historic Car Championship
Michael Bowler (Lister Jaguar)

increasing revenue to allow more professional input into running the club and its race meetings.

In the November 1981 edition of 'Recent History', Cocks explained the position. *"Motor sport in the 1980s is becoming a 'professionals only' area. To maintain our members' place as amateur participants the HSCC must organise professionally. To that end your committee has reviewed our administrative structure and is planning an improved system of operation.*

MICHAEL SCHRYVER

Racer with the club for more than 30 years

"I started racing with the HSCC in 1981; I was in my Lotus Elan and Simon Hadfield was in his Elan. We'd never met before. He was very cross because I turned up in my furniture van and he thought that was like a sort of transporter. What he didn't realise is that I couldn't afford a trailer, so I stuck the car in the back of the van. We raced against each other all year and became very good friends, and have been ever since.

"I won the Post Historic Road Sports title in my first season. I remember in my first race coming up behind a Jaguar and thinking I didn't want to overtake it in case they thought I was cheating. It was brilliant then.

"We moved on to a Lotus 23 which wasn't so good. I bought that from Brian Cocks, who was HSCC chairman. Then we got the Chevron B6, which we still have and later on won the 2-litre Historic GT title a couple of times. We moved to a Formula 2 Lotus 69, and won a championship in that. Simon raced it the year before while I was racing the Chevron.

"Then I had a Lotus 72 Grand Prix car to do the early stages of Thoroughbred Grand Prix and won the title in 1996 when it was run by the HSCC. I had to go down to Monaco to get my prize from the FIA, next door to Damon Hill who won the World Championship that season. So that was very good.

"I raced a Chevron B16 with Group 4 but I've always raced with the HSCC as well. I have a lot of fun with the HSCC. The Guards Trophy is the most reasonably priced series and prices haven't gone up as much as the other historic race series; it is such good value for money. The atmosphere is the best."

"It is no longer possible to find volunteers with sufficient spare time to cope with the requirements of running race meetings and championships, produce the Newsletter, answer daily queries from members, obtain sponsorship, etc, etc. The answer is for the club to create income from its activities to pay for the time and services of a full time organiser. To this end we are to increase our activities and our sponsorship involvement for the ultimate benefit of our members and to ensure survival of the HSCC into the 1990s."

Cocks was able to announce sponsorship for the 1982 season, notably from John Foulston's Atlantic Computers business which offered major backing for the Historic GT Championship. Part of the package was start money for the competitors and a round of the championship would be held as a support race to the British Grand Prix at Brands Hatch on 17/18 July.

Lloyds and Scottish confirmed renewed support for the Historic Car Championship in 1982 with more rounds and increased support while racer Alex Seldon pledged backing for the Classic Sports Car Championship through his air conditioning business.

The Post Historic Road Sports Championship was building support and a new Pre '65 Single Seater Championship was added to the racing portfolio. As well as the Donington international weekend on 31 July/1 August, the club's race meeting schedule was extended to include a date at Snetterton (20 June) and a joint event at Brands Hatch with the new Brands Hatch Racing Club (26 September).

The 1982 season was clearly the club's most ambitious to date with five championships. The season started with the opening Atlantic Computers round on the Silverstone Grand Prix circuit on 20/21 March, as a support race to the opening round of European Formula 2 Championship.

By March 1982 some of the club's officials had changed with Cocks taking an extended role to cover Newsletter Editor and at least some of the secretarial work as well as Chairman. Jem Marsh was now vice-chairman and Neville Heath was club treasurer. Peter Dixon remained as chief registrar while Jeremy Hall was now public relations officer and Richard Dodkins was sprint and hillclimb secretary. Eric Hall had taken

THE 1982 HSCC RACING CHAMPIONS

Classic Sports Car Championship
John Brindley (Lotus 23B)
Historic GT Championship
Richard Thwaites (Chevron B6)
Pre '65 Single Seater Championship
Mike Littlewood (BRM P261/Brabham BT2/Cooper T56)
Post-Historic Road Sports Championship
John Atkins (AC Cobra)
Historic Car Championship
Mike Salmon (Aston Martin DBR2)

on the role of social secretary and David and Pat Dawson filled the two remaining committee posts.

The Donington international Weekend featured 16 races and notable winners from Saturday's races included Alan Minshaw who won the Seldon Classic Sports Car Championship round in his Lotus 23B from the rare Ginetta G10 of Tony Hill. The Historic Sports and Single-Seater grid included racing veterans Arthur Mallock and John Pearson, while Ian Giles (Lola T212)

beat Richard Budge (Chevron B8) in the Bellini Models 2-litre Historic GT Championship round from a field that included Simon Hadfield (Lotus 47), Ray Bellm (Chevron B8), Don Cressy (Chevron B8) and David Beckett in the Astra GT.

John Atkins topped the Post Historic Road Sports in his AC Cobra while John Brindley (in the Atlantic Computers-entered McLaren M1C) narrowly headed Ted Williams (March 707) in a slender nine-car field for the Atlantic Computers Historic GT round. Brindley added a second win in the Historic Grand Prix car race in the John Foulston-entered McLaren M19A. Sunday's programme suffered several small grids, none more so than the eight-car field for the FISA Trophy Race for small-engined 1950s sports-racers.

For 1983, the club's racing programme had grown to five race meetings and six national championships. The HSCC now catered for cars up to 1971. However, it was also apparent that the club's finances were still precarious despite the sponsorship revenue generated by the racing programme. In the spring of 1983, 'Recent History' editor George Rance gave some more details.

In his editorial, Rance said: *"This issue may come as a little late but this is due in part to club finances. It has*

SIMON HADFIELD

Long-standing racer and board member

"I started racing on April 4 1981 at Silverstone in a Post-Historic Road Sports race in a Lotus Elan with Michael Schryver, who was in his Elan. It was the first time I ever met Michael and we're still huge mates today. The series allowed me to go racing in a car I could run on the road.

"That was before there were historic race meetings. It was a special time; very naïve and innocent by modern standards. I did a year with the Elan and was fortunate enough that there were still cars around that you could buy quite cheaply so I bought my Lotus 47 which we still own. I think I paid £800 for it, though it was in a bit of a

bad way. I raced the Lotus 47 in 1982 and Michael then bought a Lotus 23, which we shared.

"Everything I do today, my business and my sport, has really grown from the HSCC and I'm delighted to have seen the HSCC prosper through the years. I love the club's tag line, 'pure historic racing'. It's one of the few clubs run by the competitor for the competitor, where the worst evils of our sport haven't got in. I love the even playing field and the fun.

"More recently there was a fabulous Historic Formula Ford race at Silverstone and the podium was Westie Mitchell and his lad Ben, Nelson Rowe and his dad and Benn Simms and his dad. That there was the HSCC and that's what mattered; fathers and sons coming together for sport. There are some people within the HSCC who are worth their weight in gold!"

now been decided to produce two issues of Recent History each year and this is the first of the 1983 pair,

all of which will contain the increased number of pages to 48 as introduced last year." Rance also alluded to problems behind the scenes with the curious comment that: *"The HSCC is a good club, although it may be some way from ideal."*

SPRING 1983

A headline date of the 1983 season for the Atlantic Computers Historic GT Championship was the race at the British Grand Prix at Silverstone on 16 July, which predictably drew a capacity grid. Unfortunately, the return of John Brindley in the sponsor's McLaren M1B was short-lived as a mechanical problem pitched the car off at Stowe and it was significantly damaged. The race was a thriller as Michael Wheatley won in the BRM P154 after a final corner battle with Ted Williams in the March 707.

The International weekend at Donington was now one of the biggest events of its type on the calendar and the 1983 meeting drew over 400 entries for 18 races. The Atlantic Computers round featured a superb

38-car grid, which was split across two races, to demonstrate just how popular the championship had become.

Foulston was racing a McLaren M8C and was on his way to becoming a significant figure in the HSCC story of the mid-1980s, having become club treasurer in 1983. Ted Williams, in the mighty ex-Chris Amon March 707 Can-Am car, just beat Foulston to the flag in the race for the bigger-engined cars. The race for the less powerful cars featured another businessman who would become very important in the club story as Richard Budge won in his Chevron B8 after prolific racer Ray Bellm retired his B8 with overheating issues.

Bellm, who had started racing a couple of years earlier, also raced a Chevron B19 in the other Atlantic

---

Computers race and would later go on to win the C2 category of the World Sportscar Championship and serve as chairman of the British Racing Drivers' Club.

Other winners over the July weekend at Donington included John Atkins who won the Post Historic Road Sports race in his AC Cobra from Roger Connell's TVR. The grid for the Pre-1965 Single Seater Championship, sponsored by Freight Media, was depleted by the pair of non-starting Lotus 24s for John Foulston and his wife Mary while Bellm took victory in the Bellini Models Historic Sports Car Championship in his Lotus XI, his third car of the weekend. Mark Hales raced the mighty Attila Chevrolet to win the Seldon Trophy Race, a round of the Classic Sports Car Championship.

As well as several FIA races, Sunday's programme featured a race for 'historically interesting' Formula 1 cars but worsening weather limited the grid to just five starters after several cars were withdrawn following moments during two warming-up laps. John Brindley, in a Tyrrell 007 from Nick Mason's stable, won the shortened race from Mike Littlewood (Brabham BT42/44) and John Foulston (McLaren).

AUTUMN 1983

In autumn 1983, Cocks reported on the club's progress in the 44th issue of Recent History. *"When I was elected chairman in 1979 the HSCC had never run its own race meetings and it was my 'ticket' to undertake this operation and to re-organise HSCC racing. Five years later I am now organising five historic race meetings each year including a two-day international which is the biggest historic race meeting in the world, have established six national historic championships and negotiated and organised the 8 to 12 race programme for each of them. Quite a five-year plan, and undoubtedly what the members want, as witnessed by a substantial growth in membership."*

Cocks also noted that the club had more or less abandoned attempts to run social events and concours, which had previously been a significant element of club activity. Clearly, race and championship organisation was now the club's prime focus and marked a significant move away from the club activity of the 1970s. Cocks concluded: "Thus it seems that the Historic Sports Car Club is established as Britain's premier historic racing club and will continue its evolution along that path."

The club's 1984 racing programme started at Donington Park in April for a one-day event, moved to Brands Hatch in June for a joint-event with the Brands Hatch Racing Club, took in the two-day Donington

event in July and wrapped up at Snetterton at the end of September.

The club's seven championships featured rounds at a number of meetings organised by other clubs and, commendably, all seven had series sponsors. The full portfolio for 1984 was the Bellini Models Historic Sports Car Championship, the Rolatruc Classic Sports Car Championship, the Freight Media Pre '65 Single-Seater Championship, the John Lelliott Post Historic Road Sports Championship, the Bradburn & Wedge Pre '71 Single-Seater Championship, the Atlantic Computers Historic GT Championship and the Proflex Trophy Races for Historically Interesting Formula 1 Cars.

The 1984 International Weekend at Donington Park ran in soaking wet conditions and the slower lap times played havoc with a timetable designed around races over a set number of laps.

David Franklin's McLaren M6B at Snetterton, October 1983

Malcolm Ricketts was a winner at Donington in July 1984

International entries came to Donington Park in July 1984

John Foulston's Lotus in the rain of Donington

DON HANDS

Former vice-chairman

"I was an architect and my two business partners were vintage Bentley collectors and the Bentley Drivers' Club used to have a practice day at Silverstone. One day my partner asked me if I'd like to have a go round. I'm a died-in-the-wool Lotus fanatic so I took my Elan round Silverstone and by the time I came in I knew what I wanted to do with my life.

"I started racing in 1981 at an AMOC meeting at Brands, which was shared with the HSCC. It was such a friendly club and I was given a set of tyres because it frightened everyone to death that I was racing on Michelin ZXs. A chap called John Jarvis, who was Road Sports champion several times, gave me a set of used Dunlop R5 tyres: 'at least you won't get in our way then'. So I went out at the next meeting on these Dunlops and ran the bearings because I hadn't got a baffled sump. But that's how you learn.

"The Improved Road Sports class went from strength to strength at the time and covered 1960s and 1970s cars, but was really for 1960s. I knew Peter Dixon, the registrar, professionally and was soon on the Road Sports committee. I was given the job of trying to find sponsorship and pulled in John Lelliott to start with and then Richardson Hosken. That helped to lift the profile and we also started 70s Road Sports as an off-shoot of IRS. I was club vice-chairman for quite a while with Nick Overall.

"I remember driving down to the club office at Chippenham when Brian Cocks was in charge and just after he'd gone looking at the books and finding that we couldn't pay the wages on Friday. So it was hands in pockets time. It was that tight."

"I was very keen on endurance racing and the first race we did was the Snetterton three-hours, probably in the late 1980s. That was the catalyst for the Spa six-hours, so the HSCC was in at the start of endurance historic racing. My son Simon then raced the original Elan. I did very little racing when the recession hit as we had to focus on business and I stood down from club role.

"I'm now a scrutineer and I feel that giving something back is important. The club was a huge part of my life. I love the club and I think it has done fantastic things for historic racing. I had a great time!"

Champion in the 1984 Atlantic Computers Historic GT Championship was John Brindley in the Foulston-owned McLaren M1C. Jem Marsh won the Pre '60 title in his early Marcos GT and a later Marcos, in the hands of Roger Ealand, won the Classic Sports Championship for the second time in four years. Tony Steele claimed the Pre '65 Single-Seater crown in his Lola Mk5 and John Ward's diminutive Honda D800 topped the Road Sports. Finally, Jim Wallis was the first Pre '71 Single-Seater champion in his Brabham BT30.

As the 1984 season drew to a close, Peter Dixon resigned his post of chief registrar and was made a club life member in honour of his contribution. The initial plan from the club committee was not to replace him, but devolve some of his responsibilities to the individual championship sub-committees.

THE 1984 HSCC RACING CHAMPIONS

Pre '60 Historic Sports Championship
Jem Marsh (Marcos GT)
Classic Sports Car Championship
Roger Ealand (Marcos 1800GT)
Historic GT Championship
John Brindley (McLaren M1C)
Pre '65 Single Seater Championship
Tony Steele (Lola Mk5)
Post-Historic Road Sports Championship
John Ward (Honda S800)
Pre '71 Single Seater Championship
Jim Wallis (Brabham BT30)

5
1985 to 1989
The Foulston legacy

Pre '66 saloon car action at Brands Hatch in 1985

In the club's January 1985 newsletter, chief executive Brian Cocks announced that Atlantic Computers would be investing a six-figure sum into a Pre '65 Historic Grand Prix Championship over a three-year term. He reported tremendous competitor interest and also confirmed that Failsafe, another computer leasing company, would take over as title sponsors for the Historic GT Championship.

In 1985, the HSCC organised four race meetings, covering five days of racing. The season started with a one-day meeting at Oulton Park in May and then took in the two-day Historic International Weekend which moved from Donington Park to Brands Hatch for the weekend of 8/9 June. Then there was a long summer break before back-to-back events at Silverstone and

Snetterton in September. The Snetterton schedule included the Pre '65 endurance race.

The race meeting on the Silverstone club circuit was the first HSCC-organised event at what would later come to be the club's home venue and the day was supported by Atlantic Computers.

The Brands Hatch weekend included races for the Failsafe Historic GT Championship, an Historic F1 race supported by Waspeze, the Atlantic Computers Pre '65 Grand Prix Cars and several FIA races. Among the F1 pack was John Foulston's ex-Regazzoni Ferrari 312, Colin Poole's ex-Hunt McLaren M23 and John Brindley in a Foulston-entered McLaren M19.

The large Historic GT entry was headed by race winner Ted Williams in the vast March 707 from Ray Bellm's hard-charging Chevron B19 and David Franklin's McLaren M6B. Further down the field, current Zakspeed Grand Prix driver Jonathan Palmer raced the Aston Martin-engined Lola T70 Mk3B.

The annual cost of membership had risen to £20 for the 1985 season and the cost of the magazine 'Recent History' was a considerable expense for the club. Racer Alex Seldon took on the role of advertising manager for the magazine, while George Rance continued as editor and Ray Stewart was named as the club's race photographer.

Malcolm Ricketts in his Lotus 22 at Silverstone, September 1985

A rare Cooper T84 racing at Silverstone, 1985

The Lotus 22 of Bob Woodward at Silverstone, September 1985

Alex Seldon in his F5000 Lola T300 in September 1985

Richard Budge leads Richard Dodkins and Tim Goss in Chevron B8s

THE 1985 HSCC RACING CHAMPIONS

Pre '60 Historic Sports Championship
Peter Walker (Lola Mk1)
Classic Sports Car Championship
Tony Thompson (Lotus Elan 26R)
Historic GT Championship
Nigel Hulme (Lola T70 Mk3B)
Pre '65 Single Seater Championship
John Narcisi (Brabham BT6)
Post-Historic Road Sports Championship
John Atkins (AC Cobra)
Pre '71 Single Seater Championship
John Foulston (McLaren M19A)

For 1985, David Duffy took over as club chairman as Brian Cocks moved to the new role of chief executive, with a relevant change in remuneration. However, Duffy would serve only one year in the post before former vice-chairman Jem Marsh took over. Duffy had been racing a Jaguar D-type but switched to an ex-Rob Walker Connaught Grand Prix car.

John Foulston was now carrying out the role of club treasurer and Rob Grant handled public relations. Another new committee member was Ray Bellm in the office of club records and trophies while committee members with responsibility for specific groups of cars were Eric Hall (sports and sports-racers), Alan Putt (pre-1960 single-seaters), Jeremy Hall (post-historic road sports), Patricia Dawson (Historic GT) and David McLaughlin (pre-1970 single-seaters).

The club's committee structure was further developed for 1986 with the creation of championship chairmen roles. The Pre '60 Single-Seaters group was chaired by High Clifford and Alan Putt was registrar while John Charles and John Narcisi were the driver representatives.

Peter Walker was chairman for the Pre '60 Sports Cars, Eric Hall was registrar and driver representatives were Tim Burrett and Ken Rogers. Marcos GT racers headed up the Classic Sportscar Championship, chaired by Barry Sewell. Robin Longdon was registrar and Roger Ealand and Tony Thompson were the driver representatives.

The Post Historic Road Sports group included chairman David Barraclough, registrar Bob Pomeroy and drivers Roger Connel, Don Hands, Ian Pearce and John Ward.

Looking after the interests of the Pre '71 Single-Seater group were David McLaughlin (chairman), Alan Putt (registrar) and driver representatives Mary Foulston and Martin Steele. McLaughlin was also registrar for the Historic GT Championship, which was chaired by Pat Dawson with Chris Aylett and Martin Colvill as driver representatives. The 2-litre division of Historic GT was chaired by Don Cressy with Richard Dodkins as registrar and Peter Alderman as the drivers' representative.

In total, 36 people were named as club officials although the main committee numbered only 12 and the club office was at Brian Cocks' house, West

Historic GT variety at Snetterton, September 1985

PHRS winner Tony Ingram (Ginetta G4) at Snetterton, 29 September 1985

Tim Cairns (Lister Jaguar) in the Pre '60 race at Snetterton

Lodge at Norton near Malmesbury in Wiltshire. He had previously lived at Minsterworth near Gloucester, where he had initially run the club office.

The club's 1986 schedule was largely unchanged over previous seasons and included race meetings at Oulton Park, Brands Hatch GP, Silverstone and Snetterton. However, new was a press and test day on the Silverstone Grand Prix circuit in April and a first HSCC-organised hillclimb at Wiscombe Park in Devon in mid-October.

Sadly, the Wiscombe hillclimb was poorly supported by competitors and the event was not repeated. Just 28 cars gathered at the scenic venue for two practice runs and up to five timed runs. Richard Brown needed only four runs to claim fastest time of the day in 40.33s and win the Church Green Engineering Trophy from Dr Roger Willoughby (March DG84) in 40.84s and Bill Morris (March) in 40.85s. Class winners were Clive Richards (Frazer Nash Le Mans Replica) with a best climb of 51.77s and Paul Channon (AC Cobra) in 45.22s. Regular racers who took part included Stephen Curtis (Jaguar D-type), Terry Sanger (Healey Silverstone), Julian Balme (Lotus Elan +2) and Martin Steele (March 702).

New for the 1986 season was the Historic GT Championship for up to 2-litre cars. As interest in the main Historic GT Championship continued to build, and bring out more and more 5-litre and 7-litre cars, the club formed a stand-alone 2-litre championship

which also enjoyed support, albeit only for 1986, from Atlantic Computers. The inaugural champion was Simon Hadfield in Michael Schryver's Chevron B6, who was closely pursued by Frank Sytner.

The club's racing year opened with a one-day meeting at Oulton Park in May and, remarkably, the Pre '71 Single-Seater Championship featured two Lotus 72s in the five-car entry list with cars for Mary Foulston and David McLaughlin.

Among those entered at Oulton Park, some were still racing 30 years later including Sid Hoole (Cooper Monaco), John Harper (Cooper), Robin Longdon (Lotus Elan) and Ted Williams (Lola T160). Michael Schryver (Chevron B6) and George Douglas (Ginetta G12) were still racing the same cars three decades on.

The big event of the club year in 1986 was the Atlantic Computers International Historic Weekend on the Brands Hatch Grand Prix circuit on 31 May/1 June. To celebrate his recent acquisition of Brands Hatch, Oulton Park and Snetterton for £5.25million, Foulston threw a party in the Brands Hatch Kentagon on the Saturday night of the race weekend and all HSCC members were invited.

When Eagle Star Holdings announced plans to sell the tracks, it received many approaches and not all of them would have preserved the venues for motor racing. Fortunately, it was decided that John Webb, long-time manager of the operation, would be given

April 1986: a Lotus Elan Road Sports battle at Silverstone

The BRM P154 of Mike Wheatley heads the Historic GT pack at Brands in June 1986

September 1986: Jim Wallis (McLaren M8E) at Silverstone

Silverstone 1986: March 702 versus Lotus 69

Mallock U2 and Brabham battle into Woodcote Corner at Silverstone

the opportunity to find a financial backer to ensure the tracks remained. Webb approached Foulston and a deal was done, thus ensuring the tracks remained active and critical to the on-going health of the sport in Britain. Webb managed the tracks until 1990 when Foulston's daughter Nicola took control.

As well as a full line-up of HSCC championships for the Brands Hatch weekend, guest races for the FISA Trophy, FISA GT Cup and Steigenberger Hotels Trophy gave the event international status. The Steigenberger race was a round of the International Super Sports Cup, which would ultimately absorb the HSCC's Atlantic Computers GT Championship and the Brands Hatch entry comprised most of the regular HSCC entry from both the Atlantic Computers and 2-litre GT series. Overseas visitors amounted to just four German drivers, however. The FISA GT Cup had grown significantly, with a 50-car entry from all over Europe.

THE 1986 HSCC RACING CHAMPIONS

Pre '60 Historic Sports Championship
Denis Welch (Austin-Healey 100/6)
Classic Sports Car Championship
Tony Thompson (Lotus Elan 26R)
Historic GT Championship
David Franklin (McLaren M6B)
HSCC 2-Litre GT Championship
Simon Hadfield (Chevron B6)
Pre '65 Single Seater Championship
John Jarvis (Brabham BT14)
Post-Historic Road Sports Championship
Roger Connel (TVR Griffith)
Pre '71 Single Seater Championship
John Foulston (McLaren M19A)

At Silverstone on 13 September, the race for 'Historically Interesting Formula 1 cars' featured 10 cars from eight manufacturers including the two-year old turbocharged Toleman TG184 of Pete Hammond.

The 1986 season ended on a controversial note, but not on a racing topic. The club's annual dinner dance featured some behaviour that was considered inappropriate involving shaving foam and soda syphons, but it was a performance from a stripper that caused the most outrage, albeit without the prior knowledge of club officials. Strong letters in the next newsletter showed the scale of offence caused and prompted a letter from club chairman Jem Marsh to re-assure members that such events would not be repeated.

New for the 1987 season was the introduction of a racing membership fee at an additional £15 on top of standard membership. In his editorial in the December 1986 newsletter, Brian Cocks noted that the club office was now mailing over 20,000 items of mail each year and the new charge would help cover ever-increasing postal charges.

The 50th edition of Recent History was published in the spring of 1987, which would prove to be a pivotal year in the club story. New for the 1987 racing season was the Novice Championship supported by Classic and Sportscar Magazine. Aimed at newcomers in road sports cars produced between 1960 and 1970, the new series fulfilled a clear gap in the market as a place where novice racers could get started in a less-pressured environment and it would run for five seasons before the pool of potential newcomers dwindled to uneconomic levels. However, in those five seasons from 1987 to 1991, the Novice Championship introduced dozens of drivers to historic racing and many of them went on to race extensively with the club.

For 1987, Cocks laid on a slightly enlarged racing schedule with club race meetings at Oulton Park (in May and August), Brands Hatch GP, Donington Park, Silverstone and Snetterton. The two day international event at Brands on 6/7 June was once more the season highlight.

June 1987: Lola T210 and McLaren M6B in Historic GT

Road Sports battle: Lotus Europa, Datsun 240Z and Lotus Elan

Ted Williams (McLaren M8C) in Historic GTs at Brands, 1987

June 1987: Classic Sports action at Druids at Brands Hatch

The Hon Andrew Fellowes (Brabham BT30) at Silverstone in 1987

Paul Weldon's TVR Griffith in Post-Historic Road Sports, 1987

Classic Sports action with a Marcos GT and MGA

1-litre F3 cars raced in the Pre '65 Single-Seater Championship in 1987

Ted Williams and David Franklin battle in the rain at Silverstone

Tony Mitchell (MGC) and Roy Jordan (Chevrolet Corvette)

The Historic GT Championship again had a round at the British Grand Prix at Silverstone over the weekend of 10/11 July, with extended backing from Atlantic Computers. Meanwhile, company boss John Foulston had added Cadwell Park to his portfolio of tracks.

Other news for the 1987 season included new sponsorship for the Classic Sports Car Championship from Guildford Estates, the company of racer Nick Overall. The sponsorship was primarily aimed at promoting the Muscular Dystrophy Group, which was a charity close to Nick and his family.

September 1987: Cyril Baxter (Marcos) at the Snetterton Bombhole

John Foulston at Silverstone in his McLaren M8F

Roly Nix (Chevron B8) leads the 2-litre GT race at Snetterton

John Foulston racing the M19 at Snetterton

The Pre '65 Single Seater Championship was expected to grow following the addition of a class for Historic F3 cars and a further 10 cars were due to join the grid. Remarkably, 200 people applied for details of the new Novice Championship and a dedicated test day was arranged for them at Castle Combe in early April. The club's main press and test day was 10 days later on the Silverstone Grand Prix circuit.

The novice championship was a great success in its inaugural season, with 27 drivers scoring points as Ronnie Farmer took the overall title in his TVR Griffith

with a straight run of six wins. Other novices enjoying their first season of racing included Rory Fordyce (Ferrari 246 and 330), Allan Cameron (Austin Healey) and Lotus Elan racers Tim Wright and Chris Holland.

Tragically, the club's 1987 racing season was darkly overshadowed by the death of John Foulston when testing a McLaren M15 Indy car at Silverstone on Tuesday 29 September. It appears that he had been having problems with the 900bhp Offenhauser engine cutting out and it then re-fired and the throttle stuck open. The car plunged off the track at Club Corner

Foulston in the M8F two days before his death

and Foulston died instantly. It is clear that Foulston made a major contribution to the development of the HSCC; as a racer and a championship sponsor as well as a club benefactor.

The club's races for Historic GT, 2-litre Historic GT and Pre '71 Single Seaters planned for the annual Silverstone finals' meeting at the end of the week were cancelled as a mark of respect. Two days before his death, Foulston clinched the club's Historic GT Championship title with another win at Snetterton in his McLaren M8D.

Foulston had been a controversial figure in the computer industry, having founded Atlantic Computers in 1975. He built it into the UK's biggest computer leasing company and by 1987 pre-tax profits had hit £40 million. His business success allowed Foulston to indulge in his passion for historic race cars and he owned an extensive collection of cars, many of which he raced.

John and Mary Foulston

In a letter to the club office on 1 August 1987, less than two months before his death, Foulston spoke about his plans for the 1988 racing season. He had ordered a new Spice Fiero DFL for use in the World Endurance Championship with Mike Wilds and John Brindley sharing the driving. He also planned to continue racing his McLaren M8D in the Historic GT Championship, which would again be sponsored by Atlantic Computers. Sadly, those plans were never realised.

Brian Cocks wrote an obituary in his editorial for the October 1987 club newsletter. "JGF was one of life's winners, as a dedicated, determined competitor and a brilliantly decisive and generous man. He was a great benefactor, who worked hard to earn his fortune, and then used it well. His saving of Brands Hatch will go down in history. His loss to motor racing in general, and the historic scene in particular, is enormous."

During 1987 the club acquired permanent headquarters at Kington Langley near Chippenham in Wiltshire. The building was sited next to the A420 and was only five minutes from junction 17 of the M4. Offices, a conference room and a library were all part of the package and a report in 'Recent History' reported that a recent boom in property prices along the M4 corridor meant that the office had tripled in value almost overnight. This bold claim seems to have later been shown to be rather over optimistic.

THE 1987 HSCC RACING CHAMPIONS

Pre '60 Historic Sports Championship
Denis Welch (Austin-Healey 100/6)
Classic Sports Car Championship
Tony Thompson (Lotus Elan 26R)
Historic GT Championship
John Foulston (McLaren M8D)
HSCC 2-Litre GT Championship
Michael Schryver (Chevron B6)
Pre '65 Single Seater Championship
Chris Smith (Chevron B17)
Post-Historic Road Sports Championship
Kevin Irons (Datsun 240Z)
Novice Championship
Ronnie Farmer (TVR Griffith)
Pre '71 Single Seater Championship
Mike Pendlebury (Lotus 69)

The club's racing portfolio had been the subject of vigorous debate through the middle of 1987 and by early September the club office set out the plan for 1988. The biggest debate had centred on the Road Sports classes, with a proposed split at 1965. However, after a lot of competitor feedback, the Post Historic Road Sports Championship was re-branded as the HSCC Road Sports Championship with two races planned for each event; one for large capacity and plastic-bodied cars and one for metal-bodied cars.

There was also a change in the Pre '60 Championship, which for the 1988 racing season would evolve into a joint promotion between the HSCC and the Aston Martin Owners' Club.

Reporting on 1 December 1987, treasurer Peter Walker explained a profit of £7497 for the 1986 accounting year, down from £12,494 a year earlier. The club's reserves stood at £23,111 at the end of 1986. The support of sponsors was cited as the main reason for a fair financial position and expenses had not grown noticeably. Walker pointed to a stronger result for 1987 following an influx of new members for the Novice Championship and increased sponsorship revenue. "The increased volume of activity and membership will mean a significant rise in expenditure is expected, but I am confident at this stage that the Club's profits and its retained cash deposits will both show a very healthy increase over 1986 levels," concluded Walker.

The income and expenditure account showed just how heavily the club was relying on sponsorship. For 1986, membership fees amounted to £10,348 and race meetings made a loss of £12,393 on an expenditure of £54,310. At a total of £55,871, sponsorship was the over-riding factor in the club's profitability.

The 1988 race programme started at Oulton Park at the end of April and then took in race meetings at Cadwell Park, Brands Hatch GP, Donington Park, Oulton Park, Thruxton (in partnership with the BARC), Silverstone and Snetterton.

By 1988 the club had ownership of eight championships, but that included the Historic F1 Championship which would later evolve into Thoroughbred Grand Prix and break away from the HSCC. Meanwhile, the Pre '60 Historic Car Championship was shared with the Aston Martin Owners' Club and the Atlantic Computers Historic GT Championship was destined to merge with

TREASURER'S REPORT - YEAR ENDED 31st DECEMBER 1986

This month will see the conclusion of my first year as Treasurer of the Historic Sports Car Club, having taken responsibility from John Foulston at the beginning of 1987, which I deemed to be somewhat of an honour.

During the four years of John's holding the financial reins the Club's finances had gone from strength to strength, resulting in the peak profit of £12,494 recorded in 1985. At the December 1986 Annual General Meeting the then Treasurer commented that "the current year should see a profit of at least £10,000 being recorded". This comment turned out to be somewhat optimistic since when John and our Auditors finalised the accounts for 1986 the profit had fallen to £7,497 from the previous years result of £12,494.

The main factors underlying this fall in profits were: A reduction in race income of almost £10,000; lower sales of regalia; a lower amount of bank interest received on deposits; and a provision for doubtful debts of £2,875, which amount has had to be subtracted from 1986 income.

However the good news from 1986 is that the Club's cash deposit balance has increased substantially and the net current assets stood at £23,111 at 31st December.

You will also note from the Annual Income and Expenditure Account that the Club's expenditure did not rise substantially in 1986 over the 1985 level, which is an encouraging trend.

The overall financial result in 1986 was helped substantially by the contributions of the Club's many sponsors and advertising supporters and thanks is due to these companies and individuals for their continued loyalty in supporting the sponsorship of the many championships and events now being organised.

Turning for a moment to the activities and outlook for 1987, the year which is under my own financial control I can see an even stronger picture emerging for the Club in the current year. Membership has risen substantially in 1987 with many of the new members coming from the popular Novices Championship enrolment. More race events were organised in 1987 and income from sponsorship shows a substantial increase this year. The increased volume of activity and membership will mean a significant rise in expenditure is expected, but I am confident at this stage that the Club's profits and its retained cash deposits will both show a very healthy increase over 1986 levels.

Peter Walker
Treasurer

1st December 1987

the pan-European Supersports series and move away from the club.

That left five championships at the heart of HSCC racing. Roadsports, Classic Sports, Pre '65 Racing Cars, Pre '71 Single Seaters and the 2-Litre Championship were the staple diet for 1988.

The pre-season test day was held on 11 April and offered a day on the Silverstone Grand Prix circuit for £48 which, as Cocks pointed out at the time, represented excellent value against regular test day prices that ranged from £55 to £85. The race entry fee for the season-opening race meeting at Oulton Park was £45.

There was reason for optimism as the 1988 season got underway, with nearly 400 registrations for the club's eight championships. Even the Historic Formula 1 Championship, which had struggled for support for a couple of years, was looking more healthy according to championship chairman David McLaughlin, who reported the potential for 20-car grids on a regular basis.

By the spring of 1988 the club officers were working from the new office at Kington Langley with Cocks as chief executive supported by Sue Walton as office manager and Tina Cocks taking on the role of race meeting executive. Peter Walker had taken over the role of treasurer following the death of John Foulston. New for the 1988 season was a John Foulston Memorial Trophy, which would be awarded to the driver scoring the most points across the HSCC championships.

In the early summer of 1988 the seeds for change in Road Sports were being sewn and a drivers' meeting on 24 July gave unanimous support to splitting the Road Sports Championship in two for 1989; one for Standard Road Sports and one for Improved Road Sports, which would run to the existing Road Sports regulations. The new Standard category would be for cars in very much production specification and other ideas floated at the meeting were to impose a ban on trailers and mandate road tyres only for the Standard category. In fact, these were the norm for the Novice championship and for 1989 the rules for the Standard Road Sports Championship did indeed mirror those for the successful novice series.

By the late summer of 1988, there was a wind of change at the head of the club. Both chairman Jem Marsh and treasurer Peter Walker confirmed that they would be resigning from their posts at the Annual General Meeting on 4 December. The retiring main committee announced that it would unanimously recommend Don Cressy for the role of chairman.

On the track, the 1988 season delivered plenty of good racing from generally strong grids. Bodo Linhoff had an exemplary season to win the Classic & Sportscar Novice title in his Lotus Elan, though Chris Pearce (MGC) ran him close on points and Geoff Ironside twice headed Linhoff in the battle of the Elans.

Kevin Irons moved from the Post Historic Road Sports title in 1987 to win the John Lelliott-supported Road Sports crown in '88 in his Datsun 240Z from the similar car of Dave Jarman, while Roger Connel's TVR Griffith headed Aidan Mills-Thomas (AC Cobra) in the big banger class.

Over 40 drivers scored points in the Classic Championship, including Gerry Marshall and Bob Birrell in MGBs, Simon Hadfield in a Lotus Elite and drivers like John Chatham and Roly Nix in Austin Healeys. Denis Welch over-steered his Healey 100/6 to the first of three Classic titles but was matched for points by Tony Thompson's Lotus Elan 26R. Thompson had won three titles in a row from 1985 to 1987.

Support for the joint HSCC/AMOC Pre '60 Historic Car Championship remained patchy and hit a low in September when only four drivers scored points at Thruxton. Other rounds enjoyed better grids, but the picture was still not rosy as David Beckett (Lister Chevrolet) won the crown with a race to spare.

The Pre '65 Racing Car Championship covered both single-seaters and sports cars as well as a class for Historic F3 cars and it was Lotus 23B racer Steve Hitchins who won the title as Mike Freeman (Brabham BT14) and Peter Farrer (Lotus 22) headed the single-seater classes. The Pre '71 Single Seater Championship

THE 1988 HSCC RACING CHAMPIONS

Historic Formula 1 Championship
Don Wood (Arrows A3)
Pre '60 Historic Sports Championship
David Beckett (Lister Chevrolet)
Classic Sports Car Championship
Denis Welch (Austin-Healey 100/6)
Historic GT Championship
Colin Pool (Chevron B19)
HSCC 2-Litre GT Championship
Michael Schryver (Chevron B6)
Pre '65 Single Seater Championship
Steve Hitchins (Lotus 23B)
Road Sports Championship
Kevin Irons (Datsun 240Z)
Novice Championship
Bodo Linhoff (Lotus Elan)
Pre '71 Single Seater Championship
John Beasley (Lola T300)

covered F1, F2 and F5000 cars with John Beasley's Lola T300 scooping the title, with chief executive Brian Cocks second in the F5000 class in his rare Crossle 15F.

The 2-litre GT Championship had a good season with the overall title going to the former F100 Royale RP4 of Martin Edgerton. At the head of the races, Richard Dodkins (Chevron B6) was the best of 18 such cars in Class A. In the Atlantic Computers Historic GT Championship, Colin Pool (Chevron B19) took the title from Class C as Richard Eyre (McLaren M8C) topped the bigger cars.

In all, 15 Historic F1 cars raced during the season in their championship and it was Don Wood (Arrows A3) who won the title from Tony Gordon and Urs Eberhardt in Williams FW08s. Others to race during the season included Fredy Kumschick (Lotus 81B), Alo Lawler (McLaren M30), David McLaughlin (Tyrrell 012 and March 711) and Richard Peacock (Surtees TS9B).

Little more than a year after the death of John Foulston, the club lost another key figure when treasurer Peter Walker died suddenly at only 46 years of age. His death, three days before the annual dinner dance in early December 1988 was described by Brian Cocks as an 'unbelievable bombshell'. Walker had joined the club in 1982 to race a Jaguar E-type and later won the FIA European Historic Championship in a

May 1988: Novice Championship Lotus Elan of Bodo Linhoff at Cadwell Park

Tony Thompson's Classic Championship Elan at Cadwell Park

The Novice field heads into Coppice at Cadwell Park in 1988

September 1988: George Douglas (Ginetta G12) at Silverstone

A Classic Sports Car Championship Morgan in the Silverstone rain

Steve Hitchins (Lotus 23B) won the 1988 Pre '65 title when sports-racing cars were admitted

A rare Costin-Nathan running in the Classic Championship

The ex-Mike Hailwood Surtees TS9 F1 car at Silverstone in 1988

Brabham versus Lotus in the Pre '65 Championship

Roger Connell's Road Sports TVR Griffiths

Formula 5000 McLaren versus Formula 2 March in September 1988

Lola Mk1. At the time of his death, Walker was further expanding his extensive business commitments and Cocks noted that: 'his death brings a sad lesson to us all not to over extend ourselves.'

The Annual General Meeting followed on the day after the dinner dance and, as Cocks reported, was a very muted affair in the absence of the treasurer. "Jeremy Hall's annual attack on the Committee brought only a numbed response from the rostrum," said Cocks in the club newsletter. The new club officers were duly elected as Don Cressy (chairman), Mike Freeman (vice-chairman) and Ray Hunter (treasurer). Topics discussed at the AGM included the question of the club becoming a limited company and the motion that all championship rounds should be run over a minimum distance of 10 laps. The new committee pledged to consider both ideas.

As the 1989 racing season opened there was uproar that the RACMSA had approved a recommendation from circuit owners that certain historic classes should be silenced. While the club's road sports classes were already silenced to MOT regulations, the move to extend silencing into other historic classes caused a furore. History shows that the matter was later resolved to the reasonable acceptance of the historic racing community.

JOHN JARVIS

Former champion and friend of Brian Cocks

"I met Brian Cocks in 1973. He was living in Minsterworth in Gloucestershire and we lived near Gloucester as I worked at Birdseye Walls, the ice cream company.

"A chap there knew I was dead keen on racing and his wife was a cleaner for the Cocks. He asked if I wanted to meet Brian as he went racing. I'd done a bit of rallying by then.

"Brian lived in this lovely Victorian house, called Severn Bank, on the side of the River Severn. It had stables, garages and a couple of acres of land going down the river. I met him and we clicked straightaway, but he was the complete opposite to me. As soon as he opened his mouth, he commanded attention and he spoke so well. He was educated at Dulwich College, where his father was a tutor.

"Brian's main income at the time was making fireproof overalls under the Briokay brand. James Hunt came to the house to be measured for his overalls and another time he brought Lord Hesketh with him.

"He was running a Formula 1300 with the 750 Motor Club at the time and was having problems with it and wanted some help. I'd worked on Ford engines so I went and had a look at it. I took it apart four or five times and eventually found out what was wrong with it. So I sorted it out.

"Then he got a Lotus 23B as a bare chassis and a load of bits and he asked me if I could build it up. We built that into a winner and all the time he'd been pushing me into driving and then we had Lotus Elans and that was what I raced mainly. I won a championship in that car. Wherever we went, he paid for me. I always drove it to the races with Sadie and our two sons in the car.

"My wife Sadie worked in the office with Brian and his wife Tina. He was a very charming man. He did an awful lot for the HSCC and didn't get paid a lot for what he did. He was a really good organiser and a brilliant bloke. He never let me down and he got me into racing when I could never have afforded to; he gave me a helmet, overalls and all sorts.

"Next we built a Lotus 30 but that was the worst car I ever drove. It was quite frightening because it twisted so much that it picked the opposite wheel up off the ground. The engines were a problem and he must have blown three up and I blew one up at Silverstone when he insisted I race it even though I told him the engine was knocking.

"Then he bought a Crossle Formula 5000. He always raced as car number 61 as that was the number on his MSA race licence. Later on we did a Ford Mustang to race in Europe and ran it from a converted coach. We went all the way to Paul Ricard with a gearbox problem on the coach which meant we could only do a top speed of 48mph.

"After he finished with the HSCC he went into golf and he did a lot for the Conservative Party, with business dinners at the Houses of Parliament. He lived until he was in his late 70s and stayed living in Wiltshire."

The club's 1989 programme started with the Silverstone GP circuit test day in mid-April and had grown to nine race meetings, including a July visit to the newly-opened Pembrey circuit in South Wales. The Welsh track only hosted its first race meeting in May 1989 after the track was developed on the former RAF airfield, more recently used as a chicken farm.

Heading into the new season, championship registrations were looking healthy and included 36 new drivers for the Novice Championship. Among those destined for a long racing career were Jim Woodley (Jaguar XK140), Matthew Truelove (Triumph GT6), Tim Bryan (Lotus Elan), Philip Nelson (Lotus Elan) and Paul Smeeth (Lotus Elan). The Road Sports registrations included 10 Datsun 240Zs, seven Honda S800s and 18 Lotus Elans.

Nearly 40 drivers registered for the Pre '71 Single Seater Championship before the end of March and a number of them were, or would be, central to the organisation of the club. They included John Harper (March 701), David McLaughlin (March 711), Bob Birrell (March 712), Simon Hadfield (Lotus 69), Nick Overall (Brabham BT35), Lincoln Small (Brabham BT35) and Brian Cocks (Crossle 15F).

Richard Peacock's F1 Tyrrell 010 at Oulton Park in 1989

Ted Williams (Arrows A4) in an Historic F1 race at Oulton Park

Pre '65 Championship variety at Brands Hatch, June 1989

Simon Hadfield in Michael Schryver's F2 Lotus 69 in 1989

THE 1989 HSCC RACING CHAMPIONS

Historic Formula 1 Championship
Richard Peacock (Tyrrell 010)
Classic Sports Car Championship
Tony Thompson (Lotus Elan 26R)
Historic GT Championship
Colin Pool (Chevron B19)
HSCC 2-Litre GT Championship
Michael Schryver (Chevron B6)
Pre '65 Single Seater Championship
Martyn Smith (Brabham BT15)
Standard Road Sports Championship
Bodo Linhoff (Datsun 240Z)
Improved Road Sports Championship
Julian Dodd (Fairthorpe Electron)
Novice Championship
Martin Cliffe (TVR Tuscan)
Pre '71 Single Seater Championship
Rick Hall (McLaren M10B)

Peacock in the F1 Tyrrell, this time at Silverstone in September

Towards the end of the 1989 season, the club' main committee confirmed that it considered December 1971 as the end of the historic period. This kept the club in line with FIA Group G regulations and, by a unanimous vote, it was decided that there would be no extension to the cut-off date for any of the club's championships for at least five years. The only exception was for the Historic Formula 1 Championship, which, from 1990, would be open to all naturally aspirated cars with a maximum capacity of 3-litres, thus removing the more recent turbo cars from the grid.

Two 2-litre Lolas at Silverstone, September 1989

The 1989 on-track activity proved very successful with good support across nine championships, although the club's involvement in the Pre '60 Championship was rested. TVR Tuscan racer Martin Cliffe took the Novice Championship title while former novice champion Bodo Linhoff hopped up to the Standard Road Sports Championship and made it back-to-back titles in his Datsun 240Z. Julian Dodd's rare Fairthorpe Electron clinched the Improved Road Sports title.

Despite having over 30 registered contenders, the Historic Formula 1 Championship struggled to achieve double-figure grids and peaked when 14 cars raced at the Brands Hatch Super Prix round in early June. The series also visited Pembrey on 1 July when eight cars contested what may well be the only Formula 1 race ever held in Wales. Richard Peacock's Tyrrell 010 was the clear title winner.

More than 80 drivers signed up for the Classic Sports Car Championship and Tony Thompson made it four overall titles in five seasons in his Lotus Elan 26R. The Pre '65 Single-Seater Championship was rather less well supported and only the 1-litre F3 class was contested on anything like a regular basis. On his way to the overall title, Martyn Smith won the F3 class in his Brabham BT15 from the BT21B of Robert Baker-Carr.

Nick Overall and Ian Giles in a Pre '71 battle at Oulton Park, 29 July 1989

Preparation ace Rick Hall scooped a perfect score with five wins in his Formula 5000 McLaren M10B to win the Pre '71 title from F2 class winner Simon Hadfield (Lotus 69).

The twin Historic GT championships went to Michael Schryver, who again headed the 2-Litre Championship in his Chevron B6, and Colin Pool who retained the Historic GT title in his Chevron B19. However, support for the former Atlantic Computers series was dwindling as the pan-European Super Sports Cup drew the cars away from the domestic series. The UK season started badly with just six cars at Oulton Park and only picked up a little for the higher profile meetings. For 1990, the Historic GT schedule would be pared back to just three

JOHN BRINDLEY

Successful historic racer and HSCC champion

"In 1979 I had a Lotus 23B and won the first race at the first HSCC meeting at Donington Park. Then in 1980 and 1981 I had the Lotus 22 Formula Junior and the 23B together. They were very good days and that's what I liked to do best and I was very fortunate to be quite successful.

"One year, in 1981 or '82, I picked up six trophies in one night at the awards' dinner; how fortunate was that? I knew Martin Covill very well and John Foulston asked Martin who he would recommend to drive for him. Martin suggested two people and I met John one lunch time. He asked me what my favourite lunch was and I said a cappuccino coffee and a smoked salmon sandwich. He said that's exactly what he liked and about 40 minutes later he said I was going to drive for him. It was a great opportunity and I said I'd do my best.

"John Foulston really resurrected the club. He put a lot of effort, a lot of time and a lot of money into the club. I raced for John for six years up until his death. I raced the Can-Am cars for John and it was fantastic.

"He bought this McLaren M16 and I told him it was lethal. I tested it for him twice. I still get quite upset about it and the day he was killed was the first time he went testing without me. I'd been there every time he went testing. After two years with him, he wouldn't drive a car unless I'd got it set-up to suit his driving style.

"Every car we had set up with the master switch on the same place on the steering wheel and I told him if he ever got into any trouble at all, hit that switch and dip the clutch and then get on the brakes and normally you'll come out okay. But he crashed at Club, which was the fastest corner at Silverstone. If you were brave back then, you didn't even change down for Club.

"When he died, in his safe were five letters and five cheques and his wife Mary said mine wasn't the biggest cheque but it was the nicest letter. It was addressed to 'a dear friend who taught me to race and win'. He was pretty brave and determined to do well. In my opinion he taught the city a few lessons. I was very fortunate to get to know him and race with him."

races, two shared with the 2-Litre Championship and a Donington Park race run in parallel to a round of the International Super Sports Cup.

The year-end accounts for the 12 months to 31 December 1989 showed a modest profit of £1662 compared to a loss of £4631 for the previous year. Membership revenue for 1989 was down a little, while sponsorship income £41,000.

The end of 1989 marked the finish of an era for the club when Brian Cocks left the role of chief executive after four years in the role preceded by six years as chairman.

Nick Overall was on the main committee at the time and recalls that Cocks' departure was simply a financial matter when terms for an extension of his employment could not

be agreed. Although it cast a shadow over his time with the club, there is no doubt that Cocks played a central role in developing the club though the 1980s. When he first became chairman, the club did not organise any race meetings and only had a small number of championships, but when he left his role at the end of 1989, the HSCC was running seven or eight race meetings a year and had a portfolio of nine championships, including the fledgling Historic Formula 1 Championship.

Writing in a newsletter, regular correspondent 'Kermit' paid tribute to Cocks. "It is with some regret that I learned that Brian Cocks was to leave the Club at the end of 1989. Brian, in my mind, has served us well as a race organiser and ambassador outside the Club. A fine disciplinarian, he has fully supported the Club's rules and marshalled fair play within those constraints."

6 1990 to 1996
The Lydon legacy

John Harper (Lola T300) at Oulton Park, May 1990

The new decade began with the club under new management as Steve Lydon was appointed to replace Brian Cocks and he took up his role at the Kington Langley office early in 1990.

Don Cressy introduced Lydon in the January 1990 newsletter. "He has a lot of experience to offer us having been an active member of the BARC South West Centre involved in the running of Gurston Down hill climb and in the negotiations and running of the sprint course in Southampton. Stephen is currently chairman of his centre and was intending to stand for the main BARC council until his appointment with

us. He is well known to John Felix, the Clerk of the Course at our meetings, and is also a personal friend of Autosport's Marcus Pye."

In February, Lydon wrote his first editorial. "My involvement with motor racing spans 18 years, mainly with the BARC. I would freely admit that my knowledge of historic racing is not as broad as that of my predecessor, but I am learning fast!"

Changes for the club's 1990 race programme included dropping one Oulton Park event when the planned date clashed with the BRDC's new historic festival at

Jon Reakes (Surtees TS5) at Oulton Park in May 1990

*May 1990: the Lotus Elan
of Richard Overall*

Silverstone. The 28/29 July event was the first edition of what grew to become the Silverstone Classic. The club also decided not to run its own race meeting at Pembrey, although some of the club's championships were given a slot in the Jaguar Drivers' Club event at the Welsh track. The Brands Hatch Super Prix had a different look as it did not feature rounds of the club championships, but instead offered members with FIA papers for their cars a chance to run in some international races.

The club's full 1990 programme started with the novice test day at Castle Combe and the annual Silverstone test day in April, albeit on the national circuit this time. Race meetings followed at Cadwell Park and Oulton Park in May and then came the Brands Hatch Super Prix in early June. The major Donington Park weekend ran in late July, and included

a Friday test day as well as a celebration of Chevron, and there was then a lengthy gap until one-day events at Silverstone and Snetterton in the autumn.

There was tragedy during the later part of the 1990 season, first when John Saphir suffered a fatal heart attack when driving his Williams FW07 on the Silverstone Grand Prix circuit. Saphir had become a popular club member when racing his Lola T160 in Historic GT races and served on the club's main committee to represent Historic GT. He was just 43 when he died.

Barely a month later, Phil Cooper was killed when testing his Improved Road Sports Lotus Elan at Silverstone the day before the penultimate race meeting of the season. He was a very popular character within Road Sports and was still declared

The McLaren M8F of Charles Agg at Donington Park in 1990

THE 1990 HSCC RACING CHAMPIONS

Historic Formula 1 Championship
Alan Baillie (Penske PC3)
Classic Sports Car Championship
Simon Hadfield (Lotus Elan)
Historic GT Championship
Richard Arnold (Chevron B19)
HSCC 2-Litre GT Championship
Michael Schryver (Chevron B6)
Pre '65 Single Seater Championship
John Narcisi (Brabham BT6)
Standard Road Sports Championship
Simon Park (Lancia Fulvia)
Improved Road Sports Championship
Aidan Mills-Thomas (AC Cobra)
Novice Championship
Guy Evans (Lotus Elan)
Pre '71 Single Seater Championship
Rick Hall (Surtees TS8)

class C champion at the end of the season. Tragically, his brother Barry had succumbed to leukaemia only a couple of months earlier.

Other issues keeping the committee busy through 1990 included a heated debate on the merits of permitting Road Sports competitors to use trailers to get their cars to and from meetings. There were passionate pleas from both sides of the argument. Then, a proposal was received for the club to run some pilot races for 2-litre sports cars from up to 1975. The idea was put forward by Historic F1 racer Don Wood, who also offered sponsorship through his company. In due course, the committee decided not to take the idea forward into 1991 as it went against the decision to limit the club to pre-1972 cars.

Efforts were being made to make the club more attractive to non-racing members in a bid to take membership up to around 1500, while the September 1990 newsletter would be the final one in the current format as plans were unveiled for the launch of a new club magazine, which would replace both the sporadic 'Recent History' magazine and the monthly newsletter.

'Histrionics' was the name for the new magazine and it was launched with the issue of December 1990/January 1991.

1990 Historic F1 champion Alan Baillie receives his awards from Don Cressy (L)

Don Cressy (L) presents Pre '71 Single-Seater champion Rick Hall with a framed photo of his F5000 Surtees

The impressive 40-page four-colour magazine was edited by Steve Lydon and included features, news and advertising.

The 1990 champions included Simon Hadfield who took his Lotus Elan to the Classic Sports title and Michael Schryver who added a fourth 2-Litre GT title in five seasons. Alan Baillie topped the Historic Formula 1 Championship in his Penske PC3 and Richard Arnold won the Historic GT title in his Chevron B19. This would prove to be the final year of the Historic GT

Championship as ever-falling grids made the series economically unworkable.

Simon Park (Lancia Fulvia) and Aidan Mills-Thomas (AC Cobra) won the Road Sports titles and Guy Evans (Lotus Elan) topped the Novices Championship, which included a race debut for Carol Spagg in an Alfa Romeo. However, support for the Novice series was significantly reduced and the feeling was that the great success of the preceding three years had substantially mopped up the available pool of likely novice racers. Single-seater titles went to John Narcisi (Brabham BT6) and Rick Hall (Surtees TS8), but neither the Pre '65 nor the Pre '71 category was particularly well supported.

News for the 1991 season included the club's first away fixture in the form of the Irish Historic Superprix at Mondello Park on 13/14 April. During 1990, the club's Historic Formula 1 and Improved Road Sports Championships visited the Naas circuit and that trip was deemed successful enough for the club to take a full programme of races to the 1.25-mile track. The 1990 Historic F1 race was the first race for Grand Prix cars in Ireland since before the Second World War. In addition, the 1991 event would include a race for the Pre '75 2-Litre Group 6 Challenge, which was to be administered by the club office but not run as a club championship.

Sadly, with a few weeks to go to the planned event, the Mondello weekend had to be cancelled as too few drivers had entered to make it viable. Only around 30 cars were committed to the meeting and it seems that the cost, distance and time involved in getting to the circuit was too much for most club members. The background of the early 1990s recession was cited as a factor in the lack of support.

In May, the club joined forces with the Donington Park promoters, Two Four Sports, to organise a major Formula 1 retrospective race meeting to mark the 25th anniversary of the inception of the 3-litre Formula 1 regulations. Displays, demonstrations and star guests were promised along with a full support programme of HSCC racing. Appearances from Jody Scheckter, Sir Jack Brabham, Denny Hulme and John Surtees were expected.

Another change for 1991 was the re-introduction of a Pre '60 Championship for single-seaters and sports cars after a two-year sabbatical, which would again be jointly organised by the HSCC and AMOC. The new competition secretary of the AMOC was Richard Culverhouse, who filled the slot left by the departure of Alan Putt. Developments included a change of name for the Pre '71 Single-Seater Championship to the Historic Formula Racing Car Championship and the resting of the Pre '65 category after a disappointing season in 1990.

In the early summer of 1991, the club unveiled plans to create a Pre '71 Formula Ford 1600 category. Unlike the existing Pre '74 category, run by the BRSCC, the new series would require cars to run in proper period specification with relevant bodywork and radiator position. The launch of the series was planned to coincide with the 25th anniversary of the creation of Formula Ford, back in 1967. Chris Alford became a prime mover for taking the idea through to the reality of what ultimately became one of the club's most successful categories.

The Donington Formula 1 celebration event ran very well and some of the famous drivers took part in what was supposed to be a steady demonstration run but soon got quite competitive. Jean-Pierre Jarier drove his 1979 Tyrrell 009, Paul Stewart drove Tyrrell 003 on behalf of

Nick Savage in his Road Sports Alfa Romeo Giulia at a 1991 Castle Combe test day

Jack Brabham driving Lincoln Small's Brabham BT35

Donington 3-litre F1 celebration 1991: back row (L-R) Guy Edwards, Jean-Pierre Jarier, Jody Scheckter, Denny Hulme, Bette Hill, Jack Brabham, Derek Bell, Richard Attwood; front row (L-R) Howden Ganley, Brian Henton, Jean-Pierre Beltoise, Paul Stewart

his father Jackie, Jody Scheckter handled a Ferrari 312T3 from Nick Mason's stable and Denny Hulme drove Lorina McLaughlin's McLaren M23. Jack Brabham (aged 65) was due to drive an F1 Brabham but when that car developed problems he was quickly able to switch to Lincoln Small's F2 Brabham BT35. Jean-Pierre Beltoise, Brian Redman, Guy Edwards, Brian Henton, Derek Bell, Richard Attwood and Howden Ganley were all on hand.

"It was a great weekend," said Brabham. "I enjoyed very much catching up with all the old friends and meeting new ones." Hulme, similarly, enjoyed the occasion. "To me it was like a time warp; those present, including the mechanics, just haven't changed."

The club's other major Donington Park race meeting on 21/22 July was a double celebration. On the back of the success of the Chevron theme for the 1990 event, the '91 edition celebrated the Lola marque and 25 years of the HSCC. The focal point of the weekend was a Lola parade spanning as many cars as possible from the company's 33-year story with company

founder Eric Broadley as guest of honour. Guy Griffiths was also invited to the event as a special guest in honour of the 1966 race at Castle Combe that led to the formation of the HSCC.

Club vice-chairman Mike Freeman won the 25th Anniversary Race at Donington in his Lister Costin and accepted an award from Guy Griffiths, who presented a framed photograph of Betty Haig at the wheel of her Frazer Nash.

Towards the end of 1991, the club confirmed that it had applied to the RACMSA for approval to run a Group 6 Championship in 1992. The series of pilot races run in '91 had gone well and the drive of Mike Pendlebury in particular had encouraged a growing number of cars onto the grid. A six-race series was

Jeremy Broad (L) and Guy Griffiths at Donington in 1992

Historic F1 action at Brands Hatch in 1991

Historic Racing Saloons at Mallory in 1991; the series joined the HSCC in 1994

planned for 1992, with dates organised to avoid the Steigenberger Super Sports Cup.

In confirming the new series, chairman Don Cressy acknowledged that the new series would take the club beyond the existing 1971 cut-off date but he explained that it was not the start of a blanket move to allow any pre-1975 cars into the club.

Committee changes at the end of the 1990 season centred on vice-chairman Mike Freeman standing down after three years' service and he was replaced by Nick Overall following a postal ballot. Roly Nix and John Harper stood down as category representatives on the main committee and were replaced by Lincoln Small and David Hudson, while Mike Pendlebury was also elected to represent the new Group 6 category.

The club's championships winners at the end of the 1991 season included Road Sports aces Kevin Irons (Datsun 240Z) and Aidan Mills-Thomas (AC Cobra) who each took another title and Denis Welch (Austin Healey 3000) who won the Classic Sports crown for the second time. Lotus Elan racer Steve McKechnie won the Novice title but with less than 20 drivers scoring points this would be the final year of the championship.

Chevron B8 racer Phil Buck won the 2-Litre GT title as Michael Schryver only contested a couple of races, while March 712 racer Paul Gardener won the newly-titled Historic Formula Racing Car Championship.

Looking ahead to 1992, Lydon confirmed a new plan for an overseas trip. Despite the disappointment of the enforced late cancellation of the 1991 Mondello Park meeting, the club was pushing ahead to take several championships to the tight little track of Croix-en-Ternois in Northern France. The event would be a joint venture with the Vintage Sports Car Club over the weekend of 9/10 May. Profits from the event would go to a new charity set up to help drivers and officials injured and disabled through motor sport and the president of the charity was former Grand Prix driver Phillipe Streiff who was seriously injured and left quadriplegic following an F1 testing accident in 1989.

Mike Freeman (centre) receives the Full Bore Trophy for 1991 from John Surtees and Don Cressy

John Surtees (L) presents Phil Stott with the 1991 Jaguar Trophy

Denis Welch collects the award for winning the 1991 Classic Championship

THE 1991 HSCC RACING CHAMPIONS

Pre '60 Historic Sports Championship
David Beckett (Lister Chevrolet)
Classic Sports Car Championship
Denis Welch (Austin Healey 3000)
HSCC 2-Litre GT Championship
Phil Buck (Chevron B8)
Standard Road Sports Championship
Kevin Irons (Datsun 240Z)
Improved Road Sports Championship
Aidan Mills-Thomas (AC Cobra)
Novice Championship
Steve McKechnie (Lotus Elan)
Historic Formula Racing Car Championship
Paul Gardener (March 712)

In the March 1992 Newsletter, an attempt to re-energise races for pre-60 sports cars was announced under the title of the 'Chairman's Invitation'. The plan was to rekindle the original spirit of the club with occasional fun races and Ray Hunter was the man asking for interest from potential competitors. Races for pre-55 cars were also planned while the new series for Formula Ford 1600s was gathering a lot of support and 40 driver had expressed an interest in taking part, including Road Sports front-runner Gary Smelt. The first race was scheduled for Mallory Park on 17 April.

Changes to the 1992 calendar came at a late stage when Donington Park took a late decision to promote a round of the World Sports Car Championship and the club's regular two-day meeting was the major casualty. The planned two-day meeting in July was replaced by a one-day meeting in September and hasty plans were arranged to replace the lost track time with a meeting at Pembrey in August. However, this event was later cancelled when the club's board deemed that the level of competitor support would probably mean a significant loss if the meeting went ahead.

Guy Evans spins his Lotus Elan in the Standard Road Sports at Donington in 1992

The struggling 2-Litre Historic GT Championship continued in 1992 and was joined by the new RJB Mining Group 6 Championship for pre-1975 cars. Cars from Chevron, Osella and March were among those pledged along with rarities like the Gropa of Malcolm Ricketts and the Toj of Ian Giles. Inevitably, the two series shared a grid through 1992 and for 1993 the partnership became a full marriage under the RJB title.

The 1992 season started at the annual Brands Hatch Super Prix (30/31 May), which had new support from the Visage TV production company. There was a fresh look for the Super Prix in '92, with no FIA championship rounds this time. Instead, guest races would include

Thankfully, the pack just about missed the spinning Elan

European Historic Formula 2, the Healey Driver International Club and a visit from the German Open Championship. Also on the schedule was a race for the new QED Seven Club Challenge for pre-1973 Lotus 7s, which was being administered from the club office.

VISAGE SUPER PRIX ACTION

Writing in the July/August edition of 'Histrionics' chairman Don Cressy wrote of the rising track hire costs faced by the club. *"However, indications are already coming to us that further large increases in track rental are on the horizon for the 1993 season, and your committee is holding a special meeting to decide which tracks we can afford to run meetings at next year and what level the entry fee will be. Obviously we have applied to the circuits for similar dates to those which we have arranged for the current season, but there comes a point at which the arithmetic does not add up correctly for each circuit; i.e. Cadwell Park – always very popular with the drivers, but not usually well attended."*

At the close of the 1992 season, Don Cressy ended a four-year term as chairman and this quiet, but determined gentleman had skilfully steered the club through some difficult times following the death of John Foulston and then the end of Brian Cocks' term as Chief Executive. Steve Lydon wrote about the retiring chairman in his magazine editorial. *"Apart from those on the main committee I think very few members will ever realise what I debt the club owes to Don and of course to Betty (his wife). Both of them have given freely of their time and they have both contributed an enormous amount in many ways to the success of the*

club. Don has to be one of the most diplomatic and successful negotiators I have ever witnessed and our current standing amongst other clubs and circuits is due almost entirely to Don's efforts."

Cressy's term of office came to a close at the AGM and Dinner Dance

THE 1992 HSCC RACING CHAMPIONS

Classic Sports Car Championship
Denis Welch (Austin Healey 3000)
HSCC 2-Litre GT Championship
James Watt (Royale RP4)
RJB Mining Championship
Mike Wilds (Chevron B31/36)
Standard Road Sports Championship
Guy Evans (Lotus Elan)
Improved Road Sports Championship
Aidan Mills-Thomas (AC Cobra)
Historic Formula Racing Car Championship
Michael Schryver (Lotus 69)

at the end of 1992 and the couple received a standing ovation when new chairman Richard Arnold presented them with a framed Craig Warwick artwork of Don's Chevron B8 in period action at Kyalami. Arnold was elected, unopposed, to the role of chairman and Nick Overall continued as vice-chairman.

The champions of the 1992 season included former Grand Prix driver Mike Wilds who took the first of his RJB Mining titles at the wheel of Richard Budge's Chevron, while James Watt sealed the final 2-Litre Historic GT title in his Royale RP4. Aidan Mills-Thomas (AC Cobra) and Guy Evans (Lotus Elan) each won a Road Sports title while Denis Welch retained his Classic Sports crown with his ever-oversteering Austin Healey 3000. Michael Schryver won the Historic Formula Racing Car Championship in his Lotus 69, raced by Simon Hadfield the year before, and then announced plans to step up to Historic F1 in an ex-Reine Wisell Lotus 72.

Major news announced at end of 1992 included confirmation that John Surtees would be the star guest at the Visage Historic Super Prix at Brands Hatch the following June. Plans for the weekend included demonstrations of cars and bikes from his career on two and four wheels along with a couple of races for classic motorbikes, which would be a first at an HSCC race meeting.

In the same issue of 'Histrionics' came some intriguing comment about the club and a possible tie-up with Goodwood. Launched for June 1993 was to be the

Lincoln Small clambers out of his F2 Brabham at Thruxton

first hillclimb on the drive of Goodwood House, though it had been used for a similar event in 1935. The entry was to be limited to around 70 or 80 classic and historic cars and the HSCC would be responsible for assembling a representative field for what would quickly grow to become the Festival of Speed.

Lydon went on to reveal that discussions between the club and Goodwood had gone further. "The current Earl of March is very keen to see the circuit re-established as motorsporting venue and to this end he has invited the HSCC to consider the possibility of becoming a resident club at the circuit. Various options are being examined and negotiations are continuing and members will be advised as soon as the main committee reaches a decision." Clearly, history shows that the idea did not progress, but had it come to fruition, the move would surely have shaped the club very differently.

The 1993 schedule was topped by the Brands Hatch weekend in June and started at Mallory Park in May. Other race meetings were at Oulton Park (July), Cadwell Park (August), Silverstone (September) and Snetterton (October), while a two-day Donington Park

meeting in early September included rounds of the FIA Historic Championships.

The championship and series line-up for 1993 was extended to nine in total, though the Historic Formula 1, Historic FF1600/Formula Junior and QED Club Challenge were all run as series rather than full championships. The HSCC/AMOC Historic Car Championship was back for one more try, while the five staples were QED Standard Road Sports, Barley Construction Improved Road Sports, RJB Mining Group 6, Classic Sports and Historic Formula Racing Car Championships. In the office, club secretary Ruth Hibberd left in April 1993 ahead of the birth of her baby and was replaced by Emma Marshman.

Meanwhile, at the end of the year, Ray Hunter stood down after five years as treasurer and was replaced by Trojan Formula 5000 racer John Narcisi. On reporting for the year ending December 1992, Hunter recorded a surplus of £2374 against a loss of £5546 a year earlier and the club had cash reserves of £20,000. An increase in support from a major sponsor, thought to be RJB Mining but not identified in the accounts

1993 awards: Mike Wilds (L) collects an award from Stuart Turner

1993 awards: David Hudson (L) and George Douglas collect RJB awards

Simon Hadfield (L) picks up a 1993 award

1993 awards: Helen Bashford collects an award from Stuart Turner

narrative, took sponsorship income from £34,000 to £60,000 and proved critical in the club being able to return a small surplus.

A year later, in December 1994, Narcisi reported on the finances for the year to December 1993 which showed a remarkable surplus of £34,248. This sum, it appears, resulted largely in an agreement with one circuit over the waiving of the circuit hire fee. No more details were given to explain this unusual situation, which contributed to a surprising set of results when compared to a budgeted surplus of £9000. As a direct consequence, the club's cash reserves grew to £38,925 and total assets were listed at £72,541. Narcisi then projected a break-even for 1994 as recession took a grip on the UK economy. However, a year on, the 1994 results showed a loss of £3761, partly due to changes in VAT rules that led to a higher VAT liability for the club.

Champions from the 1993 season included John Jarvis (Classic Sports), Northern Irishman Arnie Black (HFRC), Antony Ross and Guy Evans from the Road Sports categories and Ian McCullough who took the RJB title with his Crossle C9S. The Doncaster school teacher ran

the Crossle on the tightest of budgets and the start money made available from the RJB backing was vital to his campaign.

For the 1994 season, the Pre '65 Single Seater Championship returned after a three-year sabbatical

THE 1993 HSCC RACING CHAMPIONS

Pre '60 Historic Sports Championship
Andrew Wilkinson (Lotus XI)
Classic Sports Car Championship
John Jarvis (Lotus Elan)
RJB Mining Championship
Ian McCullough (Crossle C9S)
Standard Road Sports Championship
Guy Evans (Lotus Elan)
Improved Road Sports Championship
Antony Ross (Alfa Romeo Spider)
Historic Formula Racing Car Championship
Arnie Black (Crossle 19F)

and a re-work of the Road Sports classes was confirmed. The existing Improved and Standard categories were replaced by two age-related championships for Historics (up to 1969) and 70s (up to 1979). The new 70s Road Sports series was sponsored by Classic and Sportscar magazine. It proved to be a real success and before the end of 1994 it was confirmed that RACMSA championship status had been awarded for 1995.

The 1994 season also marked another landmark for the HSCC as it first ran a series for touring cars. In previous seasons, the ICS Historic Touring Car Championship had become a popular and permanent support race to the British Touring Car Championship. However, car specifications were constantly moving on and costs escalated.

As a reaction to this, the Historic Racing Saloon Register was formed and ran a series of races away from the BTCC schedule, initially under the wing of the British Racing and Sports Car Club. Before long, the ICS series withered and died and for 1994 the HRSR joined forces with the HSCC at the start of what has proved over the years to be a very successful partnership.

At the time, HRSR spokesman and Fiat racer Tony Castle-Miller said: "We really wanted to put the word 'historic' back into our racing and for that reason we are delighted to be associated with a historic club as well respected as the HSCC." An eight-event series was created for the 1994 season.

In the final reckoning for the 1994 season, it had clearly been a good year for Datsun 240Zs as both the Improved and Standard Road Sports titles went to the Japanese machines in the final year for both championships. Barley Construction again sponsored the well-supported Improved Road Sports Championship with well over 50 drivers scoring points as Vernon Taylor took the overall crown in his 240Z. Others to score points included Kevin Kivlochan, William Jenkins and Peter Shaw. In stark contrast, the QED Standard Road Sports Championship enjoyed limited support as Paul Stafford took his 240Z to the title. Only 15 drivers scored points in the final season for the class.

Trupart sponsored the Historic Formula Racing Car Championship and the overall winner was Michael Schryver in his first season with his sensational Lotus 72. His rivals included Nick Overall and Mike Whatley in Formula 5000s and Arnie Black, Martin Birrane, Peter Hannen, Paul Bason and Lincoln Small in 1600cc and 2-litre cars. Mark Gillies took the Pre '65 Single-Seater title by a tie-break from Tony Steele and David Methley won the Classic Sports Car Championship in his Marcos GT.

THE 1994 HSCC RACING CHAMPIONS

Classic Sports Car Championship
David Methley (Marcos GT)
RJB Mining Championship
George Douglas (Ginetta G12)
Pre '65 Single Seater Championship
Mark Gillies (Lotus 22)
Standard Road Sports Championship
Paul Stafford (Datsun 240Z)
Improved Road Sports Championship
Vernon Taylor (Datsun 240Z)
Historic Formula Racing Car Championship
Michael Schryver (Lotus 72)

Richard Budge gave the club significant support

NICK OVERALL

Former Club Chairman

"I started racing in 1968 with an Aley Mini at a cost of £400. I remember being on the grid at Silverstone alongside a Dutch lady called Liane Engeman and she was very attractive and very quick. The flag went down and, of course, I was looking at her and not the flag and I think I came last in that race.

"Then I moved on to Formula Ford like everybody did in those days, with an Alexis in a team with Ian Ashley. Then I did a bit of Formula 3 with Alexis. I drove a Formula 2 Brabham BT36 in what was then the Jaybrand Formula Libre Championship, which was all at Silverstone.

"Ron Dennis was running a Formula 2 team with a Brabham BT38 and I had a sponsor and my sponsor was all ready to buy that car. Then this Surtees TS8 came up through Bell and Colvill and, stupidly, I plumped for the Formula 5000 Surtees. That was in 1974 and 1975 towards the end of Formula 5000. It went quite well but then I had a huge crash at Maggotts at Silverstone. I raced a Chevron B21/23 in the middle 1970s then sponsors dried up and I stopped.

"A few years later in 1983 or so I had a good friend called Alex Seldon and he suggested I tried the Historic Sports Car Club, which I'd never heard of. Brian Cocks was running the club from his house at Minsterworth and I joined the club and bought myself a Diva. Brian was chairman and Jem Marsh was vice-chairman. That was my start in historics.

"The Diva was a great little car and I was then asked by Tony Thompson and Barry Sewell if I'd be interested in joining the Classic Sports Car committee. That was about 1986 and that's how it all started. Brian Cocks went from being chairman to Chief Executive Officer and later on, unfortunately, we couldn't agree new terms with Brian for him to continue in the role.

"I was on the Classic Sports committee in 1988 with Tony Thompson, Denis Welch and Barry Sewell. Then Jem Marsh was chairman and Alex Seldon was vice-chairman and Peter Walker was the treasurer. I was on the committee for quite a few years through various ups and downs for the club. I guess you'd describe them as growing pains. It was expanding quite quickly.

"Jem retired in 1989, I think. Then Don Cressy was voted in as chairman and he was an absolute gentleman and he did an awful lot at the time when Brian Cocks was trying to re-negotiate his contract and the main board said no. It was completely a financial decision.

"Don was a brilliant chairman. He was a very modest man and he was the master diplomat and brought back harmony. Mike Freeman, who is also a good racer, became vice-chairman and they balanced each other perfectly. That was in 1990.

"At that time Steve Lydon joined the club to replace Brian Cocks. Mike Freeman did two years as vice-chairman and in 1992 said he was stepping down. At the dinner dance Tony Thompson and a couple of others told me they'd put me forward for vice-chairman, and I was elected.

"Steve was full of enthusiasm, but he was not everyone's cup of tea. He introduced a tape recorder for all board meetings, which we'd never had before. The arguments got quite intense.

"Don Cressy did four years and had done a lot of good work. By then he'd had enough and it was then presented to the board that Richard Arnold would become chairman for two years. I continued as vice-chairman. But Richard was very busy with his own business so we never saw him and I chaired most of the meetings. When Richard stood down I took over as chairman.

"Then I looked at the accounts and the full extent of the situation became clear. It was horrendous. We were well in debt and the office at Kington Langley was falling apart. We should never have bought it. It was bought outright in Brian Cocks' time. Thank god we managed to sell the property.

"Technically, when I took over as chairman and saw the figures, the club was bust. Probably from a legal point of view we should not have been trading. It was that bad. One of my first actions was to say we had to sell the office and move. It was bought for over £80,000 and sold for middle £40,000. At that time we also recruited a new accountant, a man called Derek Downing. He went through the books with a fine toothcomb.

"I was keen to move the club to a race track and I was introduced to John Fitzpatrick at the BRDC by Chris Alford. He was very accommodating and we moved into the old farm building to begin with. Then we had

a building next to the Silverstone Club, and then the current building near the main entrance.

"We had to accept what had gone on before and move ahead. We owed £37,500 to a range of creditors and that's where I came in. We were very lucky to have Richard Budge from RJB Mining who put £30,000 into sponsorship and that went straight into the club funds. That sort of balanced the books and gave us some breathing space but it was a very dodgy time.

"Steve did do good things for the club and he then moved on to run Thoroughbred Grand Prix with Bob Berridge, but that was quite short-lived. TGP had started and grown with the club and at the time we did not have the funds to take it forward. We were broke, but thankfully very few people knew that at the time. This was around 1996 and 1997.

"With the sale of the property at Kington Langley and the RJB sponsorship, the club was solvent. We then recruited a chap called Joe Keech to be the club manager. It started well enough but it became apparent fairly early on that Joe wasn't going to be a CEO. I remember talking to Lincoln Small and others and saying we needed to find someone for the role of CEO. Grahame White's name came up through Lincoln.

"I met Grahame and went through it with him and he thought about and then turned me down. It took me about a year to convince him to take the job. I just kept on badgering him and in the end he gave in. I was absolutely certain that if there was one man for the job, it was him. Eventually I managed to persuade him. Other than selling the club office, it was the best decision I made as chairman.

"When Grahame first came on board it was for a couple of days a week. But then Joe Keech left and Grahame moved into a full time role. We could then start to manage the better progress of the club and I knew I could back out of a lot of things and leave it to Grahame.

"By now things were starting to look more rosy. Derek Downing then left and he'd been a key element for several years in getting the club back on its feet and getting the books straight. Martin Atack came after Joe Keech for a fairly short period.

"Initially Don Hands became vice-chairman and then Stephen Minoprio took the position. Stephen had come back to racing much later in life after being a rising star in the early 1960s. He was racing a Marcos and took over from Don Hands to be vice-chairman for most of my time as chairman. When I decided to step down, and I'd made that decision two years earlier, Richard Thorne threw his hat into the ring with Mike Southin to stand for vice-chairman.

"Stephen Minoprio decided not to go for the post of chairman and Anthony Goddard, who'd taken over as treasurer, suggested Chris Sharples and he agreed to stand. That went to a full postal vote and Chris was elected as chairman with Chris Alford as vice-chairman.

"Once I got involved, the passion grew to the point where I was so involved with the club that I just couldn't help myself. You couldn't abandon ship and there was a burden of responsibility. When I saw the figures there was no way I could walk away. I love challenges and I never give up. I have an emotional attachment to it.

"Right at the end, when Grahame was there and Anthony was treasurer and we had a good board which was pretty free of politics, I felt that here was something that had been worthwhile doing. I am proud of where the club is now. But I think it cost me quite a lot of money in my own business and without a doubt my business suffered. Particularly at the start of the venture, it needed full time attention to put the club back into a good situation. I had to do it and looking back I do see it with a sense of achievement.

"Everybody played their part in turning the club around and Grahame has played a massive part. Thankfully the politics started to disappear; otherwise there wouldn't have been a club."

CHRIS ALFORD

Former Vice-Chairman

"My first involvement with the HSCC was in 1983. At that time I was racing in Sports 2000 and I'd always fancied having a bash at historics. One of my main competitors in Sports 2000 was John Brindley and he also had a Lotus 22 Formula Junior and a Lotus 23 sports-racing and he was winning a lot of historic races.

"I met Cedric Selzer, who was Jim Clark's mechanic, and I was pretty much on my beam end in terms of racing budget. I'd always loved the Lotus 23 and Cedric had been restoring one for a sponsor of mine from Sports 2000 and invited me to race it in 1983. That led to me driving a Lotus 24 that Cedric also restored and, some years later, a Lotus 25 that he restored. Jim Clark was my great hero so that was very special.

"In the late 1980s I started wheeling and dealing in historic cars and I used to sell Formula Juniors. Formula Ford, at the time, was not historic although there was the Pre '74 category. I had this guy in Japan who wanted to buy old single-seaters and selling them to people to hang on their walls. It was a wonderful deal for me and I must have sent 10 or 12 cars out there.

"Then John Harper and the board of the HSCC said that historic racing cars were getting too expensive and we needed something for our members to race, so let's do Historic Formula Ford. The price of cars started to rise and it built from there. One year, maybe 1994, I had six or seven cars in stock and I would get people in them to give the category a helping hand.

"I love the cars and still think it is the biggest bang for your buck. I think the most I ever sold a Formula Ford for was about £15,000. That model of Merlyn now changes hands for up to £30,000.

"I was vice-chairman for 11 years until 2016 and I started when Chris Sharples became chairman. I replaced Don Hands as vice-chairman. Chris and I helped build the club, but when you really come down to it, Grahame White made it happen. When Grahame took over the club was not in good shape.

"When I first joined the board I was looking after Formula Ford and in those days we were based in Kington Langley at our own premises, which were awful. The club's finances weren't good.

"One thing I can take credit for is that one day we were sat around the table at Kington Langley trying to decide what to do and I'd been at Silverstone the weekend before chatting to John Fitzpatrick of the BRDC. I said there were some premises at Silverstone we could have and so Nick Overall went to see John the next week and we moved to Silverstone. It was a very smart move.

"Initially we moved into the farm building for a year or so and then to a porta-cabin round by the Silverstone Racing Club. Then we moved to the current premises, which was the old Sterling Helicopters office. It's an old RAF dispersal hut.

"The HSCC means a hell of a lot to me. I'm incredibly proud to be a member of the two best motor racing clubs in Britain; the BRDC and the HSCC. The club is on a far, far better footing in 2016 than it ever was. It is a fantastic club. I've raced for over 50 years and I've never had as much fun as I do with the HSCC."

*Retiring chairman Richard Arnold and wife flank
Nick Overall in 1994*

Paul Stafford receives the SRS spoils from Simon Park (L)

*Chris Burbury (L) receives the David Barraclough
Trophy from Don Hands*

*1994: Philip Walker (L) receives the Goodwood Trophy from
race commentator Ian Titchmarsh*

*David Methley with his trophy haul and Ian
Titchmarsh (L)*

1994: George Douglas collects the RJB title

Nearly 40 drivers scored points in the RJB Mining Group 6 Championship and it was George Douglas who took the title in his Ginetta G12. Former champion Mike Wilds started the season in the Chevron B31/36 of Richard Budge but then suffered a terrible accident at the Goodwood Festival of Speed and serious leg injuries put him out for the rest of the season. Willie Green took over the Chevron for the balance of the season. David Beckett in the Nerus Silhouette was the closest rival to Douglas on points while other class champions included Chevron racer Richard Evans.

In the December 1994 issue of Histrionics, retiring chairman Richard Arnold warned members that the upcoming Annual General Meeting would report a less favourable financial report, largely due to the loss of one of the Club's major sponsors. Arnold went on to confirm that RJB Mining's support for the club would continue in 1995. A small saving was made when the planned number of magazines was cut in 1994 as Steve Lydon spent some of the year in hospital.

There was a major development in the club's programme for the 1995 season with the formation of the FIA Cup for Thoroughbred Grand Prix Cars. The FIA-sanctioned championship emerged from the club's Historic Formula 1 Championship, which had grown and evolved over the preceding eight years.

During 1994 support for the club's series of races for Historic F1 cars had developed well and was topped by a superb 28-car grid at Donington Park in early September. Drivers on the grid during the 1994 season included Simon Hadfield, Mike Littlewood, John Fenning, Urs Eberhardt, Geoff Farmer, Ian Giles, Sean Walker, Bob Berridge and Lorina and David McLaughlin. Max Samuel-Camps was championship chairman and acknowledged the work of David McLaughlin in building the category.

A sign of the growing status for the Historic F1 movement was the fact that the 1995 championship was officially launched at Williams Grand Prix

Engineering in Oxfordshire on Wednesday 26 April. It was an impressive affair as a five-race season was confirmed, taking in races at Donington Park (May and again in September), the Nurburgring (June), Brands Hatch GP (July) and a season closer at the spectacular Brno circuit in the Czech Republic at beginning of October.

Former BRM and Lotus engineer Tony Rudd was appointed as Technical Registrar and the championship was administered by Steve Lydon from the HSCC office at Kington Langley.

Commenting in the club magazine at the end of 1994, chairman Richard Arnold pointed out the significance of this development. "This demonstrates the level of satisfaction that the RAC and the FIA have in the HSCC's proven ability to run such a prestigious series, which we are sure will be a flagship for the club."

Mike Littlewood on the podium

Donington 1995: the start of the TGP race

Martin Stretton (5) and Geoff Farmer (3) head the pack

Stretton went on to win the overall title

JPS Lotus in the TGP race at Donington Park in 1995

Mike Littlewood heads the field into Redgate

Mike Littlewood (Williams FW07)

Bob Berridge was now a driving force in the development of TGP

Martin Stretton in Tyrrell 005

Another addition for the 1995 season was the Toyota Formula 3 class when the category's association voted in a majority to join forces with the HSCC. The successful category for cars from the 194-1980 F3 era, originally conceived by people like Tony Broster and Marcus Pye, would join the HSCC roster for a series of dates in the 1995 and the Toyota Formula 3 Association confirmed plans to have competing cars returned to period livery over the coming 12 months.

In September 1995 the club moved from the office at Kington Langley to a temporary base in the farm buildings at Silverstone. In January, the office moved again to a building next to the Silverstone Club on the outside of Woodcote Corner. The story behind the move is detailed in the column from Nick Overall, club chairman of the time.

A direct consequence of the office move was the loss of Debbie Wilson-Smith as the office manager as she decided not to move to Silverstone. For the closing weeks of the 1995 season the club office was in turmoil but it was hoped that the arrival of new staff early in 1996 would improve the situation.

THE 1995 HSCC RACING CHAMPIONS

FIA Cup for Thoroughbred Grand Prix Cars
Martin Stretton (Tyrrell 005)
Classic Sports Car Championship
David Methley (Marcos GT)
RJB Mining Championship
Peter Lee (Chevron B8)
Pre '65 Single Seater Championship
Tony Steele (Lola Mk2)
70s Road Sports Championship
Richard Thorne (Alfa Romeo GTV)
Historic Road Sports Championship
Paul Howarth (Lancia Fulvia)
Historic FF1600 Championship
Bryan Hayward (Lotus 61)
Historic Formula Racing Car Championship
Arnie Black (Crossle 19F)

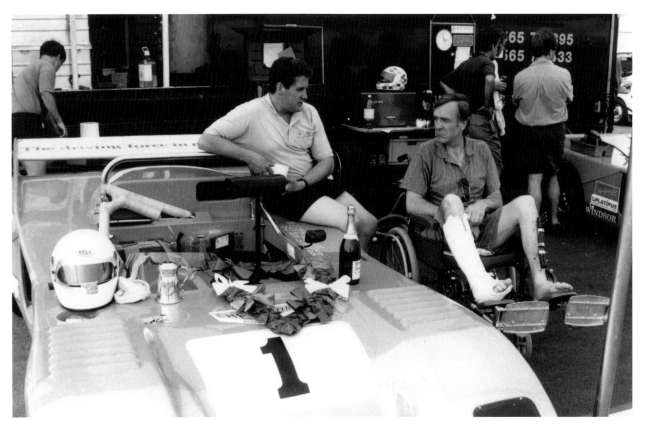

Mike Wilds, still recovering from his leg injuries

Paul Howarth (Lancia Fulvia Zagato) won the 1995 Historic Road Sports title

Among the 1995 champions was novice racer Brian Hayward who won the Historic Formula Ford 1600 title as the class enjoyed championship status for the first time. From the novice class, he scored just one point more than Keith Norman.

Chevron B8 racer Peter Lee won the RJB Group 6 crown in his Chevron B8 as Mike Wilds made a popular return to racing as he continued his recovery from the Goodwood accident. Meanwhile, the young Richard Evans was impressive in his Chevron B26 and marked himself as a rising star of historic racing.

JiJim Evans (Alfa Romeo GTA) at Mallory Park, September 1995

Martin Stretton won the inaugural FIA Cup for Thoroughbred Grand Prix Cars and at the club's annual awards' dinner Mike Whatley won the John Foulston Trophy for the highest number of outright wins in the season.

In the final season for the Pre '65 Single-Seater Championship, Tony Steele took a narrow championship victory in his Formula Junior Lola Mk2. The Pre '65 cars often shared a grid with the Historic Formula Racing Car Championship where Crossle stalwart Arnie Black commuted across the Irish Sea to take the title.

Paul Howarth used his nicely restored and rather rare Lancia Fulvia Zagato to win the first Historic Road Sports title and Richard Thorne took the 70s Road Sports title in his Alfa Romeo GTV after a tie-break with Peter Gregory (Datsun 240Z). David Methley retained his Classic Sports Car title.

The TGP circus at the 1995 final at Brno

In his summary of the 1995 season, chairman Nick Overall described it as a 'busy and hectic' year. "On the whole entries were slightly up on last year but we did have to amalgamate many races. Circuit owners insist on full grids so if we want the meetings we really do not have any choice. I am hopeful that in 1996 we will see grid sizes increase again and to this end I can confirm that it is not our intention to increase entry fees, subject to other costs remaining the same."

Significant changes were made to the club's single-seater portfolio for the 1996 season, which included the re-branding of Toyota F3 into Classic F3 and the introduction of a class for the 1600cc F3 cars raced from 1971 to 1973. Previously, these cars had run with the British Automobile Racing Club. Dwindling support for both the Pre '65 Single-Seaters and the Historic Formula Racing Car Championships was another problem and neither class had delivered strong enough grids to retain MSA championship status.

The solution presented to the annual drivers' meeting was to make a clear split between the two groups and introduce the newly-titled Classic Racing Car category for non-winged cars running on treaded tyres with a late 1960s cut-off. The HFRC would continue in a revised format for cars with slicks and wings built for any international single-seater category up to the end of 1979.

For 1996, along with the FIA Historic Formula 1 Championship, the club ran another nine championships and series. For the club's 30th season, there were championship titles for Richard Hayhow

A board meeting from 1996 including Steve Lydon, Nick Overall, Lincoln Small, Bob Birrell and Chris Alford

Paul Sleeman on his way to the 1996 Historic FF1600 title

(Lotus Elan) in Classic Sports, Mike Wilds (Chevron B31/36) with a second RJB Group 6 crown, Andy Shepherd (Lotus 7) and Chris Horner (Turner Mk1) in the twin Road Sports series and. John Narcisi (Trojan T101) in the final year of the Historic Formula Racing Car Championship.

Michael Schryver won the FIA Cup for Thoroughbred Grand Prix Cars in his Lotus 72 while Paul Sleeman (Jamun T2) won the first of four Historic FF1600 titles in five seasons.

Sleeman had made his racing debut in an FF1600 Lotus 51 at Lydden in 1972 and raced extensively in the category. "I thoroughly enjoyed myself with the HSCC and it is an excellent club to race with," said Sleeman as he reflected on his incredible run of success in the club's Historic Formula Ford 1600 Championship.

Historic Touring Cars, Classic Racing Cars and Classic Formula 3 all ran for a final year as a series rather than a championship, but all three classes gained full championship status for the 1997 season. However, there were much bigger changes around the corner for the HSCC.

THE 1996 HSCC RACING CHAMPIONS

FIA Cup for Thoroughbred Grand Prix Cars
Michael Schryver (Lotus 72)
Classic Sports Car Championship
Richard Hayhow (Lotus Elan)
RJB Mining Championship
Mike Wilds (Chevron B31/36)
70s Road Sports Championship
Andy Shepherd (Lotus 7)
Historic Road Sports Championship
Chris Horner (Turner Mk1)
Historic Formula Racing Car Championship
John Narcisi (Trojan T101)
Historic FF1600 Championship
Paul Sleeman (Jamun T2)

Mike Wilds won the 1996 RJB title in the sponsor's Chevron B31/36

7

1997 to 2002
The White stuff

By early 1997 Steve Lydon had left the club and had effectively taken the FIA Thoroughbred Grand Prix Car Championship with him to run it on behalf of a group of competitors led by Bob Berridge.

For 1997, the HSCC continued to hold the championship permit but it was little more than a flag of convenience and the organisation and promotion of the championship was contracted over to Thoroughbred Grand Prix Limited, a company set up and owned by a number of competitors. Berridge went on to win the 1997 title in his March-inspired RAM 01.

It was a time of turmoil for the club as detailed by Nick Overall and the club officials did not particularly fight the departure of the F1 series. There were plenty of fires to be put out within the club's bread and butter race programme and many felt that losing the main responsibility for TGP would allow the new club officials to concentrate on core business.

Joe Keech was appointed Club Manager from the office at Silverstone and brought experience as a marshal and race car preparer. Working alongside him was Club Treasurer Derek Downing and administrator Marilyn Watkins.

One of the significant changes for the 1997 season was the re-branding and re-styling of the club's major

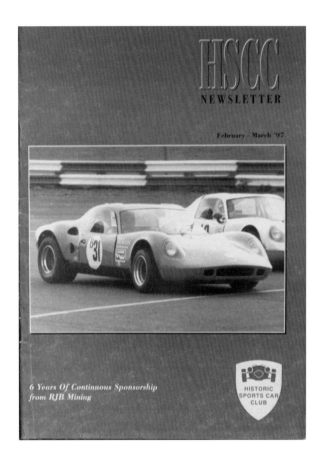

HSCC NEWSLETTER

February - March '97

6 Years Of Continuous Sponsorship from RJB Mining

HISTORIC SPORTS CAR CLUB

single-seater series. The Historic Formula Racing Car category had suffered a thin time in the middle 1990s, but was re-packaged for 1997 as the Derek Bell Trophy. A class for Classic Clubmans cars was added to accommodate a slowly growing number of pre-1980 front-engined sports-racing cars. The Classic Clubmans idea had sparked during Steve Lydon's time at the helm of the HSCC and racer David Childs took up the idea from within the Clubmans Register.

Another significant development for 1997 was the appointment of Sir Stirling Moss as the club's first Patron. The arrangement came about through the efforts of board member David Pratley and it was

Helen Bashford-Malkie in her Chevron B19 at Silverstone in May 1997

John Burton (Chevron B26)

The Nerus Silhouette of Alan Philips

Mike Campbell-Cole (Martin BM8)

Andrew Schryver (Chevron B8)

Barry Hargraves in his Formula Ford Lotus 61

The Elden Mk8 of Chris Alford

Kevin Stanzl (Merlyn Mk20) at Silverstone in May

Brian Jones interviews Damon Hill at Brands, watched by a young Matt James from Motorsport News

Hill present the laurels to Rob Hall

hoped that Sir Stirling would be able to visit some of the club's race meetings. On the magazine front, Hazel Clements and Sarah Thomas from Hawk Racewear took over production of 'Histrionics'.

At the annual Brands Hatch Super Prix in July, reigning World Champion Damon Hill was the guest of honour and ran some demonstration laps in his 1997 Arrows A18.

On-track in 1997 there was plenty of good racing as championships were won and lost. Peter Gregory and Paul Stafford battled season-long for the 70s Road Sports title in their Datsun 240Zs and it went down to

the wire in the final round at Snetterton when Gregory finished four seconds ahead to clinch the crown.

The first year for Classic F3 with championship status went well and the overall champion in the Oregon Timber Frame Homes-supported category was Terry Nightingale in his front-engined Mallock Mk11B from the 1600cc class. His main rival was Winston Bunn in his Ensign LNF3 while Rob Moores won the 2-litre class in his Chevron B38.

Former hillclimber Tim Barrington won the Classic Racing Car title in a Brabham BT21C, but only after a stern challenge from instructor and driver coach

Duncan Rabagliati in the Alexis at Donington on 1 June

Lawrence Suffryn's Formula Junior Terrier

Formula Junior Lotus 22

Frank Sytner (Jaguar D-type)

Alan Minshaw's Lister Chevrolet at Silverstone in May

John Harper (Cooper Monaco)

Lola T240 at speed at Donington

Malcolm Ricketts (Lotus XI)

THE 1997 HSCC RACING CHAMPIONS

FIA Cup for Thoroughbred Grand Prix Cars
Bob Berridge (RAM 01)
Classic Sports Car Championship
David Methley (Marcos GT)
RJB Mining Championship
David Hudson (Sturdgess SL1)
Classic Racing Car Championship
Tim Barrington (Brabham BT21C)
70s Road Sports Championship
Peter Gregory (Datsun 240Z)
Historic Road Sports Championship
Mike Eagles (Turner Mk1)
Derek Bell Trophy
Nicholas Pearce (Delta T78/79)
Historic FF1600 Championship
Paul Sleeman (Jamun T2)
Historic Racing Saloon Championship
Nevil Smith (Ford Lotus Cortina)
Classic Formula 3 Championship
Terry Nightingale (Mallock Mk11B)

Malcolm Smith in the Gold Leaf-liveried Lotus 59 1-litre F3 car owned by James Wigmore.

In the RJB Mining-backed Group 6 Championship, David Hudson ran his Sturdgess on the smallest of budgets and actually came out of the season ahead once the start money from RJB was factored in. The season included away dates at Castle Combe and the spectacular Phoenix Park track in Dublin and

it was Mike Wilds who did most of the winning in the sponsor's Chevron B31/36. Unfortunately, lack of class rivals cost Mike full points in some races and any chance of fighting for the overall title.

Paul Sleeman retained his Historic FF1600 title by a handsome margin over the Merlyns of Keith Norman and Kevin Stanzl, with championship sponsor Chris Alford fourth in his Elden Mk8. The novice award went to Frank Lyons after his first season of racing in his Merlyn Mk11 but he only beat the similar car of John Bladon by a single point. Sleeman also won the John Foulston award for the 1997 season for the greatest number of outright wins.

Peter Goring's HRSR Ford Mustang at Mallory Park in 1997

Robin Stainer in his AC Cobra at Mallory

Paul Sleeman on his way to another Historic FF title

Mike Eagles won the Historic Road Sports title in his Turner, David Methley (Marcos GT) topped the Classic Sports and the Formula Ford 2000 Delta T78/79 of Nicholas Pearce won the Derek Bell Trophy as Keith Norris (Chevron B28) topped seven Formula 5000s in the big class.

In his address to the Annual General Meeting in early December, Nick Overall reported on a challenging year for the club. *"1997 was a year of change in which Stirling Moss has become our first ever Patron. Grahame White joined us as our new Executive Director and major changes in the office will mean a new approach to our race management strategy.*

"With ever escalating costs of circuit hire meaning increased entry fees, which nobody wants but without which we could not afford to hire even the smaller circuits let alone such expensive venues as Brands Hatch Grand Prix circuit, it is imperative to give greater value for money than ever before. This is a view shared by everyone in the office and we will be working hard to ensure that all our members see the benefit of this.

"Outsourcing of race organisation has not been an unqualified success but was necessary for this transitional year. This year (1998) we will be bringing race organisation back in-house. We are confident that with Grahame White now in overall charge of our racing programme, our members will reap the benefits and hopefully have a much better organisational set-up."

The problems experienced during the 1997 season had clearly caused Overall and the board some concern and he went on to identify some of the improvements expected during 1998. Key aims for the new season included an earlier closing date for race entries to ensure that final instructions and passes could be sent out in good time, avoiding shortened races due to lack of time, a rather less rushed atmosphere at events, variation of race meeting timetables and to bring more variety to club events. Initially, Grahame White's arrangement with the club covered two or three days a week but it soon developed into a full time role.

The club's finances continued to be in a perilous state as Derek Downing reported at the Annual General Meeting in December 1997. During 1995 and 1996 the club had made a total loss of over £25,000 with the 1996 accounts showing income of £84,698 and expenditure of £99,661. Net assets were accordingly reduced to £43,292.

Downing detailed the forecast for 1997 as being between break-even and a £5000 loss, citing improved race meeting profitability as the main factor. Only the race meeting at Croix-en-Ternois made a loss during 1997. In his report, Downing discussed the club's future.

"For a number of years the Board's strategy has been to hold down subscription costs and entry fees in order, as far as possible, to alleviate racing costs to entrants and competitors, with the ongoing philosophy of obtaining sponsorship income wherever possible. Overhead and running costs have been constrained to the lowest feasible level.

"This strategy has produced losses in every year since 1993, during which time the club's accumulated profits fund has dropped by almost half from £70,000 to a likely £35,000 at December 1997.

"Whilst as a members' club, there should be no generalised ambition to make significant profits, there is still a need to maintain a sound financial base for the club's well-being; the recent history of losses therefore needs to be arrested.

THE 1998 HSCC RACING CHAMPIONS

FIA Cup for Thoroughbred Grand Prix Cars
Bob Berridge (Williams FW08)
Classic Sports Car Championship
Sid Marler (Lotus Elan)
RJB Mining Championship
Mike Wilds (Chevron B31/36)
Classic Racing Car Championship
Alan Baillie (Jovis)
70s Road Sports Championship
Jason Kennedy (Lancia Beta Coupe)
Historic Road Sports Championship
Mike Eagles (Turner Mk1)
Derek Bell Trophy
Nick Shrigley-Feigl (Chevron B28)
Historic FF1600 Championship
Benn Simms (Merlyn Mk20)
Historic Racing Saloon Championship
Peter Wray (Ford Lotus Cortina)
Classic Formula 3 Championship
Winston Bunn (Ensign LNF3)

Gary Pearson heads Simon Hadfield at Oulton Park

*Chris Alford in an FF
Merlyn at Thruxton*

*"There is at the same time an equally pressing
need to improve services to members at all levels
and particularly to provide better value for money to
competitors at race meetings."*

In conclusion, Downing reported that changes to
the club management would enable race meeting
organisation to come back in-house and that, unless
significant new sponsorship was secured, entry fees
would need to be increased. Despite his relatively short
time in the role of treasurer, it was clear that Downing
had acquired a firm grasp of the issues facing the club
and his professional diligence and wisdom brought
great benefit to the HSCC at a critical point in the
club's history.

The 1998 programme took in seven HSCC race
meetings, topped by the Brands Hatch Super Prix
on 4/5 July. Two weeks later the club again headed
for northern France and the Croix-en-Ternois circuit
while some HSCC championships featured in a BRSCC
meeting at Castle Combe on 8 August. The season
started with a two-day Silverstone meeting in early
May and included one-day events at Mallory Park,
Cadwell Park, Snetterton and then Silverstone in
October for the finals' meeting. A three-hour race for
Appendix K GT and touring cars was planned for the
Brands Hatch Super Prix, building on the success of
previous races over recent seasons.

Aside from the Thoroughbred Grand Prix Car
Championship, the club confirmed plans for a further
nine championships and series for the 1998 season.
Only the Derek Bell Trophy would run as a series
alongside championships for Historic Formula Ford,
Classic Sports, 70s Road Sports, Historic Road Sports,
Historic Racing Saloons, Classic Racing Cars, RJB
Thundersports and Classic Formula 3.

In the middle of 1998, the club's magazine took on
a new look with the first issue of HSCC News. The
editorship was a joint venture between Grahame White
and racing journalist Paul Lawrence and a front page
story reported on a very successful season opener at
Silverstone. The club management's pledge to deliver

GRAHAME WHITE

Chief Executive Officer, 1997 to date

"I was a founder member of Sevenoaks and District Motor Club with my father and just did local motor sport events. My father was Chairman of the club for a while. We did trials, driving tests and rallies; all the usual bits and pieces. That's how it all started for me in motor sport.

"In the same village was a man called Basil Tye, who worked at the RAC, and he and my father became good friends. I used to go to Goodwood occasionally with Basil in his beautiful bright red Jaguar XK120. We drove all the way along country roads with the hood down and I was just in heaven. I'd have been a young teenager then.

"One day my father said to me that Basil had told him the BARC was looking for someone to work in the competitions department. I'd followed my father into the insurance world in the City. I arranged an interview and went to the very posh offices at 55 Park Lane in London.

"Soon after the interview they offered me a job. The boss then was John Morgan who had been running the club for a while and was also the owner of the Steering Wheel Club. I didn't really know quite what to expect. Although I'd been involved in all sorts of motor sport I hadn't started to race at that time. I soon had to learn. That was in 1962.

"It was a massively steep learning curve, but very enjoyable. The BARC was a big club then with 16,000 members and was probably the biggest such club in the world. On the committee were people like Colin Chapman, Tony Brooks and Gordon England and for the first few committee meetings I sat in, I wondered what I was doing there!

"Because of all the events the club organised, the responsibilities were divided north and south and I looked after the southern circuits like Goodwood, Crystal Palace and Brands Hatch. A guy called Ken Yates was given the northern circuits. I became responsible for everything to do with running a race meeting.

"I had lots of things happen at Goodwood. I was there for a test day and the works Lotus team was there with two Lotus Cortinas for Jim Clark and Peter Arundel. I heard Colin Chapman say to Jimmy: 'Well, go out and see if you can find the limit of the car.' Two laps later he rolled it at Madgwick and came walking back and said to Colin: 'I've found the limit!'

"Roy James, one of the Great Train robbers, was down there to do a race meeting and practised on the Friday. Then he heard that the police were after him and disappeared. The police were all over Goodwood on the Friday night after he'd gone. Someone rang the circuit and asked to speak to me as I was running the race meeting. They talked to me as though I was a mate and I was totally naïve, not knowing that it was the Daily Telegraph, chatting about Roy because I didn't know what had been going on. That weekend I'd borrowed a Rolls Royce to use as a course car and I got back to the circuit quite early on Saturday morning. I drove in and parked on the startline, there was a group of marshals waiting and as I got out of the car there was a great chant about me being a friend of Roy's and the Rolls Royce being a present from him! I didn't know what they were talking about until someone showed me the front page of the Daily Telegraph, where I was quoted at length.

"Another day at Goodwood I got a call in race control from Ken Tyrrell who was looking for a young driver and he understood he was at Goodwood. Ken said: 'I think his name is Stewart and do you know if he is there?' I'd talked to him earlier so I knew he was there so Ken asked me if I could find him. So Ken held on the line and I went to find Jackie in the paddock and said: 'There's a bloke called Ken Tyrrell on the phone'. Jackie said: 'I wonder what he wants?' That was the start of it all.

"It was a different era back then. Jimmy Clark had made his name by then, but he hadn't changed at all. He was just a lovely guy. One Easter we were all staying at the Chichester Motel down on the roundabout and I remember going up to my room after dinner and trying to get into my bed. Someone had made what we used to call an 'apple pie bed' and you couldn't get into it. I was walking through the paddock the following day and Jimmy came by and asked if I'd had a good night's sleep. It had been him!

"We used to spend a lot of time chatting because he was a farmer and I always wanted to be a farmer. What a super guy. I was at Hockenheim when he was killed and had breakfast with him that day. It wasn't a good weekend because I was at Silverstone on the Saturday and there had been a fatal accident when Robin Smith in a Ford Mustang went straight on at Woodcote. I'd been asked by the RAC to be the steward for the race at Hockenheim so after the meeting at Silverstone I drove to the airport and flew out to Germany and booked in to the hotel where Jimmy was staying. We had breakfast on Sunday morning and were organising presenting him with a BARC Gold Medal at Thruxton the following weekend at Easter.

"He'd been out of the country for tax reasons and he was explaining his travel arrangements between Hockenheim and Thruxton. He'd just picked up his new twin-engined aircraft as well and was due to fly back to Scotland the day after Hockenheim. It was just awful.

"In race control after the accident happened it was a little difficult because no one seemed to speak English, so all our conversations had to be in French. They were very reluctant to tell me exactly what had happened and that Jimmy had been killed. They sent his body to hospital because the doctor could not accept the fact that noting could be done, because of who it was.

"I went to the scene of the accident and saw the car. Then the race officials asked if I would tell the team what had happened. Eventually I went over to the team and I told Graham Hill, who was Jimmy's team-mate. We were sitting in the cab of the Lotus team transporter and Graham wouldn't believe me. That was his reaction and Graham was a very strong character. He was almost forcing me to tell him it wasn't true, and I can totally understand his reaction as they were such good mates. Jimmy was so special and Graham insisted I went back to race control and got confirmation. He would not accept it. I think we all went numb with the shock.

"Colin Chapman wasn't there as he was skiing in the Alps and he borrowed a VW Beetle and drove all the way to Hockenheim. There was nothing he could do, but he just wanted to be there. He turned up at the hotel on the Sunday evening and we were all just sitting about, not talking and just completely numb. No one could believe it.

"Formula 2 has always been a favourite for me. I was very fortunate in that I was organising all of the Formula 2 races in the UK and it was at a time when most of the Grand Prix drivers were also doing Formula 2. The pressure was off, they could have a great time and the cars were very competitive. They were going to nice places and there were probably less than 10 Formula 1 races on the calendar. The drivers were more relaxed and it was a friendly atmosphere, so you got to know Grand Prix drivers where you wouldn't have done otherwise. I had some great times in Formula 2 because I was often a steward at the continental events and we had some fun times.

"I first met Jochen Rindt when he was racing in Formula Vee and he was a little bit similar to Jimmy. He couldn't understand what all the fuss was about, because he was naturally talented like Jimmy. He loved what he was doing but he was not the typical superstar and we'd chat about all sorts of things. But he was so talented.

"The day he was killed at Monza I walked into the paddock not knowing what had happened and there was a rather strange atmosphere. The first person I bumped into was Jackie Stewart and he told me what had happened. It happened too often in those days.

"I left the BARC in 1973 and went to work with Chevron for three years as sales manager. I had a great time during 10 years at the BARC and started as an assistant in the competitions department. Then I became competitions secretary and then general secretary and it was very enjoyable. But after 10 years it was probably time for a change and a new challenge.

"Derek Bennett at Chevron was just different and very likeable. He was very, very talented but very modest, both as an engineer and a driver. But he didn't really want to know about all the fuss and didn't really want to talk to the teams and sponsors. That's really why I went there.

"I was still running my own property business so I never joined anyone full time. I was doing quite a lot of stewarding for the RAC and I had a couple of years looking after the PR side of Silverstone. I was very good friends with Richard Lloyd from way back when he was racing a Triumph Spitfire and we used to race against each other occasionally.

"Into the 1980s he said he was thinking about joining the World Sportscar Championship with a Porsche 956 and would I be interested in helping to run the team. Of course, that was most enjoyable and we did around 10 years with lots of different sponsors. We had lots of drivers including Jonathan Palmer and Jan Lammers who are both still good friends now.

"We did the World Championship for many years and Richard and I travelled together to events. We had some great times in lots of different countries with a lot of success. As a private team in Group C you could compete pretty well with the works teams. You were always two or three developments behind but not too far and the Porsche factory was pretty helpful to the privateers. We won a few races and were on the podium a few times.

"You get to know the drivers so much better when you are spending a week at a time with them. One race I remember was the 1983 Nurburgring 1000kms and the people from the Porsche factory said they had a driver they couldn't fit in for various contractual reasons and wondered if we could run him. That was Keke Rosberg. He was the current Formula 1 World Champion and had said to Frank Williams that he wanted to race on the Nordschleife before the circuit was closed, which seemed likely at the time. Keke was quite persuasive and Frank Williams allowed him to do the race.

"The Porsche factory made sure we had a good engine. I knew Keke from Formula 2, of course. He didn't do any testing and he'd never driven a 956 before and the Nordschleife is not really the place to learn a car. Anyway, he went out and did two or three laps in practice and when he came in we were all waiting for him to say do this or do that. But he got out of the car and said he didn't want to change anything and he'd drive it absolutely as it was. He had a ball racing it with Palmer and Lammers and we finished third behind the works car of Jochen Mass and Jacky Ickx and the Joest car 956 of Bob Wollek and Stefan Johansson.

"After Group C I was really concentrating on the property business through the 1990s and I also had a farming interest. I still went to Le Mans with Richard with the Audis and the Bentleys, but it wasn't a full time role. I was heavily involved in quite a big property project and that needed some of my time. I enjoyed doing that and although I'm not a qualified architect I can do designs and plans. Converting farm buildings is one side of that.

"It was Lincoln Small who made the first contact about the HSCC. We were staying with some friends in France and he asked me to give him a ring when I got back. I'd been out of organising race meetings for a long time and I didn't know if I really wanted to get back into it or whether I could commit the time. Initially, they asked if I could come in one or two days a week, just to see what I thought to the club's situation. I don't think they realised how much of a mess it was in. You have to spend some time going backwards and forwards to find out what is going on.

"Fairly soon I realised that a lot had to be done to try and put it on a more professional footing and also a commercial footing. That was in 1997 and I had absolutely no intention of staying so long. I could only really commit to spending more time with the club as two or three of my property projects completed successfully.

"We've achieved lots of different things in that time and we've put the club on a very sound financial footing. I was rather pleased the first time I saw a bank statement saying the club had over a million pounds in the bank. We've achieved that amount by working to achieve it; it is not a windfall and has been raised by running the club properly and commercially. But it is not something we shout about. It is much better to be able to negotiate with organisations if you are financially sound and run a professional operation. Of course, there might be a rainy day at some stage and maybe one day we will need to buy some premises or we could have a disastrous race meeting.

"We're not trying to make huge profits out of anyone and that money has been built up over a long time, nearly 20 years. I think that for every race meeting I've been responsible for, we've made a profit. Everything we do is for the good of the club and the members and there is no personal gain in this. It is about the enjoyment of driving out of a paddock on a Sunday evening when you think you've put on a good race meeting and people wave and say thank you. That is worth a huge amount.

"We run a tight ship with a small staff and the people we have are tremendous, they really are. I've been fortunate to find good people and it is a nice little team with a great atmosphere.

"I think we've established ourselves as a good and sound organising club. But we have been fortunate that this has all been going on at a time when historic racing has blossomed. But the challenge is to keep up and never stand still. Racing has changed enormously over the last 20 years. We try and keep our entry fees at a very competitive level.

"In terms of other achievements, I think it was nice when we were asked to run the support race at the British Grand Prix. We also ran an invitation race at Macau and we have a very nice working relationship with Jaguar Land Rover, which is good for the club. We're represented on FIA and MSA committees and the club has a good standing in the industry.

"I still thoroughly enjoy what I'm doing. The 50th anniversary season has been a big landmark and I'm pleased to have been around while the club is enjoying that milestone."

a more relaxed atmosphere and better value for money was achieved with longer races throughout the weekend for 350 entrants. The response from members was very positive as the influence and experience of Grahame White started to become apparent.

Long-standing racer and HSCC member John Harper summed up the impact made by Grahame White's appointment. "I've been racing since 1963 and I've raced all sorts of things. I was heavily involved in the HSCC at one stage and I was on the committee for quite a while in the 1980s and I was there when we took Steve Lydon on," said Harper. "The club went through the doldrums for a while, but since Grahame White has been at the helm it has become a very, very professional club. He's done a wonderful job with the club."

The 1998 Brands Hatch Super Prix was headlined by the FIA TGP race which drew a record field of 25 cars to the grid and ended in a commanding victory for Bob Berridge in the ex-Rosberg Williams FW08B. On the same programme, Benn Simms topped a 38-car Historic Formula Ford field and the TVR Griffith of Joe Ward and Chris Conoley won the three-hour sports and GT race from a 45-car grid. In total, the meeting drew over 430 entries which was deemed to be a new record for the club and a major boost for the club's finances and reputation.

At the close of the 1998 season, nine champions were confirmed including racing veterans Mike Wilds (RJB Group 6), Alan Baillie (Classic Racing Cars) and Sid Marler (Classic Sports). A youthful Benn Simms won the Historic Formula Ford title and Jason Kennedy and Mike Eagles each took a Road Sports crown, while Nick Shrigley-Feigl (Derek Bell Trophy), Peter Wray (Historic Saloons) and Winston Bunn (Classic F3) were the other big winners. Many of the winners from the season were presented with their awards by Derek Bell, who was guest of honour at the annual dinner dance.

Season-end reviews for each of the championships were generally upbeat with steady or, more likely, increasing grids being reported across the spectrum. From struggling to make double figures a year earlier, the Derek Bell Trophy ended the season with a 40-car entry at Silverstone. The numbers reflected the fact that the club had turned a real corner under the direction of chairman Nick Overall and new chief executive Grahame White. While long-standing categories like Road Sports were in continued good

health, more recent additions like Formula Ford, Historic Saloons and Classic F3 were all playing a part in the renaissance. Critically, the club now had enough content to confidently plan a racing programme based mainly around its own categories.

Sure enough, as the club office planned the 1999 season there was a clear sign of optimism about the club's improving financial position and expected level of competitor support. The 1999 calendar was to be the biggest yet with nine race meetings at seven venues along with three more invited events at circuits including Spa-Francorchamps. The new season would include continued support from Richard Budge at RJB Mining.

That optimism was underlined by comments from treasurer Derek Downing in the pre-Christmas 1998 magazine. "Following the sale of our old premises at Chippenham, which allowed the bank loan to be repaid, and two years of reasonable excess of income over expenditure, the balance sheet at 31 December 1998 will reflect a much healthier position than that previously reported." The next AGM would be in March 1999 following a decision to move it from the traditional December date.

In his report at the AGM, Nick Overall highlighted the turn-around in the club's performance. *"The Club has made many improvements in the past year, lots of them badly needed and to achieve this is due in no small way to the efforts of our executive director Grahame White and the club's manager Joe Keech. Our race meetings are better organised, sticking to the timetable and not shortening races, regulations and passes are sent out earlier and the general atmosphere seems to be much more friendly – we didn't have a single protest last year. The office works better and we now have a much improved and more regular newsletter.*

"We have also had a much better financial year than in the past – providing a reasonable surplus with both grid numbers and membership up. I believe we can now start to build on this and create a sensible reserve of funds for the future. Derek Downing, our treasurer, deserves our utmost thanks for all his help in this matter."

Alongside the expanded race programme for 1999 came news of two new race series. A new series for Historic Sports-Racing Cars was to run over six races and was open to cars built up to 1965, including the type of cars that raced in the club's very early

HSCC News
JOURNAL OF THE HISTORIC SPORTS CAR CLUB   Issue Seven August 3/1999

Brands Hatch
Superprix -
'the best ever!'

Spa-
Francorchamps
- the world's
finest track

For the full
report from
Brands, please
turn to pages
eight
and nine.

Geoff Farmer on his way to the 1999 CRC title

years. Meanwhile, Grahame White had come to an agreement with the Jaguar Enthusiasts' Club for the HSCC to run the JEC XK Series Sports Car Challenge for examples of the Jaguar XK120, 140 and 150. The six-race series was a joint venture between the two clubs and all cars were required to be road-registered and road legal.

A total of 11 race meetings made up the 1999 schedule, along with a single-seater race at Spa in September. A two-day Croft meeting in May and visits to Croix-en-Ternois and Mondello Park made up a busy season. By the middle of the season, Joe Keech had decided to move on and left the club, while Grahame White's initially part-time role was now confirmed as a full-time position.

Early season meetings in 1999 included the season-opener at Donington Park (18 April) where thick fog hung over the circuit and forced the club to run qualifying sessions behind the safety car. Thankfully, the fog cleared in time for racing to go ahead as

planned and winners included Paul Sleeman (Macon MR8) in Historic Formula Ford, Geoff Farmer (Brabham BT18) in Classic Racing Cars and Richard Evans (Chevron B34D) in the Derek Bell Trophy. Those three drivers all won again during a successful two-day meeting at Silverstone in May when the European Formula 2 field was a guest race. Bob Juggins won both races in his Lola T240 with series organiser Freddy Kumschick on the podium for both races in his March 712.

The standing of the annual Brands Hatch Super Prix was higher than ever in 1999 with guest races for TGP, European Historic Formula 2, HGPCA Pre '66 Grand Prix cars and the BRDC's 1950s Sports Car Championship. At the time, plans were being made for the Kent track to host the British Grand Prix under a new multi-year deal between Formula 1 and Octagon, the track's new American owners. There were fears that such a move would mean a major re-work of the track to suit modern Grand Prix cars and thus take away the true driving challenge of a track largely unchanged since it was extended in the early 1960s.

The lead story in the June 1999 issue of HSCC News previewed the Super Prix. "Recent news about the proposed return of Formula 1 racing to the famous Kent track is going to change the face of the circuit forever. If the plans reach fruition, the Grand Prix circuit will alter drastically over the next couple of seasons. This is set to be one of the last chances for

Road Sports action at Castle Combe, August 1999

drivers to tackle the unique challenge offered by the current lay-out."

The TGP entry for the Super Prix totalled an impressive 34 cars, including Michael Schryver (Lotus 72), Duncan Dayton (Brabham BT33), Martin Stretton (Tyrrell P34), John Narcisi (Trojan T103), Bob Berridge (Williams FW08), Joaquin Folch (Lotus 91) and Helen Bashford (Shadow DN9B). In the race, Berridge led until his engine cut-out and so Stretton took over to win and give the six-wheeled Tyrrell its first win since 1977. At the end of 1999, the three-year deal for the HSCC to remain involved in TGP, and receive an annual fee, came to an end.

The three-hour sports and GT race at Brands Hatch was won by a trio of Minshaws as Alan joined his sons Jon and Jason in the winning Jaguar E-type, while

Frank Sytner's Cooper Monaco topped the BRDC Historic Sports. A serious accident in the Historic FF1600 race sent Stuart Kestenbaum to hospital, from where he pledged to return to racing as quickly as possible. However, the driving standards in the race and lack of attention to flag signals earned the drivers a briefing on the grid from clerk of the course John Smith before the race was re-started.

Other news from the second half of the 1999 included the appointment of Peter Dixon as the club's Chief Registrar, while former treasurer Ray Hunter suffered a massive accident at Spa in his Turner. He was hospitalised in Belgium for a month but was later transferred to a hospital in London to continue his recovery. It was four months before Hunter finally returned home, but the doctors were unable to save his leg, which was badly damaged in the accident.

Classic F3 action from the Silverstone Finals meeting

The roll of honour at the end of the 1999 season celebrated 10 champions including Bob Berridge, who won the TGP crown for a third time in a row. Graeme Dodd, back racing after a gap of more than 20 years, won the Alfred Blackmore-supported Historic Racing Saloon Championship in his Jaguar Mk2 while another racing returnee, Mike Campbell-Cole, took the Classic F3 title. It was also a good season for Geoff Farmer as he won the Classic Racing Car crown in Roger Swanton's Brabham BT18 and then won at Goodwood in the ex-Rob Walker Lotus 49, recently restored by Simon Hadfield.

Prolific racer Nicholas Pearce won the RJB title from the Sports 2000 class in his Tiga SC79 and in the process beat Mike Wilds in the Richard Budge-owned Chevron B19 to the crown. Thirty years earlier, the young Nicholas had been a gofer on Mike's racing programme and they had remained friends ever since. An invitation class catered for the over 2-litre cars, but none of them raced regularly.

After a year off from racing in 1998, Paul Sleeman bounced back to win the Historic FF1600 title for a third time, this time at the wheel of a Macon MR8 rather than the Jamun T2 he used to win back-to-

THE 1999 HSCC RACING CHAMPIONS
FIA Cup for Thoroughbred Grand Prix Cars
Bob Berridge (Williams FW08)
Classic Sports Car Championship
Sid Marler (Lotus Elan)
RJB Mining Championship
Nicholas Pearce (Tiga SC79)
Classic Racing Car Championship
Geoff Farmer (Brabham BT18B)
70s Road Sports Championship
Des Fitzgerald (Lotus Elan)
Historic Road Sports Championship
Kevin Kivlochan (TVR Griffith)
Derek Bell Trophy
John Robinson (Reynard SF78)
JEC XK Series Sports Car Challenge
Chris Jaques (XK120)
Historic FF1600 Championship
Paul Sleeman (Macon MR8)
Historic Racing Saloon Championship
Graeme Dodd (Jaguar Mk2)
Classic Formula 3 Championship
Mike Campbell-Cole (Brabham BT41)

HRS racing at Silverstone

back crowns in 1996 and 1997. The novice class title was hotly contested by Paul Smith, in the ex-Sleeman Jamun, and newcomer Chris Sharples in his Palliser.

While the racing had been very good through 1999, there was equally important good news on the club's finances, which continued to improve markedly under Grahame White's guidance. At the AGM in the spring of 2000, Derek Downing reported a year of sound financial performance. Income was up by 8% and expenditure rose by 5%, with an increase of membership and racing registrations and a small increase in sponsorship revenue. In his report, Chairman Nick Overall commented: "We have again achieved a reasonable surplus and we are now beginning to build a reserve for investment and for the future of the club."

At the same time, the club launched its own website for the first time and Mark Lowrie joined the staff to help with race meeting administration. By the spring of 2000, David Addison had taken over as magazine editor as Paul Lawrence stood down due to other work commitments within the sport.

In revealing the 2000 season, Grahame White confirmed continued backing from RJB Mining for what was now titled the RJB Thundersports Championship for the new season along with a mini-series of hour-long, pit-stop races for Historic Saloon Cars, with races planned at Silverstone, Brands Hatch and Spa.

The calendar included a return to Cadwell Park in May and some classes would make guest appearances at Thruxton and Castle Combe in the summer. Key dates for the club's own race meetings were a season-opener at Donington Park (16 April), a two-day Silverstone (May 27/28), the Historic Super Prix at Brands Hatch (1/2 July) and the championship finals meeting at Silverstone on 14 October.

Unfortunately, due to a shortage of available days on the Brands Hatch Grand Prix circuit, the Super Prix was consigned to the Indy circuit this year. From a 15-race programme, notable winners included David Methley (Marcos GT), Miles Townshend (Ford Mustang) and Richard Thorne (Morgan +8) while in the Formula Junior race Paul Dudley just beat Michael Hibberd in a Lotus battle.

A little later in the year, came news that Richard Budge would join Stirling Moss and Derek Bell as a patron of the club. Richard Budge joined his family business in 1966 and later developed the group's mining activities through the 1970s. He headed a management buy-out in 1992 and became Chief Executive of RJB Mining PLC, the largest coal mining operation in the UK by 1994. At the time, the company operated 13 collieries and a similar number of opencast sites, producing around 25 million tonnes of coal a year with a turnover of £700 million and employing 8000 people. He raced Chevrons, in particular, with great success in the early 1980s and was a tremendous supporter of the club through some of its most

Paul Smith heads a pack at Thruxton

*Des Fitzgerald made his
FF debut at Thruxton*

challenging times. Indeed, without his support, the club may not have survived through the 1990s.

Towards the end of 2000, it was confirmed that Formula Ford 2000 and Formula Super Vee cars would be admitted to the Classic Formula 3 Championship as grids of F3 cars had struggled through the season. This was a pilot idea for the final two races of the season but was due to be extended into 2001. The cars were still able to race in the Derek Bell Trophy alongside F1,

Formula 5000, Formula 2 and Formula Atlantic cars as well as Classic Clubmans.

Winner of the Derek Bell Trophy for 2000 was John Bladon in his Formula 5000 Surtees TS11, while Paul Sleeman made it four FF1600 titles in five seasons with nine wins from 10 races and Paul Heywood-Halfpenny topped the Historic Racing Saloons in a Lotus Cortina. The Classic F3 contest went down to the wire at Silverstone and Neil Dunkel did all he

THE 2000 HSCC RACING CHAMPIONS

Classic Sports Car Championship
David Methley (Marcos GT)

RJB Mining Championship
Steve Mills (Tiga SC80)

Classic Racing Car Championship
Richard Urwin (Brabham BT28)

70s Road Sports Championship
Adam Bagnall (Triumph GT6)

Historic Road Sports Championship
Justin Murphy (Alfa Romeo Giulia)

Derek Bell Trophy
John Bladon (Surtees TS11)

JEC XK Series Sports Car Challenge
Chris Jaques (XK120)

Historic FF1600 Championship
Paul Sleeman (Macon MR8)

Historic Racing Saloon Championship
Paul Haywood-Halfpenny (Ford Lotus Cortina)

Classic Formula 3 Championship
Peter Williams (Argo JM6)

Classic Sports action from the Silverstone Finals' meeting

could by winning the race, but fellow Argo racer Peter Williams drove a measured race to finish second and win the championship.

The end of the 2000 season also heralded some changes in the club's line-up of championship officials. After nearly a decade as 70s Road Sports chairman, Richard Thorne stood down as did David Pratley from Classic Racing Cars and former vice-chairman Don Hands. New names joining the board included Andy Shepherd (70s Road Sports) and David Pullan (Classic Racing Cars).

It was calculated that the club's race meetings had drawn a total of 2000 entries across the 2000 racing season. The financial report pointed to another profitable year and increases in membership income, despite static fees, almost offset the loss of revenue following the agreed end of the TGP contract. Treasurer Derek Downing reported that: '2000 will show another solid profit to further boost the club's improving financial resources'.

For 2001, there was little significant change to the club's portfolio of championships, but the race calendar included a return to Mallory Park and Oulton Park for one-day meetings. The trip to Croix-en-Ternois, which had never drawn big grids despite being enjoyed by those who made the journey, was dropped from the schedule. The 2000 event was reported as making 'an unacceptably high loss' and would not be repeated.

There was also some concern about the finances for 2001, which centred on increased circuit hire charges. After being unsuccessful in trying to move the British Grand Prix to a re-developed Brands Hatch, US-based Octagon Motor Sports Ltd had to do a deal with the British Racing Drivers' Club to use Silverstone and one of the consequences of this was an immediate hike in circuit hire fees for Silverstone. In the final accounts for the year to December 2001, the club showed a small loss, the first for six years and it was largely attributed to rises in circuit hire charges.

In the club office, Mark Lowrie moved on in the spring of 2001 and was replaced by Phillip Parfitt. In the chairman's report in the magazine of Spring 2001, Nick Overall was upbeat in his assessment of the club's position. *"Now that we have begun to achieve what I set out in my AGM report of 1996, to have sufficient reserves, I believe the time is right to start the next stage of investing more in the Club's future and we will be looking at better publicity, upgrading our website and regalia in particular.*

We shall also throughout this season, be asking members for their view on the long term future of the Club. I feel we are the most understated Club in racing - this we must change."

The 2001 season opened at Donington Park and it was journalist and

THE 2001 HSCC RACING CHAMPIONS

Classic Sports Car Championship
Mark Ashworth (MGB)
RJB Mining Championship
Lawrence Benson (Chevron B8)
Classic Racing Car Championship
Ed Mercer (Palliser WDB2)
70s Road Sports Championship
Charles Barter (Datsun 240Z)
Historic Road Sports Championship
Mike Eagles (Milano GT)
Derek Bell Trophy
John Crowson (Chevron B40)
Historic FF1600 Championship
Neil Fowler (Lola T200)
Historic Racing Saloon Championship
Simon Garrad (BMW 2000Ti) and Graeme Dodd (Jaguar Mk2)
Classic Formula 3 Championship
Peter Williams (Argo JM6)

Marcus Pye (right) tells Ian Titchmarsh (left) of his dramas as car owner Paul Smith looks on

commentator Marcus Pye in the news and on the front page of the magazine. Pye had accepted an invitation to race one of two Jamun T2s owned by Paul Smith and backed by Dupaul Engineering. The Historic FF1600 race was all going well until a tangle of wheels pitched Pye's car over at the chicane from which he fortunately escaped muddy but otherwise largely okay despite his crash helmet taking a hit during the spectacular incident. Marcus then walked into the pits and was able to give commentator Ian Titchmarsh a detailed description of the shunt.

Pye remembered the incident clearly. "It was my first FF1600 race in towards 10 years and I qualified really well - eighth or so - in a big field and climbed to third at one point. I recall the Jamun's owner Paul Smith's words before I went out. 'Drive it like you stole it,' and the following week him being taken aback when he learned that I'd called Tony Mundy on the Monday morning and bought a new upright to replace the smashed one.

"A couple of other things were interesting: Classic F3 Chevron racer Martyn Porter ran up to the medical centre to examine my wrists as he is an orthopaedic surgeon and Alan Baillie drove the car back from the scrutineering bay with the rear corner out of kilter."

Elsewhere at Donington there were good entries and close racing and friends Graeme Dodd (Jaguar Mk2) and Simon Garrad (BMW 2000Ti) battled against Richard Evans (Alfa Romeo GTA) in Historic Racing Saloons and it was Garrad who won after a glorious contest. James Murray won in Historic FF1600 and Charles Barter took his first race win in 70s Road Sports with his Datsun 240Z. Another first-time winner was former bike racer Chris Lillingston-Price who took a debut win in the non-championship Historic FF1600 race despite starting from the back of the grid.

Early in May, the club went to Cadwell Park for a one-day meeting that came close to being cancelled due to a shortage of marshals. The numbers were okay in the run-up to the meeting, but a number of cancellations meant there were not enough marshals to man the circuit. After some quick thinking, the racing was moved to the shorter 1.5-mile club circuit as there were enough marshals to man the shorter track.

In June, the club's visit to Snetterton included the first revived Autosport Three-Hour race and marked a return to running endurance races. Michael Schryver and Simon Hadfield dominated the race in Michael's Chevron B16 and won four laps.

THE 2002 HSCC RACING CHAMPIONS

Classic Sports Car Championship
Chris Reece (Lotus Elan)
Classic Racing Car Championship
James Long (Brabham BT15)
70s Road Sports Championship
Adam Bagnall (Triumph GT6)
Historic Road Sports Championship
Nick Adams (Lotus Elan)
Derek Bell Trophy
Nick Crossley (March 73A)
Historic FF1600 Championship
Neil Fowler (Lola T200)
Historic Racing Saloon Championship
Adrian Oliver (Hillman Imp)
Classic Formula 3 Championship
Neil Dunkel (Argo JM3)

In mid-season, the annual Brands Hatch Super Prix drew an entry of more than 400 cars and a total of 13 red flag incidents certainly kept the team in race control at full stretch. Race winners included Michael Hibberd (Lotus 27) in Formula Junior, young Neil Fowler in Historic FF1600, Steven Worrad (Brabham BT28) in Classic Racing Cars and Nick Crossley (March 73A) in the Derek Bell Trophy.

Future club chairman Chris Sharples did some excellent negotiation to get the Historic Formula Fords a slot on the Silverstone Historic Festival over the August Bank Holiday weekend and a fabulous 44-car grid turned on a stunning race as new pretender Neil Fowler beat established ace Paul Sleeman after a mighty contest. It was the first race to be titled the Walter Hayes Trophy and was the club's first significant on-track involvement in an event that would later become an important date on the HSCC calendar.

The season's champions included FF1600 ace Fowler who broke Sleeman's dominance of the category and racing newcomer Charles Barter after an excellent debut season in 70 s Road Sports. Ed Mercer was a

Touring Car action at Silverstone

Classic Clubmans at the Finals' meeting

delighted winner of the Classic Racing Car title in his Palliser and the duelling Simon Garrad and Graeme Dodd could not be separated in Historic Racing Saloons and were declared champions. Though fierce rivals on-track, they were good friend off-track and earlier in the year Graeme had been best man at Simon's wedding.

The big news for the 2002 season was the revival of the Oulton Park Gold Cup, to give the Cheshire track a major historic festival for the first time. With Octagon Motor Sport managing the track alongside its contract at Silverstone, this was effectively a case of moving the Silverstone Historic Festival to Oulton Park. The August Bank Holiday date was retained and the HSCC was appointed race organiser.

Grahame White explained the deal in the April 2002 edition of 'HSCC News'. "As a result of negotiations with Octagon Motor Sport they have agreed we should run this event. We are the only club dedicated to running just historic motor racing, so I am sure this has helped. We are working with Octagon to ensure that it is an excellent meeting."

Plans for the weekend included a full programme of HSCC races, two races from the HGPCA, a drum-braked sports car race and a BRDC Historic Sports race. The last time the Gold Cup had been run for historic cars was in 1981 when it was won by John Surtees in a Maserati 250F.

Later in the season it was confirmed that Sir Jack Brabham would be the guest of honour at the Gold Cup in celebration of his four wins in the race in the late 1950s and mid-1960s. His wins in 1964, 1966 and 1967

Graeme Dodd fends off Simon Garrad at Silverstone

all came at the wheel of his own cars. Added to the race programme was a Lurani Trophy Formula Junior race, the only FIA historic championship event in the UK that year, and a FORCE race for pre-1974 Grand Prix cars.

The connections with Octagon brought further benefit when the club was asked to organise a race for historic sports cars as a support race to the 2002 British Grand Prix at Silverstone on 7 July. Cars from the 1950s and 1960s were to share the grid and the race was heralded as adding further to the HSCC's reputation and its involvement with Octagon, promoters of the Grand Prix.

Colin Blower won the race in the ex-Denny Hulme Lola T70 Spyder after a battle with Simon Hadfield's Lotus 30. Up into 16th place at the finish was club patron Sir Stirling Moss in his Cooper Monaco. The race was a big success with a capacity grid of varied cars and close racing all down the order.

Other developments for the 2002 season included a two-day Snetterton meeting which would feature longer races, with hour-long contests for Classic Sports and Historic Racing Saloons and a race for RJB-type sports-racing cars even though the RJB-backed

championship had been laid to rest at the end of 2001 due to lack of competitor support. Lawrence Benson (Chevron B8) was the final champion as the long-running RJB sponsorship finally came to an end.

The Classic Sports Car race enduro at Snetterton had several leaders and both Chris Reece (Lotus Elan) and Philip Nelson (Marcos GT) retired near the end of the hour to leave the way open for Jamie Boot to win in his TVR Griffith). Neil Fowler beat Paul Sleeman by a fraction of a second after a fierce 30-minute Historic Formula Ford race, while Win Percy won the BRDC Historic Sports Car Championship round in Nigel Webb's Jaguar D-type.

By the end of the 2002 season, the titles were won and lost and it was Adrian Oliver who gave the Hillman Imp its first overall victory in the Historic Racing Saloon Championship. Neil Fowler retained his Historic FF1600 Championship and Nick Crossley's rare March 73A won the Derek Bell Trophy. Lotus Elans took the Classic Sports title with Chris Reece and the Historic Road Sports crown with Nick Adams, while Adam Bagnall won his second 70s Road Sports Championship title in his Triumph GT6 after Charles Barter's 2001 victory.

8

2003 to 2007

Building in the new millennium

Edwin Jowsey heads the DBT field at Donington, April 2003

The club went into the 2003 season with eight core championships covering Historic Road Sports, 70s Road Sports, Classic Sports, Derek Bell Trophy, Classic Formula 3, Classic Racing Cars, Historic Formula Ford and Historic Racing Saloons. In addition, the Jaguar XK Series was now running with the club and a growing number of Formula Junior championship dates were at HSCC race meetings.

Laurence Bailey's TVR leads at Donington

A new sponsor was announced for the 70s Road Sports Championship as Lotus Esprit racer Andy Reeves supported the category through his Wesprey Castings business. Millers Oils was the sponsor of Historic Road Sports, a deal arranged by racer and agent Robin Longdon, while Retro Track and Air supported Classic Racing Cars. Matthew Watts, from the aircraft and race car restoration operation, would race his Brabham BT16 in the championship.

An attempt was made to create a 70s Road Saloons category, but the concept never really got off the ground despite the efforts of series chairman Richard Thorne. One or two cars did appear, including the Ford Escort RS2000 of Bob Trotter, but the idea was quietly shelved and the cars that emerged were absorbed into the 70s Road Sports category.

The season started with race meetings at Donington Park and Cadwell Park in April before a new-look Silverstone weekend in May. At the instigation of venue operator Octagon Motorsports, the 17/18 May weekend featured a series of Vintage Sports-Car Club races alongside the regular HSCC categories and the action moved to the International Circuit layout.

In the April 2003 edition of HSCC News, the thinking behind the event was explained. "Our first Silverstone meeting could well turn out to be the start of something big. Octagon Motorsports has played a part in creating this idea and we look forward to it working well and perhaps growing into the Classic Festival for 2004. It is no secret that Octagon wants a major historic meeting at Silverstone again, as Brands Hatch and Oulton Park both have one, and this is possibly the embryonic event." Since the US-owned organisation had moved the former Coys Festival to Oulton Park to

Historic Road Sports at the Mallory hairpin

Dodd chases McWhirter in XKs at Mallory Park, May 2003

become the Gold Cup, Silverstone had been without a headline classic festival. However, history later showed that independent promoter Roger Etcell and his Motion Works operation came forward to organise a new event under the Silverstone Classic brand.

In the club office, Philip Parfitt was into a relatively brief term as competitions' secretary and would soon be replaced by Martin Atack, who joined the club in January 2004. Emma North (later to become Emma Jemmett) joined the staff at Silverstone to look after the club's finances and accounts as club treasurer Derek Downing announced that he would retire from office at the 2003 Annual General Meeting. There was also a plan for another move of club office, away from the building adjacent to the Silverstone Club. The plan

was to stay at Silverstone and move to bigger premises with space for a board meeting room.

The end of Downing's term as treasurer marked an important period in the club's finances as resources were rebuilt from the perilous situation of the mid-1990s. Chairman Nick Overall paid tribute to Downing's role in that recovery in his AGM report in the spring of 2003. "On behalf of all the members, Derek, I cannot thank you enough for your support

Ollie Smith and Paul Sleeman battle in HFF

Fellow HRS competitors help to fix the Turner of Dick Coffey

ANTHONY GODDARD

Former club treasurer

"My father was a sponsor of Mike Spence and he was my cousin, so it started with him. I wasn't allowed to go motor racing as I was considered far too precious by my father, which is difficult to believe. It was shocking when Mike was killed at Indianapolis in 1968.

"It was really Andrew Schryver, my wife's cousin, who got me into racing. We were talking at a funeral and he said I should get into historic racing and that was about 20 years ago.

"I started with Historic Formula Ford, which is a super formula, and I consider it's where I really belong. I'm an accountant by profession and from a very early time I thought I could possibly offer something to the HSCC. I'm quite nerdy with spreadsheets and for the first couple of years I spent a lot of time there and was working three days a week for the club developing the systems of which remnants are still used to this day.

"It was about 2000 when I took over the role of club accountant. I can claim a little bit of credit in what we did making entry forms easier to use. If you've got an entry form and all the information is there and you've just got to sign it, that's a lot less effort than trying to find all the information.

"Grahame White had arrived not long before me and it was his efforts that really got the club out of the mire. All I did was record the fact that the club was doing better than before. The club has prospered mightily in the period since Grahame has been there. I was able to record some good years. It was a case of getting the club properly structured and getting internal record keeping sorted out and into the 21st century.

"I did some stuff at home on the Isle of Wight and would go to Silverstone once or twice a week. In those days it wasn't quite the pain to be travelling that it is now. I used to keep a car on the mainland so it wasn't that bad.

"Through that time I was racing in Formula Ford and then went to Classic Racing Cars and amazingly won the championship in 2007 with my Merlyn Mk9. It was mostly by sand-bagging and making sure I finished. It was certainly not a reflection of my talent.

"I've loved my racing and made lots of good friends. The Cooper T56/59 Grand Prix car I've raced this year has been two years of constant problems and I blew up three engines not realising that I had no oil pressure going round left-hand bends. Eventually the penny dropped and we got the oil system sorted. We still had an electrical fault, but we eventually re-wired the whole thing and now it goes like a train. The Alfa Romeo engine in it is delightful.

"Bill Hemming leant me his Elfin 300 at Philip Island. That was a fabulous car and what a pleasure to drive down there and to cap it all, he leant me another Elfin to do the support race for the Australian Grand Prix at Melbourne. I've been able to race at Imola, Nurburgring and Zandvoort and all these fantastic places where you can feel the ghosts of drivers past."

and expertise. You will be a hard act to follow. I have enjoyed working with you. The Board takes great pleasure in offering you life membership together with some tokens of our gratitude."

In his final report as treasurer, Downing reflected on the success of the plan to attain and maintain a sound financial base for the club. Despite further increases in circuit hire costs, the accounts showed a small profit on the 2002 season. Downing's commentary was: "I am very pleased that, due almost entirely to the

Club having its most successful racing season ever, in financial terms as well as in the prestige brought to the Club, that any loss was avoided, and a small profit resulted." Historic Formula Ford racer Anthony Goddard took over the role of club treasurer from the 2003 AGM.

At the club's Snetterton meeting on 21/22 June, a special new award was presented in memory of Peter Swinger. As a long-standing club steward, Peter was a regular official at HSCC race meetings and died suddenly after attending the 2002 Oulton Park Gold Cup. In his earlier years he raced a Lotus 7, but that was sold to help with the deposit on a family home, so he stayed involved in the sport as a volunteer official. The first recipient of the Peter Swinger Trophy was young single-seater racer Edwin Jowsey from the Classic Racing Car grid.

Over the weekend of 5/6 July the annual Brands Hatch Super Prix was a resounding success with 470 entries for races that included guest grids for the Orwell Supersports, Gentlemen Drivers and BRDC Historic Sports Cars. Richard Eyre (McLaren M8F) won both Supersports races while the hour-long Gentlemen Drivers race fell to the Jaguar D-type of Win Percy and Gary Pearson. Notable winners from the HSCC championships included Laurence Bailey (TVR Griffith) in Historic Road Sports, Ian Jones (Lotus 59) in Classic Racing Cars after a mighty battle with Edwin Jowsey, Charles Barter (Datsun 240Z) in 70s Road Sports and Martin Stretton (Lotus Elan) in Classic Sports.

The weekend's final race was a round of the Legends-supported Historic Formula Ford 1600 Championship, which featured a tremendous battle between Oliver Smith (Merlyn Mk20) and Neil Fowler (Lola T200). Smith just got the verdict after a fine contest as Jason Minshaw, Paul Sleeman, Stuart Tilley and James Murray rounded out the top six.

In mid-August, more than 50 club members took their cars to Dublin for the annual Phoenix Park road races with non-championship grids for closed and open wheel cars. Local racer Tom McKinney won the first open wheel race from John Bladon and Robin Longdon, while local legend Tommy Reid won the second race in his slick-shod F2 Brabham. Chris Ball recovered from a

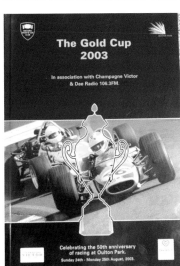

couple of moments in the opening race to take his Brabham to second ahead of Bladon. Double closed wheel honours went to John Monson's Elva, with Bruce Stapleton second in his Morgan Plus 8.

At the drivers' briefing, the clerk

of the course commented: "It's a dangerous circuit and we will probably run a bit late, but that's normal here." Everyone came home unscathed from a very enjoyable and sociable weekend.

Later in August, the Oulton Park Gold Cup celebrated the 50th year of the venue, which hosted its first race meeting in the summer of 1953. Joining the regular HSCC categories were races for the BRDC Historic Sports Car Championship, HGPCA races for drum-braked sports and pre-1966 Grand Prix cars and a race for Historic F1 and F5000 cars from the FORCE organisation of David McLaughlin.

To mark the anniversary of the Cheshire track, and the heritage of the Gold Cup race, a star-studded line-up of guests was arranged for the weekend. HSCC Patron Sir Stirling Moss was joined by Sir Jackie Stewart, Sir Jack Brabham, Derek Bell and Roy Salvadori. Moss had an outstanding record in the Gold Cup, winning the first two editions of the original race in 1954 and 1955 and then taking a hat-trick of win in 1959, 1960 and 1961 before his crash at Goodwood in April 1962 curtailed his Grand Prix career. He later won the race again in 1981 when it ran as a one-off historic race, back at the wheel of a Maserati 250F.

The 2003 event marked the 35th anniversary of Stewart's only Gold Cup win in the Ken Tyrrell-entered Matra MS10 in 1968. Brabham won the Gold Cup four times between 1957 and 1967, while Salvadori won the 1956 race in a Cooper T41 Formula 2 car. Stewart drove Tyrrell 001 and also officially opened the circuit's new race control and media centre building.

On the race programme, Martin O'Connell (Lotus 69 in the FORCE and Derek Bell trophy races) and Edwin Jowsey (Formula Junior were double winners in single-seaters and Frank Sytner won the first HGPCA race after starting his Brabham BT4 from the pit lane when a vibration started on the green flag lap.

In November 2003 the club received a fantastic invitation to provide a grid of historic sports-racing cars for a support race at the Macau Grand Prix. The famous round-the-streets race was celebrating 50 years and the promoters wanted a historic race to add to the usual Formula 3 and Touring Car feature races.

"Barry Bland of Motor Race Consultants ran the Macau race and he was my number two at the

The Milanos of Justin Murphy and Mike Eagles

John Delane and Jackie Stewart at the Oulton Park Gold Cup

*Three former Gold Cup winners at the 2003 event:
Salvadori, Moss and Brabham*

BARC back in the 1960s," said Grahame White. "He came to me with the idea and it proved to be a very special occasion. The locals were stunned by it, as they thought the cars would be doing some gentle demonstrations but, of course, it was proper racing."

The deal for competitors was incredibly attractive and included shipping for the car, airplane tickets, race entry and hotels. The date fitted well with the end of the UK season and the race was over-subscribed for the 30 places available on the grid. For many of the drivers, it was a racing experience of a lifetime.

From a superb grid, Frank Sytner (Lola T70 Spyder) headed Simon Hadfield (Lotus 30) and Denis Welch (Lotus 23) in the first race before the top two positions were reversed for the later race. Ted Williams, Julian Bronson, Bob Birrell, Gary Pearson, Barry Cannell, John Harper, John Clark and Marshall Bailey were all on the grid.

By the end of the season, the club's eight titles were won and lost and notable champions from the 2003 season included Classic Racing Car champion Matthew Watts who took the first of two championship victories in his Brabham BT16 and Derek Bell Trophy winner Paul Smith in his Formula Ford 2000 Reynard SF79.

Historic Road Sports at Oulton Park

THE 2003 HSCC RACING CHAMPIONS
Classic Sports Car Championship
Brendan Roberts (Lotus Elite)
Classic Racing Car Championship
Matthew Watts (Brabham BT16)
70s Road Sports Championship
Adam Bagnall (Triumph GT6)
Historic Road Sports Championship
Dick Coffey (Turner Mk1)
Derek Bell Trophy
Paul Smith (Reynard SF79)
Historic FF1600 Championship
Neil Fowler (Lola T200)
Historic Racing Saloon Championship
Adrian Oliver (Hillman Imp)
Classic Formula 3 Championship
Chris Levy (March 713M)

Adam Bagnall (Triumph GT6) retained his 70s Road Sports Championship and Dick Coffey drove the doors off his diminutive Turner Mk1 to win the Historic Road Sports Championship for the first time. Both Neil Fowler (Lola T200) and Adrian Oliver (Hillman Imp) were in the middle of a run of titles in Historic FF1600 and Historic Racing Saloons respectively.

As well as celebrating the club's 2003 champions and award winners at the annual dinner dance, there was further reason to celebrate over the winter months as the club was named 'Historic Competition Club of the Year' at the inaugural International Historic Motorsport Show at Stoneleigh in February. At much the same time, the club office moved within the Silverstone site to offices that would be home for at least the next 13 years.

Important changes for British motor racing came in 2004 when Jonathan Palmer, John Britten and Sir Peter Ogden acquired Brands Hatch, Oulton

Park, Snetterton and Cadwell Park from Octagon Motorsports. After a disastrous foray into motor racing, when its fingers were burnt to a high degree over ambitious plans to run the British Grand Prix, Octagon retreated to the US. Instead Palmer's team, under the MotorSport Vision banner, moved in and quickly started to turn the business around. Immediate

The 2003 'Competition Club of the Year' award

The single-seater pack at Mondello Park in April 2004

improvements made the venues much more user-friendly and the change of ownership was seen as being very good for the sport.

The club's 2004 calendar was broadly similar to previous seasons but did include a visit to Mondello Park in Ireland in early May with some support races for British GT and the FIA Historic Championships. The Brands Hatch Super Prix moved to later in July and many of the club's championship had a Castle Combe date in early August. The season started and finished with one-day meetings at Donington Park (April) and Silverstone (October), while the Silverstone event in June was called the Silverstone Historic Tribute. Races from the VSCC as well as guest races like Group 4 and BRDC Historic Sports joined a full HSCC programme for the event that was on its way to becoming the Silverstone Classic.

Group C was a feature of the Brands Hatch Super Prix and there was a poignant demonstration session when new circuit boss Jonathan Palmer ran some laps in the Canon-backed Porsche 956 he raced to victory at Brands Hatch two decades earlier. The car was still owned by team boss Richard Lloyd and there was a further connection as club CEO Grahame White was part of the Richard Lloyd Racing team at the time. Palmer shared the car with Jan Lammers in the 1984 British Aerospace 1000kms, a round of the World Sportscar Championship.

In the racing, Gary Pearson (Jaguar XJR11) and John Burton (Chevron B26) each took a double win in Group C and Orwell Supersports, while Michael Schryver claimed Derek Bell Trophy honours on his Formula 5000 debut in a Trojan T101. Simon Hadfield charged from the back of the grid to second in his ex-Peter Gethin Chevron B37 after a late tyre change and Marcus Pye made in a complete podium for the Hadfield squad with third place in the F2 Chevron B40.

Jason Minshaw beat Neil Fowler in a tough Historic FF1600 battle and Dan Cox (Ford Anglia) saw off John Young (Dodge Dart) in Historic Racing Saloons. Other winners included Ian Jacobs (Classic F3), Andy Shepherd (Historic Road Sports) and Sean Walker with his Lotus Elan in Classic Sports.

Historic Touring Cars at Mondello

Nick Wadham's Tecno leads a DBT pack at Silverstone

Road Sports at Cadwell Park, 2004

Classic F3 battles at Brands in
July 2004

Neil Fowler and Jason
Minshaw head the Formula
Fords at Cadwell

70s Road Sports descend from Druids

Roger Godfrey's Mini at Oulton Park

Stephen Worrad leads Matthew Watts and Edwin Jowsey in CRC at Oulton Park, August 2004

Robin Longdon heads the Juniors

The 2004 Oulton Park Gold Cup, the third running of the historic festival, was once more a headline event on the calendar and featured club patron Sir Stirling Moss demonstrating a Maserati 250F to mark the 50th anniversary of his 1954 Gold Cup win. Topping the race programme were races for the Group 4 sports-prototype series, HGPCA single-seaters and drum-braked sports, BRDC Historic Sports and, for the first time at the track, Historic Formula 2. In period, Oulton Park had hosted a round of the short-lived British Formula 2 Championship, but never a round of the European championship.

At the end of the 2004 season in HSCC News, Grahame White reflected on an excellent year. "I

wanted to thank everyone who has helped make 2004 one of the most successful years in the history of the HSCC. Membership is at a high and our finances are strong and stable." He also paid tribute to the work of Emma North and Martin Atack in the club office for their dedication. By the end of the year Emma was married to Ken Jemmett and, after a honeymoon in San Francisco, returned to work for the club.

The 2004 season was an excellent year for 70s Road Sports, with a total of 68 registrations. This brought it own problems as some grids were overflowing but by splitting some classes off to race alongside other championships, the club office was able to make sure

Graeme Dodd spins out of the action at the Oulton Park Gold Cup

The closed-wheel race at Spa in 2004

everyone got to race. A season-long battle for the title raged between Richard Thorne (Morgan Plus 8) and Jai Sharma (Lancia Fulvia) but a blown head-gasket in qualifying at the Silverstone final forced Sharma to miss the race and Thorne duly took the title.

Robert Barrie was a commanding champion in Historic Road Sports in his Porsche 911 while Simon Ashworth (MGB) beat Les Ely (Jaguar E-type) to the Classic Sports title by a single point when Ely crashed out of the Silverstone final.

In Historic Formula Ford, Neil Fowler took another title in his Lola T200 from the Crossle 20F of Nigel Bancroft and the Macon of John Goldsmith with Jason Minshaw and Nelson Rowe next up despite missing some of the races. Minshaw's season was halted early by an accident at his local Oulton Park, while former Caterham racer Rowe only joined the category mid-season but immediately showed strong pace.

The Historic Racing Saloon season was tinged with sadness due to the death of prime-mover Glen Maskell who, like Ford Mustang racer Miles Townshend, succumbed to cancer. Having lost the Classic Sports title by one point, Les Ely missed this one by two points in his BMW 2000 as Adrian Oliver claimed a third title in his Hillman Imp.

John Bladon took his Merlyn Mk9 to the Classic Racing Car title and Stuart Tilley was crowned the Derek Bell Trophy winner after a season in Simon Hadfield's Modus M1. The category enjoyed a growth in support from Formula 5000s as Frank and Judy Lyons worked behind the scenes to encourage more cars onto the grid.

Classic F3 was a series of races in 2004 and the award winners were Steve Maxted (Argo JM6) in the 2-litre class and Chris Levy (March 713) from the 1600cc ranks. Formula Junior shared its season between the HSCC and the Aston Martin Owners' Club while Graeme Dodd topped the Jaguar XK series. The season's awards were presented at the annual dinner dance at the Whittlebury Hall near Silverstone and, much to his surprise and delight, Nick Overall was presented with a cheque for £6000 for the Richard Overall Trust. The money had been raised by club members for the fund set up in memory of Nick's son and would benefit those suffering with muscular dystrophy.

In his final chairman's address to the AGM, Nick Overall reflected on a very successful 2004 season.

"What a year it has been. Record grids, membership continuing to grow and our meetings the envy of other clubs. Competition comes in many forms and there are now more organisations than ever attempting to organise historic series or meetings. Our strength lies in that we genuinely try to keep the cars as they were in period and have stable sets of regulations. We must make every effort to continue this, especially in view of the new technical passport that the FIA is introducing. I cannot emphasise enough how important it is for the club's future in keeping our cars genuinely historic and the welcoming camaraderie we have in our paddocks."

Treasurer Anthony Goddard reflected on a strong year for the club's finances, with a profit of £38,000 and net assets of just under £150,000. The year had included an 11% increase in membership income and a 20% increase in race entry income. In his commentary, Goddard said: "Your board makes no apology for the reserves we have built up – it is, after all, your money. However, we think it right to be conservative. Things may be bumbling along nicely at the moment, but financial strength would enable us to ride any future changes in fortune with greater ease. You only have to look at the hard time other clubs have had.

THE 2004 HSCC RACING CHAMPIONS

Classic Sports Car Championship
Simon Ashworth (MGB)
Classic Racing Car Championship
John Bladon (Merlyn Mk9)
70s Road Sports Championship
Richard Thorne (Morgan Plus 8)
Historic Road Sports Championship
Robert Barrie (Porsche 911S)
Derek Bell Trophy
Stuart Tilley (Modus M1)
Historic FF1600 Championship
Neil Fowler (Merlyn Mk20)
Historic Racing Saloon Championship
Adrian Oliver (Hillman Imp)
Classic Formula 3 Championship
Steve Maxted (Argo JM6)

Formula Fords at Croft in May 2005

"One thing we have done this year by way of thanking those that have supported us most is to give free racing membership to those that have supported all our championship rounds bar two last year. We intend repeating this for the current year."

The 2005 AGM heralded significant changes at the head of the club as Chris Sharples moved into the role of chairman and Chris Alford took over from Stephen Minoprio as vice-chairman. Aside from representatives of each of the club's eight race categories, board members included Bob Birrell, treasurer Anthony Goddard, Andrew Schryver, Lincoln Small and, of course, Grahame White.

For 2005, the club was asked to organise the racing element of the new Silverstone Historic Festival, which ran in late July and only a week after the Brands Hatch Super Prix. New on the schedule was a trip to Croft in May and a Thruxton date in September, while both Snetterton and Cadwell Park were one-day meetings but Mallory Park was left

Three abreast in Classic F3/FF2000 at Silverstone

style of the hugely popular Tour Auto in France. The inaugural event was to start at Stratford-on-Avon on Monday 5 September and finish at Silverstone on the Thursday. It would comprise both a full competition event and a regularity rally where outright speed was not the aim.

Back in the club's regular racing activity, the crowded nature of the programme meant that both the Jaguar XK Challenge and Formula Junior Championship would have fewer races at HSCC meetings in 2005.

Changes to the club's board were announced in July when Peter Dixon retired as chief registrar after 12 years in the role. Peter first joined the fledgling club in 1969 and first became a registrar in 1972. The hugely experienced Alan Putt took over the role.

In May 2005, the club returned to Croft for the first time since 1999 and the one-day meeting was judged a success despite some smaller than usual grids. Race winners included Chris Burbury (Triumph TR5), Nigel Bancroft (Merlyn Mk20), Edwin Jowsey (Brabham BT28), James Dodd (Alfa Romeo Giulia Sprint), Frank Lyons (Lola T332) and Jamie Boot (TVR Griffith). Julian Barter (TVR 3000M) made the six-hour journey from Dorset worthwhile by scoring his first ever race win in the 70s Road Sports race.

Other notable results included a debut Formula Ford podium for series newcomer Westie Mitchell, who had

off the programme. A celebration of 40 years of the Chevron marque was planned for the Oulton Park Gold Cup, with Lancastrian racer Brian Redman as one of the star guests.

New for 2005 was Tour Britannia, a classic race and rally tour running over four days in September and open to pre-1977 cars and covering four races and a series of rally-style special stages on private roads. The team behind the event was headed by former racer and team manager Alec Poole and world-standard rally co-driver and organiser Fred Gallagher and the HSCC was appointed as race organisers, under the direction of Grahame White.

The tour was launched at the BRDC clubhouse at Silverstone and was heralded as a British event in the

70s Road Sports variety at the Brands Hatch Super Prix

Simon Hadfield leads the DBT pack at the 2005 Silverstone Classic

Edwin Jowsey heads the Formula Juniors

Nelson Rowe and Neil Fowler battle at the Silverstone Classic

transferred from racing a Frazer Nash with the VSCC. Meanwhile, David Methley was applauded for rebuilding the front of Stuart Tizzard's Lotus Elan after an off in qualifying. The work was complete just in time for Tizzard to finish second overall in the Classic Sports Car race.

Lincoln Small's Brabham BT30 at Thruxton

The gem of the mid-season period was the 16th Brands Hatch Super Prix with 15 races and 450 entries for the Grand Prix circuit meeting, while a month later the Oulton Park Gold Cup celebrated 40 years of the Bolton-based Chevron marque.

Despite some poor weather, the Brands Hatch weekend was a success with very full grids and a headline race from Group C which delivered a dramatic finish as David Mercer's Spice held off Gary Pearson's Jaguar by a tenth of a second on a drying track. Richard Piper and John Grant shared victories in the Orwell Supersports races and Neil Fowler headed Nelson Rowe in another mighty Historic Formula Ford contest. Laurence Bailey's TVR topped the Historic Road Sports and Charles Barter's Datsun 240Z was the class of the 70s Road Sports. Les Ely's BMW won the Historic Touring Cars

Steve Maxted's Argo JM6 in Classic F3

Garrad, Dodd and Cox head the Saloons into Stowe

Road Sports at Thruxton, September 2005

Neil Fowler heads the Historic FF pack into the Complex

Dan Cox leads at Thruxton, September 2005

Ian Jacobs (March 742) at the Thruxton chicane

and Steve Maxted (Argo JM6) took another Classic F3 win on his way to retaining the title.

Just a week after Brands was the newly-titled Silverstone Classic, with the Derek Bell Trophy delivering a superb field of cars for a double-header and two wins for Simon Hadfield in the ex-Peter Gethin Chevron B37. Mike Wrigley (Lola T332) was the chief rival to the flying Chevron, while the concurrent European Formula 2 contest was headed by Christian Fischer (March 772) and Martin Stretton (March 712). Nelson Rowe won a shortened Historic Formula Ford race and Les Ely recruited Simon Garrad, former owner of the BMW 2000, to help win the two-driver Historic Touring Car race.

There were many worthy champions at the end of the 2005 including Neil Fowler who completed a remarkable run of five Historic Formula Ford titles on the trot. Fowler topped Paul Sleeman's previous record of four titles in five seasons despite fierce opposition from Nelson Rowe. Four of Fowler's titles came at the wheel of his Lola T200, a car that went better in historic trim than it had in period.

Chris Horner (Turner Mk1) in Historic Road Sports

In Historic Touring Cars, Dan Cox emerged with a spectacular sideways style of driving to win the crown in his Ford Anglia and stop Hillman Imp racer Adrian Oliver building on a hat-trick of titles. It would be the first of four championship titles for the South Gloucestershire racer. The same statistic applied to the new 70s Road Sports champion John Thomason who took his Triumph Spitfire to a first title, while Frank Lyons clinched his first Derek Bell Trophy win with his Lola T332.

Ian Gray heads the open wheel race at Spa, 2005

In his report to the Annual General Meeting for the 2005 season, chairman Chris Sharples reflected on an excellent season. "2005 was a very good year for the Club. You can measure this in many ways, but to me the best indicator was the spirit in the Silverstone paddock at the end of the Finals Meeting last October. We were blessed with great weather and we had a good day of racing. Come 6pm, no-one seemed to want the day to end. Race car stayed in the paddock. Drivers had enjoyed their racing and now they were simply enjoying the company of like-minded members. As I stood alongside Grahame White in the paddock, he pointed to the sea of smiling faces and said: 'This is what the Club is all about'. It was wonderful to see and it was a fine end to a first class season." Treasurer Anthony Goddard reported on another successful season which took the club's net worth close to £200,000 for the first time.

Jaguar XKs at Silverstone in October

Matthew Watts heads a single-seater pack at Croix-en-Ternois

The closed-wheel grid at Croix

Heading into the club's 40th anniversary season in 2006, more track time than ever before was on the schedule with 14 race meetings on nine different tracks, starting at Donington Park in early April and concluding with the now-traditional Silverstone Finals Meeting in October. The Donington meeting marked the inauguration of the circuit's new pit garage complex, which replaced the original garages built soon after the circuit re-opened in the late 1970s.

At Silverstone in June, the club was asked to arrange a historic race for the British Grand Prix meeting (9-11 June) and it was decided that a grid for pre-1974 big-engined sports-racing and GT cars would deliver a fine spectacle with Ford GT40s taking on Lola T70 Mk3Bs. No one on the quality and capacity 44-car grid could match the pace of double winner Simon Hadfield, who was peerless at the wheel of Frank Sytner's ex-Sid Taylor Lola T70 Mk3B.

The Super Prix at Brands Hatch had a new date in May while the Silverstone weekend later in May would be the central point in the 40th anniversary celebrations. European F2 and BRDC Historic Sports were to be headline races while the inaugural Griffiths Formula race from 1966 would be re-visited by a race for drum-braked sports cars from the HGPCA. A return to Croix-en-Ternois

THE 2005 HSCC RACING CHAMPIONS

Classic Sports Car Championship
Simon Ashworth (MGB)
Classic Racing Car Championship
Matthew Watts (Brabham BT16)
70s Road Sports Championship
John Thomason (Triumph Spitfire)
Historic Road Sports Championship
Andy Shepherd (Lotus 7)
Derek Bell Trophy
Frank Lyons (Lola T332)
Historic FF1600 Championship
Neil Fowler (Lola T200)
Historic Racing Saloon Championship
Dan Cox (Ford Anglia)
Classic Formula 3 Championship
Steve Maxted (Argo JM6)

Road Sports at the northern France track

Chris Gawne's Lancia Aurelia at Croix

in July marked a return to an away date, albeit with races during a weekend run by a French club.

There was sad news in May 2006 when the death of former chairman Don Cressy was announced. Fellow former chairman Nick Overall paid tribute in the May 2006 issue of HSCC News. "Don was a truly delightful man who was chairman of the HSCC for four years. The club prospered under his cool and diplomatic leadership."

The May meeting at Silverstone was a success despite some poor weather and included a good grid of 1950s sports cars racing in homage to the first Griffith Formula race 40 years earlier. Jamie McIntyre's diminutive Rejo eventually got the better of the Maserati 300S of Mark Gillies. On the grid was the Allard J2X registered ORL 320, which contested the 1966 Castle Combe race in the hands of Fred Damodaran. Four decades later it was raced by then owner Josh Sadler.

Other winners across the 40th anniversary weekend included Les Ely (BMW), Ian Gray (Brabham BT30), Richard Trott (Chevron B43), Michael Hibberd (Formula Junior Lotus) and Barrie Williams (Jaguar XK120).

In September 2006, the club was involved in the second running of Tour Britannia with four days of races and special stages from an event HQ at Coombe Abbey in Warwickshire. Races at Oulton Park, Donington Park, Cadwell Park and Mallory Park all featured in the route and it was the Morgan Plus 8 Bruce Stapleton and Alastair Cowin that took overall victory from a strong field. A year earlier, the Ford

Schryver leads Hadfield in an F5000 battle in the Derek Bell Trophy

Formula Fords plunge down Paddock Hill Bend at Brands

123

Historic Touring Cars at Castle Combe in 2006

70s Road Sports off the Castle Combe grid, August 2006

Classic Racing Cars at the Oulton Park Gold Cup

The Tour Britannia race at Mallory Park September 2006

GT40 of Ray Bellm and Paul Lanzante had won the inaugural event.

At the end of another fine season of competition, the 2006 champions were presented with their trophies by Derek Bell at the annual awards dinner. Despite the best efforts of Matthew Watts in his Brabham BT16, it was the consistent pace of the similar car of Cliff Giddens that clinched the Classic Racing car title. David Randall (Ginetta G4) won the Historic Road Sports crown after a big battle with the Lotus 7 of Andy Shepherd, while Mark Dwyer capped a strong first year in his F2

CHRIS SHARPLES

Former club chairman

"From the age of 12 I wanted to be a racing driver and started subscribing to Motor Sport magazine. I never did anything about it because I went off to college, got a job, got married, bought a house and never quite got round to it.

"As I went through the male menopause I bought myself a motorbike and a guitar. I never learned to do anything with the guitar but I learnt how to ride the bike and that satisfied me for a little time but then I realised it scared my witless.

"At that point my wife, who was into horses, came back from the stable one day and said there were people who'd just got a horse at the stable and they've got a picture of a racing car on the back window of their estate car.

"So I was at the stable shovelling manure one day and the owner of the car was there and I discovered that he had a Formula Ford Nike. A few months later I went to Silverstone and saw all these people arriving back in the paddock after qualifying and when they took their crash helmets off there was a forest of silver hair. I thought to myself: 'I can do this'.

"Like everybody in those days, I bought my Palliser from Chris Alford in 1999. It was my 50th birthday present to myself and I just loved it. I've now been a racing driver for 16 years and it has been absolutely brilliant.

"After a couple of years my best mate in racing was Anthony Goddard, who was club treasurer in those days. We were sitting at the dinner dance in about 2004 and he told me that Nick Overall was standing down and he was looking for someone he felt was the right person to take over.

"We drank quite a bit that evening and by the time we finished we'd agreed that I'd stand for chairman. So I became chairman and loved every minute of it. It was not just the racing, it was being on the inside of the club and it was like I'd been invited into the sweet shop for the very first time.

"It is an extraordinary club. In the year I joined we had 667 members and by the time I left we had about 1050. Some of the most important things we achieved were to bring Formula Junior under the HSCC wing, develop Classic Sports into the Guards Trophy with full grids and, led by Grahame White, become the organising club for the Silverstone Classic, Donington Historic Festival and Walter Hayes Trophy."

March 742 by winning the Derek Bell Trophy. A nicely measured drive to second in the Silverstone final earned Nelson Rowe the Historic FF1600 title as arch-rival Neil Fowler won the final race.

In his report for the AGM in March 2007, Chris Sharples reflected on the year just gone. "2006 was our 40th anniversary year. By all measures it has been successful. We have run more races with more entries than at any time in the Club's history. It was our busiest year ever including two GP circuit meetings at Brands Hatch, the Silverstone Classic, the Gold Cup at Oulton Park, a support race at the British Grand Prix and overseas trips to Croix and Spa. I believe that the Club's founders Betty Haig and Guy Griffiths, and the hundreds of people who have worked so hard in the Club's interest through the years, can be proud of

the standing that we have achieved in the world of historic motor sport.

"This is a members' club. The only reasons for our existence are to preserve proper cars, to help our members enjoy their cars and have fun on the racetrack. We try to create the right atmosphere in the paddock. We know that camaraderie amongst competitors is a strong reason for wanting to race with the HSCC. Last year seems to suggest we are giving members what they want. The most pleasing statistic for the year was our membership roll, up by 10% to an all time high.

"We have sound finances. Our team in the office runs a tight ship. As the Treasurer will confirm we generated a £45,000 operating surplus in the year.

This sum, about 5% of turnover, will be used to strengthen reserves in our balance sheet."

The fourth running of 'Race Retro', the International Historic Motorsport Show at Stoneleigh near Coventry featured a strong presence from the Club, with officials and board members on hand throughout three days to meet current and prospective members.

April 2007: The FF2000 start at Cadwell Park

Colin Wright leads an FF2000 pack

However, the icing on the cake came on Saturday evening, when the annual Historic Motorsport Awards were presented at a nearby hotel. The Club was announced as the winner for the second time of the 'competition club of the year' award, which was a fitting way to sign off the club's 40th anniversary season.

In front of a gathering of many of the great and the good of historic motor sport, the HSCC was named as winner of the award in the face of tough competition from the AvD Germany, the Historic Rally Car Register and the Vintage Sports Car Club. Grahame White was there to collect the award on behalf of the Club.

It was largely a case of more of the same for the 2007 racing programme, with the Brands Hatch Super Prix returning to a late June date to run a month ahead of the rapidly expanding Silverstone Classic. In the club office, Alan Jones joined the team during 2006 and moved into the competition's secretary role when Martin Atack moved on. The club's core portfolio of nine race series remained largely unchanged, although Formula Junior was now officially in the fold at the start of a partnership with the Formula Junior Historic Racing Association.

THE 2006 HSCC RACING CHAMPIONS

Classic Sports Car Championship
Les Ely (Jaguar E-type)
Classic Racing Car Championship
Cliff Giddens (Brabham BT16)
70s Road Sports Championship
John Thomason (Triumph Spitfire)
Historic Road Sports Championship
David Randall (Ginetta G4)
Derek Bell Trophy
Mark Dwyer (March 742)
Historic FF1600 Championship
Nelson Rowe (Crossle 20F)
Historic Racing Saloon Championship
Mike Hanna (Hillman Imp)
Classic Formula 3 Championship
Keith White (Ralt RT1)
Jaguar XK Championship
Nigel Webb (Jaguar XK120)

Another change for 2007 was that the BRDC appointed the club to administer and organise its Historic Sportscar Championship for pre-1961 cars. Five dates were arranged, with races at Silverstone (twice), Brands Hatch, Oulton Park and Dijon.

Meanwhile, the GT & Sports Racing Championship, formerly Classic Sports, was re-badged with an iconic name from the sport's history, the Guards Trophy. The season would have a mix of sprint races and longer races, with most of the longer races being run over 40 minutes. The Snetterton race in June was to be a recreation of the Autosport 3 Hours and would be the longest historic race in Britain at the time.

For the third year running the club was asked to organise the racing element of the Silverstone Classic (July 27-29). Importantly for club members, the 22-race programme included a combined race for Historic Road Sports and 70s Road Sports, which was quite an achievement for Grahame White and the team. The response from competitors was superb and almost as soon as entry forms were published there was a full entry. For the pair of races, club patron-in-chief, Sir Stirling Moss, agreed to allow his name to be used on the winners' trophy.

The club was clearly on a roll over the opening half of 2007 as two more major developments were confirmed. First, the club agreed to take over the running of Historic Formula 2 when the previous championship promoter got into some serious problems.

The European Formula 2 Club, which had been run for several seasons by Oskar Christen, had very much helped the re-birth of F2 particularly on the continent.

However, early in the year it became apparent that the Swiss-based club wasn't going to carry on and preliminary talks took place at the first race of the series at Mugello in Italy in March. HSCC board member and EF2 competitor Lincoln Small put forward a proposal where the HSCC might be able to offer some help with the administrative side, either short term or in the future.

Lincoln and Grahame White presented a more detailed proposal to a drivers meeting held at Hockenheim in Germany in April, the result of which was that the HSCC was approved to take over all the administration of the club. "This is a good move for the HSCC, it strengthens our links with continental organisers and circuits and brings together a new group of non-UK drivers and competitors," said White at the time.

The F2 news was quickly followed by confirmation that the club had again been entrusted with organising the historic sports car race to support the Santander British Grand Prix at Silverstone over the weekend of 6-8 July. It would be for cars built between 1950 and 1970 and open to a grid of 44 historic sports racing and GT cars, with two half-hour races as well as qualifying on Friday. Sunday's race would follow the Grand Prix.

Donington Park, April 2007: Michael Lyons makes his UK race debut

"We have been overwhelmed with applications," said White. "The final selection will be extremely difficult with so many interesting cars on the list." When entries closed, 10 Lola T70s, six AC Cobras, eight E-Type Jaguars, 16 Chevrons and five McLarens were on the application list.

The season-opener at Donington in mid-April included the UK racing debut of 16-year-old Michael Lyons who raced in Classic Cars in his Merlyn Mk11A and finished fourth overall and best of the FF1600s. Michael had made his race debut in Australia in March and immediately showed his natural talent.

Following the runaway success of the inaugural Autosport Three-Hour race at Snetterton in June, the club confirmed plans to make the race an annual event. The longest race in Britain for historic and classic cars was adjudged a big success. A grid of 30 cars of the 1960s from the GT and Sports Racing Championship packed the grid, and 132 laps later, 22 of them took the chequered flag. Race winners were Michael Schryver and Simon Hadfield in the former's Chevron B6.

In period, Jim Clark won the race twice, and in 1963 his win came in the season in which he also clinched his first World Championship title for Lotus. At Snetterton 44 years earlier, Clark raced a Lotus 23B sports-racing car to victory and it was fitting that four examples of Colin Chapman's hugely successful sports-racing car design raced in the 2007 event. The best placed Lotus 23B at the finish was the car shared by Anthony Hancock and his sons Sam and Ollie.

"We were thrilled with the response to the first Autosport 3-Hours," said Grahame White. "There was a wonderful atmosphere around the event and everyone who took part loved the whole experience. We intend to make this an annual event and Snetterton is the perfect venue for such a race."

The Snetterton three-hour podium in 2007

The start of the Autosport three-hours

DBT thunder at Brands Hatch, July 2007

A month later, the club's focus was on the Silverstone Historic Sports Car Challenge at the British Grand Prix. The huge crowds that packed in to Silverstone may not have got the Lewis Hamilton victory they wanted, but two races for historic sports cars added greatly to the biggest weekend of the year for British motor racing.

Organised by the club at fairly short notice, the race for cars of the 1950s and 1960s was a big hit, with a capacity field contesting 14-lap races on both Saturday and Sunday afternoons. Sunday's race followed on from the Grand Prix and was enjoyed by a huge crowd. Both races fell to Frank Sytner's hard-charging Lola T70 Mk3B, but with battles all the way down the field, it was a fine advert for historic racing.

Club patron Derek Bell was one of the stars of the Oulton Park Gold Cup when he ran some demonstration laps in the 2003 Le Mans-winning Bentley Speed 8. He was then on hand to present awards on Monday, including to Mark Dwyer who took a double win in the Derek Bell Trophy after a mighty F5000 contest with Frank Lyons and Neil Glover. Martin Stretton and Bob Juggins shared the Historic Formula 2 spoils and young Tim Bradshaw impressed by winning the Classic F3 counter in his dad's Argo.

For three days in early September 2007, over 70 classic sports, GT and saloon cars contested the third running

Chris Sharples (left) and Paul Sleeman battle at Brands

Patrick Blakeney-Edwards and his Frazer Nash on Tour Britannia

THE 2007 HSCC RACING CHAMPIONS

Guards Trophy
Martin Richardson (MGB)
Classic Racing Car Championship
Anthony Goddard (Merlyn Mk9)
Historic Road Sports Championship
Josh Sadler (Ginetta G4)
70s Road Sports Championship
Rory Stockbridge (Lotus Europa)
Historic Formula 2
Martin Stretton (March 712)
Derek Bell Trophy
Frank Lyons (Lola T400)
Historic FF1600 Championship
Nelson Rowe (Crossle 20F)
Historic Formula Junior Championship
Sir John Chisholm (Gemini Mk3A)
Classic Formula 3 Championship
Benn Simms (March 803B)
Historic Racing Saloon Championship
Simon Benoy (Hillman Imp)

of Tour Britannia. In a tight finish, John Grant/Charles Elwell emerged victorious in their Chevron B16.

Tour Britannia was the brainchild of seasoned competitor and organiser Fred Gallagher and long-time racer Alec Poole, and was Britain's answer to events like Tour Auto and the Tour of Spain. Open to pre '76 cars, it combined races and asphalt rally stages into a three-day event, and a concurrent regularity rally caters for those who preferred their motorsport a little less high-speed, but still competitive.

As in previous years, the HSCC was heavily involved, with the club responsible for running the races. The event started at Brands Hatch with a race and then took in special stages at Brooklands and Long Cross before heading north for the overnight halt at Coombe Abbey in Warwickshire. Wednesday, day two, included timed tests at MIRA and Belvoir Castle as well as races at Donington and Mallory before returning to Coombe Abbey. Thursday's route headed north-west for a race at Oulton Park along with special stages at Cholmondeley Castle, Loton Park and Weston Park.

Road Sports racers at Spa, September 2007

The 2007 event drew the biggest entry to date. In 2006, Vin Malkie's crew turned Grant's Chevron B16 into a road legal machine, but a variety of problems hampered its progress. Undeterred, Grant returned in 2007, determined to show that the B16 could cope with three days of road driving, rally stages and races and won overall by just 13s from the Porsche 911 of Nick Whale and his fiancée Sally Wood.

The season concluded with the annual Silverstone Finals' meeting with titles won and lost on the national circuit. The final race was one of the best as 21-year-old Andrew Hibberd took Formula Junior spoils and beat his father Michael for the first time in a tremendous three-way battle with James Claridge. In fact, it was a good day for young drivers as Michael Lyons, Lee Dwyer and Oliver Thorpe all joined Hibberd in starring roles.

In Lyons, the club had seen a bright young talent develop through the 2007 season and he had raced comfortably in Historic F1 when still only 16. At Silverstone he dominated the Historic FF1600 race and put the family Merlyn Mk9 on pole for Classic Racing Cars.

Julian Barter's TVR at Eau Rouge

Running alongside Michael in Formula Renault in 2008 would be Lee, son of Mark Dwyer and another 16-year old. His DBT debut aboard his father's ex-Purley March 742 at Silverstone was a fine performance and he nearly made it two 16-year olds on the Historic FF1600 podium. Meanwhile, in Classic FF2000, 16-year old Thorpe was hugely impressive as he won the class within the Classic F3 race.

Over the first weekend of November, the club took on a new project with the race organisation of the Walter Hayes Trophy, the Formula Ford knock-out competition on the Silverstone National circuit. The event role allowed the club to offer non-championship closed wheel and open wheel races for members in a wide range of cars.

The final club magazine of 2007 detailed the 2008 racing schedule. The big news for our 2008 race programme was that, after many years of trying, the club had obtained a second date at Donington Park. It would be on 4/5 October and would allow all the club's races to have some good track time as well as including some invitation races as well.

The rest of the schedule largely kept to the successful programme from 2007, with high-profile events at Brands Hatch, Silverstone and Oulton Park through the summer months. Good news for the Oulton Park Gold Cup was that it would be a full four weeks ahead of the Goodwood Revival Meeting. Backing up the major weekends was the three-hour meeting at Snetterton and the very popular event on the Silverstone International circuit in May, which returned to a two-day format for 2008.

The 2007 year concluded with the annual dinner and awards presentation, with former sports car ace David Piper as guest of honour. Among those celebrated as champions were club treasurer Anthony Goddard who scooped the Classic Racing Car crown with his Merlyn Mk9, Historic Formula Junior winner Sir John Chisholm (Gemini Mk3A), Classic F3 champion Benn Simms and double Historic FF1600 champion Nelson Rowe. Josh Sadler and Rory Stockbridge each bagged a Road Sports title and Martin Stretton was the first Historic Formula 2 under the club's new management of the series.

The Awards Dinner and Dance was held at the Oxford Belfry Thame, on Saturday 1 December and Chairman Chris Sharples opened proceedings by making a presentation to the office staff. Grahame White received a personal photo album put together by regular HSCC photographer Charlie Wooding whilst Martin, Emma and Alan received champagne.

Michael Lyons vied with some of the more established club members for the most number of prizes to be collected in one evening. In amongst his haul of glittering pots was a new and very attractive award presented by John Monson in memory of his father Desmond. Another new prize for 2007 was awarded by the British Motorsport Marshals' Club to commemorate their 50th aniversary. This went to Sir John Chisholm for winning the UK Formula Junior Championship. David Brown, the two and four wheel motorsport enthusiast, created three new prizes for the Classic Racing Car Championship the 'John Nicol Premier Cru', 'The Quick Shift' and the Pit Star' prizes, with the highly individual awards delighting their recipients.

9 2008 to 2011
A time of further expansion

The Road Sports grid at the Silverstone Classic

The 2008 season carried on where 2007 had left off and seasonal highlights were set to include a new seven-race series for Historic Formula Ford 2000s, concentrating on the cars from up to 1981. The twin Road Sports grids got a shared high-profile race at the Silverstone Classic in July and Historic Formula 2 had an extended calendar of 18 races at nine meetings in five countries. The season started at Thruxton over Easter to celebrate the 40th anniversary of the circuit's first European F2 meeting in 1968.

There was talk of an 80s Road Sports category, but the idea failed to develop any further, and Motion

Works was announced as the new promoter of the Silverstone Classic. The HSCC would continue as the race organising club.

Saturday May 31 was confirmed as the date for the second running of the Snetterton Autosport Three-Hour race. The inaugural HSCC edition of this race, in 2007, had been won by the Chevron B6 of Michael Schryver and Simon Hadfield. In the 1960s this race was a major feature of the UK sports car calendar and it had been revived in 2007 to be the UK's longest race for historic racers. "We got a terrific response in 2007 with a big grid of Chevrons, GT40, E-types, MGBs and

The Historic Roadsports pack charges into the Redgate at Donington on 30 March

Simon Hadfield's McLaren leads Mark Dwyer and Jeremy Smith in the DBT race at Donington

Bill Coombs leads Benn Simms in the opening Classic F3 race of the season at Donington Park

Lotuses," said Guards Trophy racer Stuart Tizzard. "At the prize giving we got a round of cheers when we said we would run it again in 2008. I would like this to become a must-do part of the UK sports/GT calendar."

At Thruxton over the Easter weekend, the racing was only part of the story, as Grahame White invited a

number of former Formula 2 racers to attend and four people who were on the grid for the first Thruxton F2 race in 1968 returned to the Hampshire track, four decades later: Alun Rees, Chris Irwin, John Cardwell and Harry Stiller. In the Historic F2 races, wins were shared by Peter Meyrick and Bill Coombs, who raced John Dunham's March 712. Incredibly, for the boss of the Thruxton Racing School, it was his first win at the track.

As the guests gathered for lunch, Murray Walker said a few words about his love of Thruxton. "This is a fabulous and emotional day to celebrate 40 years of Thruxton. I've been coming to Thruxton for nearly 60 years," said Murray. "I was here for the BBC in the early 1950s, commentating from the roof of a bus in pouring rain. I saw a 17-year old John Surtees riding a Vincent Grey Flash."

For Alan Rees, a visit to Thruxton was not unusual as his son Paul, then racing in Formula Palmer Audi, had previously raced there in Formula Renault. But the 1968 Easter race was his last competitive outing at Thruxton. "The 1968 season was my last year as a driver," said Rees. "I was thinking during 1967 whether I should retire, but I decided to try one more year and that was a mistake." By the time he stopped racing, Rees was already busy with the creation of March Racing Cars as his career in the sport entered a new phase.

However, in stark contrast, Chris Irwin had seldom been to any race meetings since the terrible accident in May 1968 at the wheel of a Ford F3L sports car that ended his career. "I remember very little of Thruxton," admitted Irwin. "It was one of the few circuits in Britain that I had very little to do with. I remember the

Former F2 racers (left to right); Harry Stiller, Alun Rees, John Cardwell and Chris Irwin

Lincoln Small's F2 Brabham BT30 at Thruxton

other British circuits more than Thruxton because I did so much more racing at them."

John Cardwell was another driver to recall little of the 1968 F2 race at Thruxton, when he partnered Harry Stiller in a pair of works-entered Merlyns. In fact, the experience of racing the Merlyn at Thruxton helped him make the decision to retire from racing and by the middle of the 1968 season his racing days were over.

"I drove for Bob Gerard for the whole of 1967, but halfway through 1968 I retired," he said on his first visit to the track for 40 years. "The Merlyn I drove at Thruxton wasn't a great car and I decided I'd had enough. Thruxton at Easter 1968 was one of the last races I ever did. I walked away from racing. I think it was so bad that I have virtually no recollection of the Thruxton race. When I came third at Monaco in the F3 race, I remember every bit of that race, but because it was so bad at Thruxton it goes from your memory."

The best of the recollections of Thruxton in 1968 came from Harry Stiller. "I remember vividly that John Cardwell and I had been signed by Merlyn as the works drivers for 1968," he said from a perspective of 40 years. "But they couldn't get the cars ready and they were short of parts. It was a nightmare. They turned up at Thruxton on the morning of practice day and neither of the cars had turned a wheel. You can imagine the experience in qualifying, with two brand new cars out of the box, and we spent the whole morning trying to get the wheels pointing in the right direction.

"I think I actually finished 10th overall in the final, after getting a 60-second penalty for a push start. It was a great day at Thruxton. There was a magnificent crowd

Lorraine Gathercole guides her Lotus 18 through the Thruxton chicane

Paul Stafford in 70s Road Sports at Cadwell

Iain Rowley's FF2000 Delta at Cadwell Park's Hall Bends

*Racing returnee Rodney
Bloor died in June 2008*

*The Guards Trophy field
pours into Copse at
Silverstone, May 2008,
headed by the Chevron B6
of Will Schryver*

and we were all driven round on the back of a truck,
waving merrily. I think I had one small shot of whiskey
before I got in the car for the race. I needed sustenance."

There was sadness over the first half of 2008 as two
Club members passed away. Barry Westmoreland
suffered a heart attack while racing his Formula Junior

Lotus at Cadwell Park and recent racing returnee
Rodney Bloor died in early June after a short illness.
Rodney, of course, was best known as the entrant
of Chevrons under the Sports Motors banner. Both
drivers would go on to be annually remembered by
the Club with dedicated awards at Cadwell Park and
Oulton Park.

The Touring Cars in the 2008 British GP support race

At Snetterton, Hadfield and Schrvyer repeated their Autosport three-hour win but only after the Crossle 9S of Jon Shipman and Mark Hales suffered a stub axle failure with less than 10 minutes to run. Jack Sears was a welcome guest at the event and presented some of the awards after the race.

At the British Grand Prix at Silverstone, the Club was again invited to organise a support race and this time it was for Historic Touring Cars with a 48-car grid. Neil Cunningham beat John Young in a battle of the Ford Mustangs while Dan Cox was the best of the rest in his Ford Lotus Cortina. A week later, the Club was heavily involved in the Welsh Classic at Pembrey in South Wales. Most of the Club's classes were in action but, even though the circuit was widely enjoyed by the drivers, the event was not repeated. Classic F3 racer Bill Coombs won the Tom Pryce Memorial Trophy.

THE 2008 HSCC RACING CHAMPIONS

Guards Trophy
Robert Barrie (Porsche 911)
Classic Racing Car Championship
Ian Gray (Brabham BT16)
Historic Road Sports Championship
Colin Sharp (Triumph TR5) and
Dick Coffey (Turner Mk1)
70s Road Sports Championship
Ian Jacobs (Jensen Healey)
Historic Formula 2
Bo Warmenius (March 772)
Derek Bell Trophy
Greg Thornton (Surtees TS11)
Historic FF1600 Championship
Michael Lyons (Merlyn Mk11)
Historic Formula Junior Championship
Jon Milicevic (Lotus 18)
Classic Formula 3 Championship
Benn Simms (March 803B)
Historic FF2000 Championship
Colin Wright (Reynard SF77)
Historic Touring Car Championship
Dan Cox (Ford Lotus Cortina)

The DBT March of Richard Evans at Silverstone

Tony Keele leads Richard Kendle, Ian Gray and Antony Ross in Classic Racing Cars at Silverstone, May 2008

Stephen Gibson leads a Derek Bell Trophy battle at Silverstone

Dave Randall and Andrew Marler battle in Historic Road Sports, Pembrey, July 2008

Chris Scragg leads a Guards Trophy pack at Castle Combe, August 2008

Michael Lyons leads David Wild into Quarry in the Historic FF1600 race at Castle Combe

Ross Braithwaite leads a 70s Road Sports pack at the Oulton Park Gold Cup

Tim Bryan leads a Tour Britannia gaggle at Mallory Park, September 2008

Harvey Death's Mini at Cornbury Park during Tour Britannia

In the later stages of 2008 came news about the re-birth of racing for cars from the 1-litre Formula 3 era. The Club was working to support the development of racing for the 1-litre screamers and was planning a three-race series in 2009 for the Peter Hanson Trophy. The cars would run within Classic Racing Cars or Formula Junior events as appropriate, and ideally be involved in the May Silverstone, Brands Hatch Superprix and Oulton Park Gold Cup meetings.

In early September, Sean Lockyear and Roy Stephenson (Porsche 911RS) gave the German marque an overdue first win on Tour Britannia when the event ran for the fourth time with the Club again looking after the races. As well as the all-out competition event, which included races at Snetterton, Mallory Park, Silverstone

Dan Cox throws his Lotus Cortina through Paddock at Brands in September

The Junior pack streams down the Craner Curves at Donington, October 2008

Liza Read's Ford Anglia in the Historic Touring Car contest

Paul Aslett's Porsche 911 heads a 70s pack into Copse during the Silverstone Finals meeting, October 2008

Father and son Michael and Andrew Hibberd shared the podium at Silverstone

Paul Tooms leads James Paterson in Historic Road Sports at Donington

The 2008 champions with Tony Brooks: from the left – Jon Milicevic, Greg Thornton, Dan Cox, Michael Lyons, Ian Jacobs, Benn Simms, Robert Barrie, Dick Coffey, Colin Sharp and Ian Gray.

and Oulton Park, a concurrent regularity rally ran and was won by the Volvo PV544 of Emma Henchoz and Jeanne Taylor.

The annual classic race and rally tour, run by Fred Gallagher and Alec Poole, was a unique event on the British calendar. For three days, a convoy of pre '76 machinery took to the British by-ways as a series of races and asphalt rally special stages were linked up by some classic British countryside.

Despite the financial gloom and doom brought on by the global credit crunch, the 2008 season was typified by big grids, close racing and sporting competition across the Club's portfolio, which had now grown to 11 championships and series. It represented the biggest spread of categories in the Club's history and was set to grow further over the coming seasons.

The year was celebrated in style in November when 1950s Grand Prix ace Tony Brooks was a very special guest of honour at the annual dinner and awards evening. Swedish racer Bo Warmenius (March 772)

was a worthy Historic Formula 2 winner, while Greg Thornton topped the Derek Bell Trophy in his ex-Sam Posey Surtees TS11. Colin Wright, in his faithful Reynard SF77, was the inaugural series winner in Historic Formula Ford 2000 and Benn Simms retained his Classic F3 crown in his ex-Eddie Jordan March 803B. Former Ulsterman Ian Gray took the first of what would be three Classic Racing Car titles in four seasons with his ex-John Watson Brabham BT16, which was expertly prepared by Matthew Watts and the team at Retro Track and Air. In Formula Junior, former Caterham racer Jon Milicevic did a superb job with the ex-Henry Taylor Lotus 18 to win the championship.

In the sports car categories, there was a rare tie for the Historic Road Championship be between Colin Sharp (Triumph TR5) and Dick Coffey (Turner Mk1), while Ian Jacobs got his Jensen Healey working very well to take the 70s Road Sports crown. Robert Barrie ran a classic Porsche 911 to the Guards Trophy, while Dan Cox (Ford Lotus Cortina) took the second of four Historic Touring Car crowns.

The 2009 season approached amid a sense of doom and gloom as the full scale and ramifications of the credit crunch were being felt. The Club's management was keenly aware of the difficult times and delivered on a promise to contain the cost of going racing in the new season by holding race entry fees at 2008 levels despite increases in circuit hire and associated costs. For the opening two race meetings at Donington Park (5 April) and Cadwell Park (19 April), entry fees were unchanged and everyone was working hard to extend the situation across the rest of the 2009 racing season.

"We are going to do everything we can to help members keep racing in what is clearly going to be a difficult year," said Grahame White. "I hope our actions for the first two race meetings of the season make it clear that the interests of the members come first in the HSCC.

"The Club is very conscious of the doom and gloom over the country's financial situation at present and realises that many people will need to be a little more careful how they spend their money, so it is with this in mind that we have decided to cap entry fees at last year's level wherever possible to try and help. If we do have to increase fees at any meetings, it will be very few and very little. In the main, fees will not go up at all. Unfortunately all circuit owners have increased their hire charges and some services have also gone up, but we will not be passing this on. We hope that, as in the past, you will all support us with your entries so we will be able to pay the bills."

In addition to pegging entry fees, the Club also contained other costs for competitors by leaving annual membership fees and championship registration fees unchanged over the 2008 levels. The initial response for entries and memberships ahead of the 2009 season was encouraging. "It's going to be an interesting year ahead," said White. "Never has the country been in such a financial mess and we just do not know how many people will come out and race, but if renewed and new membership figures are anything to go by our future doesn't look too bad. Membership is holding up well, many people are talking positively about this year and we know of a number of racing car sales happening, so fingers' crossed."

Before the racing season got underway, the Club was busy with an invitation to provide a feature display of Historic F2 and F3 cars at Autosport International, held at the Birmingham NEC from January 8-11.

The 11-car display attracted a lot of visitors, both from within the sport and casual observers. The line up of cars was very impressive, and starting with the Formula

Formula 3 cars on the club stand at the NEC, January 2009

2 cars the list was Lotus 48 ex-works cars, raced by Jim Clark and Graham Hill, Brabham BT23 chassis number 001, part of a three-car works team from the 1967 season, Brabham BT30 raced originally by Club patron Derek Bell, the Lotus 69 of the Emerson Fittipaldi, and the Chevron B40 of Keke Rosberg.

The Formula 3 line up featured a number of cars from the Classic Formula 3 Association, including the Ralt RT1 raced by Nelson Piquet, the March 793 resplendent in the Unipart colours carried by Nigel Mansell, the Chevron B38 of Elio De Angelis, the March 793 in RMC livery raced in period by Kenny Acheson and the ex-Harald Ertl Lotus 69 twin-cam.

Soon after Autosport International, the Club was again prominent at Race Retro with a bigger stand and a prime position in Speed Street for a seven-car display showing the breadth of the Club's racing programme.

In his report to the Annual General Meeting in March 2008, Chairman Chris Sharples reflected on the 2008 season.

"We made further improvements to the race programme. Now titled the 'International Trophy', the Silverstone meeting in May was upgraded to two days. For its second running the Snetterton 'Autosport Three Hours' attracted an even bigger grid. We went to Pembrey in July where entries were encouraging and competitors returned with positive reports. The 'HSCC Autoglym Festival' (Superprix) and the 'Gold Cup' were well supported and in October the 'Donington Collection' meeting attracted good grids. Across the year we organised more races and took more entries than ever before.

ALAN JONES

Competitions Secretary

"My passion for motor sport goes back to 1965 when I went to Silverstone with my dad for the Daily Express Trophy. I had a little Box Brownie camera and got pictures of Graham Hill and John Surtees in their cars. I've always lived around Daventry, so Silverstone is my home track. My dad started going in 1948 when the circuit opened.

"The thing that really stands out from that particular meeting is the Ford GT40s. I was totally fascinated that the door opened and part of the roof came away. I was about nine years old at the time. I then started encouraging my dad to go to more and more races and I started getting Motoring News when I was about 12, so it's a life-long thing.

In the 1980s my wife Lynn and I started doing some photography and we were introduced to John Felix and the BMRMC, so we started taking photos for the marshals' club. We did some marshalling and from there we got involved in timekeeping. We later took a year's sabbatical and we were approached by Viv Ayres from 750 Motor Club who asked us to be club stewards.

"I joined the HSCC in 2006. Martin Atack was here at the time as Competitions' Secretary and the club was growing and it was becoming too much for Martin and Emma. The job was advertised in January or February. I went to Silverstone for an interview with Grahame and he offered me the job when I was on the club stand at Race Retro.

"Martin left in 2008 and unfortunately he left in the middle of the Silverstone Classic weekend. We got through and we were very lucky that I didn't shut the lap top computer down properly. If I'd shut it down properly I'd not have been able to get back into it as it was password protected and we hadn't got the password. The gods were on my side that weekend!

"So my role evolved into that of Competitions' Secretary. It's been good fun because I was a motor sport fan and a fan of the cars of the era that are now historic. Those 10 years have gone by very quickly and in that time the club has expanded greatly. One of the highlights has been seeing Michael Lyons develop as a racer.

"There are two circuits I really enjoy going to; Croft and Cadwell Park but the biggest event is the Silverstone Classic, which is a massive event for us and we never really get to see any racing. One of the best shows we did was the 50th anniversary display at Autosport International in January 2016."

"With longer races and the Three-Hour our Guards Trophy grids grew. For the Gold Cup we were able to run separate races for GTs and sports racers. Formula Junior was outstanding. Despite races all over the world our own grids were good and at the Brands Superprix we had 100 cars with three full Junior grids. Formula Ford was again strong and DBT saw more F5000 cars emerging. We increased our Historic FF2000 calendar from two to six meetings and there seem to be many more cars being prepared for racing. Through the year both our Road Sports championships were robust and again benefited from races at the Silverstone Classic. Historic Saloons ran as a support race for the British Grand Prix. Both CF3 and CRC had good years. For a second year we organised a calendar of European Historic Formula 2 races. After a good

start entries tailed off towards the end of the year. For 2009 we will concentrate the series with fewer meetings spread more broadly across the season.

"All of us, both in the Club office and on the Club's Board are only in this game to pursue the interests of our members. In 2008 membership fees at £150 were again held. 2009 will make eight years of stability. During 2008 we worked hard to hold down entry fees and this year we have pledged to hold entry fees at 2008 levels wherever possible.

"As the treasurer will confirm, we generated a £66,000 operating surplus in the year. It would have been more but we carry an exceptional bad debt from the Silverstone Classic, lost a small amount on

A packed Guards Trophy grid at Donington Park in 2009

John Hayes-Harlow heads a very close FF1600 pack off the line at Cadwell Park, 2009

European F2 and received no fee for our work on Tour Britannia. Steps have been taken to avoid such losses in 2009. The 2008 surplus strengthens our reserves on the balance sheet. We have worked hard through the good times to strengthen the Club's finances and are well placed to navigate the possible stormy waters ahead.

"The spirit in the Club, on the track and in the paddock is excellent. It's the members in the Club that make it so and I thank you for making 2008 a great year and trust we can make it even better in 2009."

The new season kicked off at Donington Park and among the entries was musician Chris Rea, one of a host of famous names to have raced with the Club over the years. Rea made a welcome return to circuit racing at Donington when he joined the Guards Trophy championship with his Lotus Elan 26R, which was originally raced by Australian motorsport legend Bob Jane. Rea, who unusually opted to run his car in open form, finished in mid-field.

Chevrons maintained their unbeaten record in the third HSCC Autosport Three Hours at Snetterton on Saturday May 30, but it was brothers James and Jeremy Cottingham who saw off the usual suspects amid a record entry to win a dramatic race by three laps in their DK Engineering B8.

Simon Hadfield and Michael Schryver, victors for the past two years, were out by half distance following a catalogue of problems with the latter's B6, while the Crossle 9S of Jon Shipman/Mark Hales – which came within minutes of beating it last year – suffered an identical rear hub failure after two hours.

The Snetterton three-hour winning Chevron B8 of brothers James and Jeremy Cottingham

The Historic F2 field at Monza in June

The HSCC-organised support race at the 2009 British Grand Prix: Hugh Colman (Chevron B8) to the fore

1-litre F3 cars on the grid at Brands Hatch, July 2009

1-litre F3 guests at Brands: (L-R) Chris Craft, Barrie Smith, John Miles, Tony Trimmer, Harry Stiller, Bev Bond and Dave Morgan

Scott Temple in Historic FF2000 at Brands

DBT racer Neil Glover splashes through the Oulton Park rain, August 2009

Among the entry was Warwick Banks, whose last race appearance at Snetterton was the 1963 Autosport event (won by Jim Clark in a Lotus 23B) in 'Tatty' Turner. A year later, he was crowned European Touring Car champion. Banks drove Geoffrey O'Connell's 1954 Arnolt-Bristol, while Suzanne Sears, daughter of '64 Three Hours victor Jack, was out in her MGB. Brother David, the former British FF1600 champion turned top senior single-seater league team chief came along to watch.

In June and July life was incredibly busy for the team in the Club office, with another British Grand Prix support race, the 20th annual Historic Super Prix at Brands Hatch and the Silverstone Classic: all in the space of about six weeks.

After the 2009 British Grand Prix, Nick Linney headed a Lola T70 Mk3B one-two-three at Silverstone as he headed Chris Beighton and Jon Minshaw, while John Sheldon's Chevron B16 topped the 2-litre cars with fourth overall. Notable winners at Brands Hatch included Andy Meyrick and Matthew Watts, who each took an F2 win. Richard Piper (Lola T400) won both Derek Bell Trophy races while father and son Michael and Will Schryver (Chevron B6) took the Guards Trophy race.

Andrew Tart in the Bond (25) heads a Formula Junior pack

Jonathan Rushton's Morgan in Historic Road Sports

In front of an invited group of famous former racers, the 1-litre Historic Formula 3 movement took a big step forward when 27 cars lined up to race at Brands Hatch. The re-birth of historic racing for the 1-litre 'screamers' of the late 1960s and early 1970s has been gathering momentum through the Peter Hanson Trophy mini-series as well as races in Europe, and was further boosted by confirmation of a race at the Monaco Historic GP in 2010.

Chris Craft, John Miles, Bev Bond, Tony Trimmer, Barrie Smith, Dave Morgan and Harry Stiller were all at Brands and Stiller presented a trophy to the leading F3 racer in the Classic Racing Car event, Frenchman Francois Derossi. Twenty-seven cars went out for qualifying on Saturday morning, although qualifying dramas reduced the total to 23 starters for the race. As well as the race, a fine array of cars was on display in the paddock and a total of 24 cars took part in a lunchtime grid line-up and parade lap around the Brands Hatch Grand Prix circuit.

The Oulton Park Gold Cup celebrated Formula 5000 and an array of former category drivers were on hand for an evening reception, including Gordon Spice, Bob Evans, Mike Walker, Teddy Pilette and Tony Trimmer. Not only were the old racers astounded to see the year's biggest F5000 turnout on track in the Derek Bell Trophy contests – 14 cars, bolstered by several more iconic monsters on static display – but they were delighted when period F5000 racer Trimmer finished third in the Sunday race, in a car he'd first sat in minutes before!

When the Chevrolet engine in Frank Lyons' Lola T330/332 damaged a piston in qualifying, Simon Hadfield sportingly offered the unique Chevron B37 to Trimmer – twice a Gold Gup winner in the race's British F1 era - who duly thundered from the back of the grid.

"I used to polish Tony's JPS Lotus F3 car as a lad, so it was a privilege to lend the car to a proper driver," said Hadfield, who won the race in the Hexagon Trojan T101. To cap it all, double European F5000 champion Teddy Pilette (who with Peter Gethin raced the Chevron B37 for Team VDS in 1976) presented the trophies.

In spite of the difficult economic climate, a field of over 30 cars in the competition section and another 20 in the regularity and touring events gathered at

Tour Britannia included special stages at Cornbury Park

Mark Garritt heads the Saloon pack into Gerards at Mallory Park

Simon Hadfield leads Westie Mitchell and Amanda Whitaker moments before the Mallory Historic FF accident

Jonathan Rushton: 2009 Historic Road Sports champion

Westie Mitchell: 2009 Historic Formula Ford champion

Silverstone on a Monday morning in early September for scrutineering and the start of Tour Britannia.

The competitive motoring started immediately on day one with a pair of special stages at the Porsche Centre at Silverstone. After two races on the National circuit, crews headed south to Cornbury Park in Oxfordshire for two special stages. Day two started early with a race at Rockingham followed by two runs through the special stage at Belvoir Castle. Next was the final race of the 2009 event at Cadwell Park, before a run to the second overnight halt in Harrogate.

Day three was all new, with 10 special stages at five venues across Yorkshire in a route that took in fish and chips for lunch on the sea front at Scarborough. The action started with two special stages at Harrogate Showground before two runs through a short stage at Duncombe Park. Next stop was one of the highlights of the event, two runs at the special stage on the motorcycle course at Oliver's Mount on the outskirts of Scarborough. With three hairpins and steep climbs and

THE 2009 HSCC RACING CHAMPIONS

Guards Trophy
Robert Barrie (Porsche 911)
Classic Racing Car Championship
Chris Holland (Brabham BT21)
Historic Road Sports Championship
Jonathan Rushton (Morgan Plus 4)
70s Road Sports Championship
Julian Barter (TVR 3000M)
Historic Formula 2
Martin Stretton (March 712)
Derek Bell Trophy
Neil Glover (Lola T330/332)
Historic FF1600 Championship
Westie Mitchell (Merlyn Mk20)
Historic Formula Junior Championship
Chris Drake (Elva 300)
Classic Formula 3 Championship
Bill Coombs (Argo JM6)
Historic FF2000 Championship
Neil Fowler (Reynard SF79)
Historic Touring Car Championship
Dan Cox (Ford Lotus Cortina)

descents, this was a tremendous addition to the route and the drivers loved this three-dimensional challenge.

On the route back towards the finish in Harrogate came two short blasts in the grounds of Castle Howard before a fitting finale with two runs at the hillclimb course at Harewood in a special stage that

Neil Glover: 2009 Derek Bell Trophy winner

2009 Formula Junior winners: Jon Milicevic, Duncan Rabagliati, Richard Attwood (guest of honour) and John Hutchison

ANDREW MANSELL

Board member and FF1600 racer

"I started racing in about 2006 as before that I'd not had the time or the money to do it. Someone convinced me that Historic Formula Ford was a good way of starting in terms of cost and in terms of fun. It turned out to be absolutely the case; great fun, great camaraderie and a great bunch of guys.

"I became championship chairman in 2013 and my job, really, is to keep it successful. I can then hand in over in good health to the next chairman. In 2016 most of our grids were at, or over, capacity and we were constantly asking for more track time to give our drivers the time they deserve. There are now around 100 cars that could race in the championship.

"I became a board member of the club when I took on the role of championship chairman. The most important things we work on are promoting good driving standards and then maintaining a level playing field for the cars. It is important that you can't throw money at these cars and move up the grid. If we keep those two things firmly anchored down, then the championship will run itself.

"In 2017 we celebrate 50 years of Formula Ford and we hope to put on a fantastic calendar of events. We represent the cars that started the category 50 years ago.

"The HSCC is an excellent club with really good race meetings and excellent organisation and very hard working people in the office. You couldn't wish for better."

took in the downhill run to the start as well as the climb back up the hill.

After coming close in previous years, including finishing runner-up in 2007, Nick Whale bagged victory on the fifth running of the tour. Partnered by his 19-year old son Harry, who shared the driving of his father's Porsche 911RS, they finished 1m13s up after three days of races and special stages on the unique classic race and rally tour.

The 2009 season wrapped up at Silverstone as the Club's championships were won and lost. As ever, there were tales behind the trophies and most notable was Historic Formula Ford champion Westie Mitchell, who had been hospitalised after the previous round at Mallory Park. Still not really match fit and in a borrowed car, Westie clinched the title in an emotional final race. Bill Coombs bounced back from a big mid-season accident at Castle Combe to win the Classic F3 title, while Dan Cox (Historic Touring Cars), Julian Barter (70s Road Sports), Neil Glover (Derek Bell Trophy) and Robert Barrie (Guards Trophy) were all champions.

Mitchell spent three days in hospital with a back injury after the Mallory accident and his entry for

the Silverstone final was in doubt until the preceding day. "The three days I was in a hospital bed, this was my target," said the Cirencester racer. "I was always working towards getting out at Silverstone, but I needed to see how I got on in testing."

With his own Merlyn Mk20 still damaged, Mitchell hired the ex-Tim Brise car of Mike O'Brien's Speedsport team for the final race, in which he went head-to-head with Amanda Whitaker for the title. He needed to beat the Durham lady in the race to have a shot at the title and achieved his goal as they finished fourth and seventh respectively.

"All the effort has been worthwhile," said Westie after the race. "I'm still on the mend but I'm nearly there." Whitaker was one of the first to congratulate her rival after the race. To make it a perfect day, Westie's 16-year old son Ben wrapped up the FF1600 class within the Classic Racing Car Championship in another Merlyn borrowed from Simon Hadfield.

In November, the HSCC exhibited at the NEC Classic Car show at the NEC. Aimed at the sports car owners amongst the 50,000 visitors and 200 clubs displaying at the show, the Club display focussed on Road Sports

Adam Ormandy leads an FF2000 pack at Cadwell Park, April 2010

Grahame White, Derek Bell and the famous photo

championships with Howard Bentham's Lotus Europa and Paul Castaldini's Jaguar E-type on show. Later in November, the Club's winners were celebrated at Whittlebury Hall when joint guests of honour were Richard Attwood and David Hobbs.

When reporting on the 2009 season, company secretary Anthony Goddard confirmed the best financial year in the Club's history. "As you know, the Club now operates as a 'company limited by guarantee, not having a share capital' so the old Treasurer's Report has now been transformed into this Company Secretary's Report. The content hardly changes from year to year, though, and a pattern, which was established five or six years ago, gets repeated each year. I could almost produce this report verbatim.

"Once again we have had a satisfactory year financially and our reserves continue to grow.

Highlights are as follows: Income from race meetings and their organisation rose from £132k to £220k this year. Whilst membership subscriptions and race registrations were pretty much static (an achievement against the background of the economy we keep hearing about), sponsorship income grew healthily from £14k to £26k. Bank charges (don't you just love the banks?) shot up from £7.3k to £16.8k whilst income from deposits fell by £12k. Office costs rose by 9% in general and staff costs went up by £14.8k. General overheads rose from £49.1k to £56.4k – bank charges mentioned above being a big contributor. The net result of this is a surplus of £130k for the year."

With little time to draw breath, even before 2009 season was over, the planning for 2010 was well underway and the Club unveiled what was described as its best-ever calendar for the new season, with headline events at Silverstone, Brands Hatch and Oulton Park. As well as race meetings at six venues where the focus was on racing for Club members, three higher profile events were the Silverstone International Trophy (May 15/16), the Brands Hatch Historic Superprix (3/4 July) and the Oulton Park Gold Cup (29/30 August).

In early June, the Autosport Three-Hours would run at Snetterton for cars from the Club's Guards Trophy GT and Sports Racing category. Later in June the Club planned to return to Mallory Park, while in August was a new two-day meeting at Croft. Breaking with tradition, the season would start at Silverstone in late March due to the unavailability of Donington Park,

Darren Burke flies over the Mountain at Cadwell on his way to victory

Matthew Watts (Lotus 30) heads a Guards Trophy pack at the Oulton Park Gold Cup

and the Club would return to Silverstone in October for the annual Championship Finals meeting.

Once again, the Club was to be responsible for organising the racing at the Silverstone Classic in July and at the Walter Hayes Trophy in November. "It is certainly one of the best calendars that the Club has ever had," said Grahame White. "In addition to our own race meetings, we will also have an interest in the 60th Anniversary Meeting at Castle Combe, the Spa Classic Six-Hour meeting in September, Dijon in October and five continental races for our Formula 2 Championship."

More important news was that the Club was going to run special race series in 2011, dedicated to the Jaguar E-type. As the famous model celebrated its 50th anniversary, the HSCC and the Jaguar Heritage Trust joined forces to mark the year with a series of races at high-profile historic race meetings. "We wanted to mark the 50th anniversary of the launch of the original E-type, one of the world's best loved classic cars," said Tony O'Keeffe, Curator of the Jaguar Heritage Trust.

The races were open to FIA Appendix K specification E-types and it was hoped to attract a field of over 30 cars from all over the world. The race at the Oulton Park Gold Cup meeting was particularly poignant as it was on 15

Classic F3 racer Jamie Brashaw gets his March out of shape at Lodge

Mark Jones heads the Historic Touring Car pack at Oulton Park

April 1961 that two E-types made the model's race debut at the Cheshire track in the hands of Graham Hill and Roy Salvadori. Hill went on to win the race and begin the E-type's motor sporting success story.

In January 2010, the Club celebrated Formula 5000 at Autosport International. The stand featured seven Formula 5000 cars and on the Friday morning a whole gaggle of former F5000 racers went along for a relaxed and informal re-union. Those attending included Steve Thompson, Chris Craft, Dennis Leech, Clive Baker, Mike Wilds, Bob Evans, Gordon Spice, Cyd Williams, Willie Green and Patrick Sumner, as well as more recent F5000 racers Matthew Wurr, Mick Lyons and 2009 DBT champion Neil Glover, while Lola's Bob Marston was also there.

Two real star guests dropped in to make it an even more special event. Divina Galica, British F1 racer of the late 1970s came along, while Derek Bell arrived hot-foot from a TV appointment. Bell was delighted to see his old friend Grahame White and show off a photo he had just been given. It was a shot of the young Derek with Enzo Ferrari, a photo he had never seen before. Remarkably, he did not previously own a photo of himself with the famous man.

Sir Stirling Moss, the patron of the Club, planned a return to racing at the Club's International Trophy meeting at Silverstone on 15/16 May. The news came from an interview Sir Stirling did with BBC Radio 4 about his recovery from an accident he had suffered in March 2010 at his London home.

"I hope to race at Silverstone in the Osca; that's the race I'm aiming at," Moss told BBC Radio 4 from his convalescent bed. Now 80 years old, Moss was determined to return to racing and said that the fall on 7 March would not stop him getting back into racing, 63 years after he started in the sport.

The FF2000 pack lines up at Silverstone, May 2010

The accident was the result of a lift malfunction and Sir Stirling suffered two broken ankles, four broken bones to his foot, skin abrasions and four chipped vertebrae. He had surgery to both ankles after falling 32 feet down the lift shaft and was very lucky not to suffer even more serious injuries.

"I remember the whole thing," he told Radio 4. "It was a bit of a drama, and it was very silly. I hope to be standing on my own feet by the beginning of May. It just takes longer when you are older and it's very boring." If his recovery continued to be good, Moss planned to race his beloved Osca in the first round of the Sir Stirling Moss Trophy, the race series for pre '61 sports and sports-racing cars run by Motor Racing Legends.

Sadly, Moss was not fit in time for Silverstone but did return to racing at the Oulton Park Gold Cup when he raced the Osca in the series bearing his own name. It was one of his last competitive outings in a remarkable career spanning more than 60 years. The presence of Moss, a record crowd and some tremendous racing made the Oulton Park Gold Cup meeting the best yet.

Moss reprised his 1961 Gold Cup victory by demonstrating the Ferguson 4WD, which was also part of a feature for Motor Sport magazine, and later hopped into his OSCA for the second half of the hour-long race, after the car's preparer Ian Nuthall had handled the opening stint.

The presence of the Club's patron-in-chief was the icing on the cake of a superb weekend, which drew over 450 cars to make it the biggest race weekend in the circuit's six decades of racing. Adding to a full programme for the Club's championships was an HGPCA race and a round of the GT and Sports Car Cup, while the Classic Racing Car double-header incorporated the Peter Hanson Trophy. A race for the Stirling Moss Trophy completed a mighty schedule, with a crammed timetable to keep everyone on their toes.

In Sunday's HGPCA Pre '66 race, Andy Middlehurst turned the clock back to 1963 to take victory in the ex-Jim Clark Lotus 25. The last time the car had been at Oulton Park, Clark won the 1963 Gold Cup to complete back-to-back victories in the non-championship Formula 1 race. "For me, it is the ultimate car to drive and it's a big responsibility," said

James Paterson leads Peter Shaw and Paul Anderson into Abbey during the 2010 Silverstone Classic

Guards Trophy champion Clive Wilson in his Elva at Silverstone

Tony Keele heads the CRC pack into Clervaux at Croft, August 2010

Winner Sean Lockyear on the Trawsfynydd stage of Tour Britannia

Mike Dowd slides Jeremy Cooke's Porsche at Mallory Park

Middlehurst of the car made famous by his boyhood hero. Bob Dance, mechanic to Clark in period, was there with the 25.

Moss, driving at Oulton Park for the first time in more than 15 years, contested the Motor Racing Legends race named in his honour. Up front, Jamie McIntyre was peerless in his thundering Chevrolet-powered Lister Knobbly. He out-ran his younger brother Ewen, who pushed hard to keep his nimble Lotus 15 in contention around the sweeps and dips of the Cheshire venue.

Other highlights of the 2010 season included an over 2-litre touring car race at the Silverstone Classic, with very close to a capacity 48-car field of pre '66 big bangers. Inevitably, the Mustang was the most popular choice and there were 17 of them on the entry list.

Meanwhile, in May, the Historic FF2000 movement surpassed all expectations with a capacity grid of 44 cars for the International Trophy meeting at Silverstone. Created as a mini-series of races for cars from the first seven years of the category, which was introduced in 1975, the Historic FF2000 movement was booming and the series organisers believed that there were more than 50 race-ready cars in the UK.

Sean Walker tackles the Great Orme on the 2010 Tour Britannia

Darren Burke: 2010 Historic FF1600 champion

Roger Godfrey: 2010 Historic Touring Car champion

Clive Wilson: 2010 Guards Trophy champion

"We can't quite believe how it has happened," said prime mover Alan Morgan. "The cars appeal to people; they are easy to run and have slicks and wings." After two pilot races in 2007, a mini-series was run over the last two seasons and now championship status is the target for 2011. "We came up with the idea when we were driving to Angouleme in Iain's truck," said Alan of the idea that he hatched with Iain Rowley.

It was only two years earlier that the first trial race was run at Cadwell Park and the class had a superb 30-car field at Oulton Park in August 2009. The target for Silverstone was 35 cars, so when the entry list hit 44, everyone was elated. That was possibly the biggest FF2000 grid ever and certainly the biggest as a period category.

Soon after the International Trophy meeting was the fourth annual Autosport Three Hours retrospective for Guards Trophy cars at Snetterton on June 5, which was full of all the drama for which endurance events are renowned. In the most open edition of the race to date, numerous glory bids were derailed before Gareth Burnett and Alex Ames triumphed in the Chevron B8 in which the Cottingham brothers had won a year earlier.

Announced late in 2010 was the news that the golden era of 2-litre sports-racing cars in the 1970s was to be brought back to life in 2011 with a new series of races run by the HSCC under the Martini Trophy title. The initiative, which in 2011 was expected to take in four or five events in the UK and Europe, would be for Group 6, open-cockpit, 2-litre sports-racing cars produced prior to the end of 1978.

THE 2010 HSCC RACING CHAMPIONS

Guards Trophy
Clive Wilson (Elva Mk7)
Classic Racing Car Championship
Ian Gray (Brabham BT16)
Historic Road Sports Championship
David Randall (Ginetta G4)
70s Road Sports Championship
Peter Shaw (TVR Tuscan)
Historic Formula 2
Katsu Kubota (March 712M)
Derek Bell Trophy
Neil Glover (Lola T330/332)
Historic FF1600 Championship
Darren Burke (Macon MR8)
Historic Formula Junior Championship
Jon Milicevic (Cooper T59)
Classic Formula 3 Championship
Benn Simms (March 803B)
Historic FF2000 Championship
Oliver Thorpe (Royale RP27)
Historic Touring Car Championship
Roger Godfrey (Austin Cooper S)

The new series would be open to cars running to FIA Appendix K, using Avon A11 tyres and competing in two classes. Cars with wings were to run to a minimum weight limit of 575kg excluding the driver, while cars without wings would run to a minimum of 500kg. The race format would be one qualifying session and two races of between 25 and 30 minutes each weekend. "We expect to have four or five race weekends in 2011, starting at the Silverstone International Trophy meeting in mid-May," said Grahame White.

In early September the sixth running of Tour Britannia took the event far into Wales for the first time, taking in a race at Anglesey as well as some challenging special stages. Once again, the Club handled the organisation of races at Oulton Park, Anglesey and Mallory Park.

Porsche completed a hat-trick of victories when Sean Lockyear and Ian Reed swept to victory in their potent 3-litre 911. To compound the Porsche domination of the event, the 911 of Howard Warren and Guy Woodcock won the concurrent regularity rally.

Following the event's tradition of moving around the country, the 2010 event headed to a base in Chester, which opened up a leg into North Wales on the second day. However, day one started with special stages on the remains on the Aintree club circuit before a race at Oulton Park.

Day two, Wednesday, was all new ground, starting with a real wake-up call over the narrow and bumpy roads of the Trawsfynydd ranges. The day included a race at the Anglesey track, a new challenge to most of the drivers, before the test that had the drivers truly wide-eyed. The tarmac toll road around the Great Orme at Llandudno was closed for the afternoon and the cliff-side road proved hugely popular as everyone tackled it twice. In addition, a service area on the sea front at Llandudno proved a big hit and drew lots of interests from locals and tourists. The final day took the event back into familiar Tour Britannia country, including stages at Cholmondeley Castle and Swynnerton army camp before a concluding race at Mallory Park.

As 2010 came to a close, several changes to the Club's board were announced. Anthony Goddard, after many years service as Club Treasurer and then as Company Secretary handed over the financial reigns to Crispin Schlaefli. Anthony was slimming down his work commitments to enjoy some retirement time, which was to include racing his Formula Junior in Europe.

Crispin brought an enormous amount of experience of club and motor sport accounting, having been treasurer for one of the MGCC registers for a number of years and responsible at Maranello for Club Fiorano and all its motor sport and track activities under Peter Gethin. He started racing in 1998 in the Kent County Championship with a Van Diemen RF92 and moved to the HSCC in 2003 with a Macon MR8. After many years service as the representative for Historic Touring Cars on the board, Graeme Dodd decided to step down. He was to be replaced by Ford Lotus Cortina racer Peter Hore.

In the final reckonings for the Club's 2010 racing season, Ian Gray bagged another Classic Racing Car title after some epic battles with Mike Scott's Brabham BT28, while David Methley won the concurrent Peter Hanson Trophy for the 1-litre F3 cars. In 70s Road Sports, Peter Shaw (TVR Tuscan) saw off a raft of rapid rivals to win the crown, while Dave Randall scooped Historic Road Sports glory with a hard-charging season in his Ginetta G4.

Neil Glover retained the Derek Bell Trophy after seeing off some rapid Formula 2 cars with his Formula 5000 Lola T330, while Clive Wilson (Elva Mk7) was a deserving Guards Trophy winner. Darren Burke arrived in Historic Formula Ford in a Macon MR8 from Peter Alexander's stable and dominated the season before aiming further up the racing ladder for 2011. Benn Simms took the Classic F3 crown for the third time in four seasons and Japanese commuter Katsu Kubota (March 712) scooped the Historic F2 title.

Having switched from the Lotus 18 that took him to the 2008 Formula Junior title to a Cooper T59, Jon Milicevic added another Junior title in 2010. The Towcester garage owner matched superlative pace with exemplary car control to out-gun his many rivals while young Oliver Thorpe was the top name from the Historic Formula Ford 2000 series, which was destined to gain championship status in 2011.

Roger Godfrey clinched the newly-titled Historic Touring Car Championship and, remarkably, was the first Mini racer to win the overall crown since the

Neil Fowler (left) receives the Lola Trophy from guest of honour Chris Craft

category moved to the HSCC nearly 15 years earlier. At the end of the year Chris Craft was on hand to present the annual awards, with his 1973 European 2-Litre Sports Championship-winning Lola T292 taking pride of place inside Whittlebury Hall.

As soon as the sport returned to action in January 2011 after the Christmas break, the club had a prominent stand at Autosport International at the Birmingham NEC as it celebrated the golden era of 2-litre sports car

racing. Notable period racers on hand included John Burton, 1973 European champion Chris Craft, Roger Heavens and John Miles. It was the perfect platform for the launch of the Martini Trophy, a four-event series for the 2-litre prototypes from the 1970s.

Also rapidly gathering pace was the newly-launched E-type Challenge, following an approach to the Club by Jaguar Heritage to run a series of races to celebrate 50 years of the E-type. The Club office recorded over 90 applicants from around, with many well documented historic cars coming forward to take part along with some very well known driver names.

The races would be for 3.8 litre E-Types built prior to 1966 with FIA HTP papers for either Homologation 34 or Homologation 100. Each registration was to be accompanied by a full copy of the HTP papers together with a Jaguar Heritage Trace Certificate to ensure all cars were genuine original-build Jaguars. The calendar of events for 2011 took in the Brands Hatch Historic Super Prix, the Silverstone Classic, the Nurburgring Oldtimer Grand Prix, the Oulton Park Gold Cup and the Goodwood Revival.

News about the 2011 season included the fact that the history of the Formula 3 category would be celebrated at Cadwell Park at Easter when the Club organised the Wolds Trophy Meeting at the Lincolnshire venue (Sunday/Monday 24/25 April).

The E-type Challenge started at Brands Hatch in July

Roger Cope and Steve Platts head the Historic Touring Car traffic at Brands

This new two-day historic meeting was to feature six races for Formula 3 cars, spanning 30 years of the category from the early post-war period through to the Ayrton Senna era of the early 1980s. Right through those decades, Cadwell Park was an important date on the Formula 3 schedule.

Launched at Race Retro, the Wolds Trophy was designed to be an annual historic festival for Cadwell Park to match existing high-profile race meetings at the other MotorSport Vision venues of Brands Hatch, Oulton Park and Snetterton.

"I'm delighted that the HSCC has chosen Cadwell Park for its Formula 3 celebration event," said Jonathan Palmer, Chief Executive of MotorSport Vision. "Cadwell has a long association with F3, as 500cc motorcycle-engined Formula 3 machines were the first cars to compete at the circuit in the 1950s. It's a fantastic driver's circuit, oozing with character, and an exhilarating place to drive an F3 car. I have fond memories of winning there in 1981, and of Ayrton Senna crashing at the Mountain in 1983!"

In his address to the 2011 Annual General Meeting, Chairman Chris Sharples reflected on 2010 and developments for 2011.

"Our championships grew stronger. Historic Touring Cars had a brilliant year and grids were often 20% up on 2009. Guards Trophy grids again grew. For the Gold Cup we were again able to run separate races for GTs and sports racers whilst having an invitation class for big-banger sports racers. This worked well and will be repeated. Classic Racing Cars grew with more HF3s coming out to play. Formula Junior and Formula Ford were again outstanding. Historic FF2000 had 43 cars on the grid at the International Trophy (possibly a record for the category) and is becoming a championship in 2011. Paradoxically our Classic F3 suffered a short term loss from its inclusion at the 2010 Monaco Historic with racing budgets being depleted by the cost of running at that meeting. It also saw a drop off in the HFF2000 class (with these cars having their own races). For 2011 they will be promoting their championship putting emphasis on the earlier 1600 class for the Tony Brise Trophy.

"Both HRS and 70s Road Sports championships ended the year in good health. Although the racing was often very good the Derek Bell Trophy F5000/F2 had disappointing grids. Their championship committee has made a number of changes. Classes have been expanded to allow participation from later pre-84 cars and for 2011 DBT will revert to series status.

"Historic F2, Martini Trophy and E-type Challenge; in Europe our Historic Formula 2 championship had

Charlie Kemp and Steve Hodges battle at Brands in the Martini Trophy

a good year with entries up on 2009. It drew drivers from across Europe as well as Brazil, Hong Kong, and Japan. This championship is helping the Club to grow and with the many (ownership) changes taking place in the historic scene it provides the Club with the security of having its own feature guest race at its cornerstone meetings. Late in 2010 we announced a new 2-litre sports car series, the Martini Trophy. Although in 2011 this will run mainly at UK meetings we anticipate that in future years we will be able to grow this to run alongside Historic F2. Finally we were honoured to have been asked by Jaguar to run a five race series for pukka E-types to mark the 50th anniversary of the car."

New company secretary Crispin Schlaefli reported a strong financial result, with nearly £140,000 added to the Club's reserves. "Financially the Club has had another successful year. Club turnover increased by 9%, race income was up 8% and membership fee revenue (with more members and an increased basic fee) was up 15%. However with the Club holding down the cost of race entries this increased revenue did not fully compensate for higher track costs (up 13%). Consequently net income after directs increased by only 1%.

Tim Barrington and James Claridge at Coppice in Formula 2 at the first Donington Historic Festival, May 2011

"The result has been greatly helped by overheads being down 2%. Whilst the costs of communication increased (stationery, post, photocopying) staff costs fell in the year. A further contribution from the 'Office' was that the P&L benefitted from race organisation fees and sponsorship which added £62,000 to the result. Net profit at £138,000 was 6% up on the previous year. This result is reflected in the improvement in net assets."

A piece of Club history was made early in June 2011 when total membership passed the 1000-mark for the first time in 45 years. This record-breaking level of membership was tremendous news for the Club as it came at a time when the after effect of the global credit crunch was still being keenly felt across

Cadwell Park, April 2011: Benn Simms heads the FF1600 field away

Julian Barter heads the 70s Road Sports at Cadwell

Dan Cox in typical pose at Luffield at Silverstone in his Lotus Cortina

the British economy. In 2010, total membership reached 940, but in 2011 the magic 1000 barrier was surpassed. The huge majority of those 1000 people were active racing members.

In July, Club Patron-in-Chief Sir Stirling Moss OBE finally called time on his racing career after more than 60 years of competition. During qualifying for the Le

Mans Legends race Sir Stirling made the decision to retire from the sport he loves.

"This afternoon I scared myself and I have always said that if I felt I was not up to it or that I was getting in the way of fellow competitors, then I would retire," he said. "I love racing, but now it is time to stop."

He left motor racing as one of the most recognised racing drivers in the world, having raced from the age of 18, winning the British Grand Prix twice, the Monaco Grand Prix three times, the Mille Miglia, the Targa Florio and the Tourist Trophy, as well as countless other races during his professional career.

He then went onto compete in historic racing. He was regarded as one of the greatest motor racing drivers

Ed Lovett leads the Martini Trophy pack at Silverstone, May 2011

the sport has ever known, having raced successfully in all forms of motor sport and racing not only to win, but racing because he loved the racing itself. Although he would not race again, he was sure to remain as popular and busy as ever and remained a true sporting giant.

Snetterton's new 300 circuit inspired some fine racing at the Club's Autosport 3-Hour meeting in June. After three hours of intense competition, the three-hour roll of honour featured new names on the top of the podium as Nick Fleming and Luke Stevens (Chevron B8) won the headline enduro.

A brilliant tactical call and a lucky safety car break earned Fleming and Stevens victory in the fifth historic version of the Snetterton endurance race. Their Chevron-BMW B8 became the third of the late Derek Bennett's cars to win the event, the B6 of Michael Schryver/Simon Hadfield and B8 (driven by the Cottingham brothers in '09 and Gareth Burnett/Alex Ames last year) having triumphed twice each.

Poleman Greg Caton was the hare in Brian Casey's Lenham P69 spyder, but soon after its owner took over its engine grenaded, putting the quickest Chevrons ahead to stay, with the Crossle 9S of Jon Shipman/Mark Hales in pursuit, having lost time with a stop-and-go penalty for overtaking under yellows.

A week after Snetterton was the seventh edition of Tour Britannia, which was regarded as the toughest yet as the route took in a raft of new venues. John

THE 2011 HSCC RACING CHAMPIONS

Guards Trophy
Tom Smith (MGB)
Martini Trophy with Supersports
Doug Hart (March 75S) and
Charlie Kemp (Lola T210)
Classic Racing Car Championship
Ian Gray (Brabham BT16)
Historic Road Sports Championship
Paul Tooms (Lotus Elan)
70s Road Sports Championship
John Thomason (Triumph GT6)
Historic Formula 2
Diogo Ferrao (March 712M)
Derek Bell Trophy
Michael Lyons (Lola T400)
Historic FF1600 Championship
Benn Simms (Alexis Mk14)
Historic Formula Junior Championship
Jon Milicevic (Cooper T59)
Classic Formula 3 Championship
Jamie Brashaw (March 793)
Historic FF2000 Championship
Russell Love (Reynard SF79)
Historic Touring Car Championship
Roger Godfrey (Austin Cooper S)
E-type Challenge
Jon Minshaw and John Burton

A Guinness World Record for the largest parade of Jaguars during the 2011 Silverstone Classic

that, for the first time, the event would be won and lost on the stages and not the races.

By taking the tour into South Wales for the first time, tour boss Alec Poole opened up three serious rally venues; Cwm Carn forest drive, the Epynt ranges and Caerwent military base. Suddenly, with over 60 stage miles, the rally element of the classic tour counted for more than the three races at Pembrey, Castle Combe and Silverstone. As usual, the HSCC was responsible for the running of the three races.

Clark and Emma-Jane Gilbart-Smith led from the start and were never headed in their Porsche 911. But they were under constant pressure from several rivals and only a timely off on the Epynt ranges on Friday afternoon cost Indy 500 winner and former F1 driver Danny Sullivan and Chip Connor victory in their 911RSR.

There was a major change in the format for the 2011 running of the classic race and rally tour, with a massively increased mileage on special stages meaning

From the start at Newport, crews headed straight into the Welsh valleys for two runs through Cwm Carn, with steep drops in places and low cloud shrouding the highest points of this challenging wake-up call. The expected rain set in as crews arrived and set the tone for a long, tough and wet day in Wales.

Next up was a race at a very wet Pembrey before crews headed into the Brecon Beacons for four special stages on the infamous Epynt ranges, where blind brows and jump lie in wait to catch the inexperienced or over-confident. Two short stages in Bryn Bach Park rounded out the day.

Nick Fleming heads the Guards Trophy into the rain at Croft, August 2011

Early on Saturday morning it was over the Severn Bridge for a special stage at the rain-lashed Castle Combe, then down to Weston-super-Mare for two runs along the toll road north of the town centre. Two runs through a stage in the grounds of Badminton House preceded a race at Castle Combe before the real sting in the Saturday tail; two nine-mile special stages at the Caerwent military site. This venue had a maze of roads, many with kerbs, and countless junctions. It was a fearsome test and everyone came out of it with tales of drama and excitement.

After another overnight halt in Newport, it was back to nearby Caerwent for two more stages and then up to Prescott for two runs up the hill. Two stages at Tusmore Park near Brackley were new to everyone before the final challenge, a race on the new International circuit at Silverstone, operated from the striking new Wing pit complex. "In some ways the last two days were a nightmare because we led from day one," said Clark. "I rooted the tyres completely in the race at Silverstone and it was touch and go."

The Club's 2011 racing season delivered consistently good racing from strong grids and several titles

Historic Formula Ford 'dads and lads' podium at Silverstone (left to right): Ben and Westie Mitchell, Benn and Paul Simms, Rob and Gerry Wainwright

were only settled on a bright and sunny Saturday at Silverstone in late October. Ian Gray bagged another Classic Racing Car title but only after dealing with a big challenge from the rare Crossle 12F of Paul McMorran. In Historic Formula Ford, Benn Simms

Tom Smith was superb in his MGB as he won the Guards Trophy

Russell Love: 2011 Historic FF2000 champion

John Thomason: 2011 70s Road Sports champion

clinched the title after a wonderful season-long contest with Ben Mitchell. The final podium place went to Rob Wainwright and the wonderful post-race celebrations featured three sons with their dads, Paul Simms, Westie Mitchell and Gerry Wainwright, all were all heavily involved in preparing the cars.

Sporting rivalry was just as prevalent in Formula Junior where good friends Jon Milicevic and Sam Wilson enjoyed a mighty battle as the race closed the Club season. Just as they had consistently across the season,

Milicevic and Wilson ran wheel-to-wheel yet again in the finale. This time, Milicevic led every lap, but Wilson pushed every inch of the way and ensured that the Club's fabulous 2011 season ended in style.

"Sam's a fantastic driver and it means a lot to win again on my home track," said Milicevic. Having twice lost out to Wilson during the Silverstone Classic in July, this victory was all the sweeter for the Towcester garage owner. "It's been an amazing year," said Wilson after a round of handshakes and hugs. "It was very close at times, but Jon was just too quick today." It was a proper way to close a very good season.

Guest of honour Jonathan Palmer presented the awards at the annual dinner and among the other champions and series winners to be celebrated were Paul Tooms from Historic Road Sports, Diogo Ferrao from Historic Formula 2, Michael Lyons (Derek Bell Trophy), Jamie Brashaw (Classic F3) and Roger Godfrey (Historic Touring Cars). Russell Love overcame very limited funds to win the first full Historic FF2000 Championship, while the inaugural Martini Trophy was shared between Doug Hart (March 75S) and Charlie Kemp (Lola T210). Finally, Jon Minshaw had been the class of the E-type Challenge, while John Burton took the class for more standard cars.

Jon Milicevic and Sam Wilson go wheel-to-wheel at the Silverstone Classic

2012 to 2015
The success continues

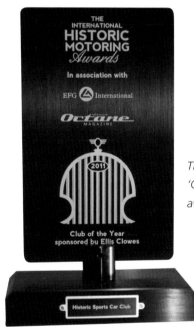

The HSCC won the 'Club of the Year' award for 2011

The 2012 season started in fine style as the Club was announced as 'Club of the Year' at the International Historic Motoring Awards. With the backing of Octane magazine, the award was presented during an impressive evening dinner in central London and was another deserved accolade for the Club.

Changes to the Club's racing portfolio for 2012 centred on the growth of Historic Formula 3 and the development of the Martini Trophy. Following the success of the Cadwell Park stand-alone races in 2011, and the growing support for the cars, the Club registered a new series with the MSA in 2012 for Historic Formula 3 Cars. The series was divided into two classes: one for the earlier side-draught cars from 1964 and 1965 and the other for the later down-draught cars from 1966 to 1970. There was a choice of treaded control tyre available and it was hoped many drivers from the continent would contest the series. This was good news for the many from within the Club who had promoted these cars including David Pullen, Steve Wilkinson, Keith Messer and Duncan Rabagliati.

More good news from the 1-litre screamer world was that a new feature film was in production, titled Rush, focusing on the rivalry between James Hunt and Niki Lauda and in particular the 1976 Grand Prix season, when Lauda returned to racing a few weeks after his near fatal accident. The film was being directed by Ron Howard, and the cast was headed by Chris Hemsworth and Daniel Bruhl.

As the story was set within motor sport, the production company had been looking for both Formula One and 1-litre Formula 3 cars of the period to help them re-tell the story. The HSCC was asked to co-ordinate some Formula 3 scenes and had been looking for some F3 screamers that would have been eligible to race prior to the end of 1970. All the cars finally selected, together with their drivers would be required to attend filming at Crystal Palace, Cadwell Park and Blackbushe Airfield.

For 2012, the Martini Trophy Series was linked with the 2-litre cars from the International Supersports Cup.

1-litre F3s filming for 'Rush' at Cadwell Park

This all happened as a result of a meeting between Grahame White and German husband and wife team Silvio and Angela Kalb. The Kalbs had been running Supersports with Orwell sponsorship for a number of years. Eligible cars included 2-litre, 3-litre and Can-Am cars but with the economic down turn the Orwell Clothing Company could not continue its support and the Can-Am cars formed an independent series so grids were reduced. It was at this point the two parties decided to join forces and restore it to 2-litre cars only.

As an experiment early Sports 2000 cars would be allowed to run at the International Trophy at Silverstone in May and Martini Trophy with Supersports, to give it the full title, was looking very promising. At Autosport International, a special award was made to John Burton as the best Chevron driver of the 2011 Martini season. Helen Bashford-Malkie presented John with a very special trophy first presented at Hockenhim in 1972 in memory of Jochen Rindt. "I've been involved with Chevrons since 1968, which is an awful long time," said John. "Martini Trophy with Supersports is a true European series and I hope we'll get many more 2-litre cars on the track. They are fantastic fun to drive and incredibly quick."

In March 2012, Chairman Chris Sharples told the Annual General Meeting that 2012 would be a year of consolidation. "In planning 2011 the Board was concerned that with a poor economic backdrop our figures would trend downwards. We now know that other clubs and championships have suffered from smaller grids. We bucked the trend. Like-for-like entries increased and our membership grew, breaking 1,000 for the first time in the Club's history. It was a record year.

"The 2012 season will be one of consolidation. We are happy with the size of the 2011 calendar. Whilst we have members who would like to race at Thruxton, Castle Combe, Mallory Park and Anglesey we have decided to hold to a roster of nine meetings albeit with Donington Park moving to two days. Similarly we continue to get requests to run other series at our meetings. We take this as a compliment but feel that with our UK championships, plus HF2, Martini and E-types, we are able to continue to give members an excellent programme with our normal level of friendly service. For now we have no plans for further expansion.

"Again we presented the Club at the NEC Classic Car Show, the Autosport Show and Race Retro. We upgraded our stands with improved display material. It is difficult to judge the effect of these shows. We take very few memberships at the shows but our judgement is that by putting on a good presentation we project the reputation of Club and have an excellent opportunity for networking.

"We have sound finances. Crispin Schlaefli (our new Company Secretary) will show we delivered a satisfactory financial result which strengthened our reserves. In 2012 the UK economy is predicted to deteriorate. Virtually all our costs are fixed within the year and any revenue loss from smaller grids falls straight to the bottom line. For instance the loss of just two or three cars from each of our grids would cut revenue by well over £100,000. We know that many clubs are cutting back their race programmes. The Board acknowledges that we may face a risk but has agreed to underwrite a calendar which is largely unchanged from 2012."

In broad terms, the Treasurer's Report confirmed a Club turn-over of £1.2 million and a net profit of £128,000, which increased net assets to the record level of £770,000.

"Whilst we are foremost a club, we are also a business," reported Crispin Schlaefli. "We continue to return a healthy surplus. It must be remembered that more than half of this surplus arises from non-core activity: that is managing events such as the Silverstone Classic and the Walter Hayes Trophy, coupled with sponsorship and advertising revenue. These extremely welcome revenue streams do create a lot of additional work for a small office team, but broadly help subsidise the overall entry fees for Club members.

"Equally we run a really tight ship in terms of staff levels and office accommodation, the surplus achieved is the result of careful cost control and massive commitment from all the staff."

In January 2012, the Club's stand at Autosport International celebrated 60 years of Formula 3 with a superb line-up of cars and visits from several former F3 racers including British champions Andy Wallace (1986) and David Brabham (1989).

The 2012 racing season started early, with a two-day meeting at Donington Park in mid-March. Young Callum Grant shot to prominence with a fine Historic

Roger Godfrey (1) heads the up to 1600cc Historic Touring Cars at Donington Park in March 2012

Paul Tooms heads the Historic Road Sports field at Cadwell Park

Ian Jones heading for a Classic Racing Car double at Cadwell Park, April 2012

John Hayes-Harlow slides his FF2000 Royale RP30 at Cadwell Park

The E-type Challenge grid at Donington Park, May 2012

David Gathercole and Silvio Kalb head the Martini Trophy grid at Silverstone

Mike Bletsoe-Brown heads Tim Barrington in F2 at Donington

Formula Ford victory on his debut race at the circuit at the tender age of just 16. His rivals included Lola team-mates David Wild and Simon Toyne and another impressive youngster, Rob Wainwright.

Others starting the season with a win included Paul Conway (Morgan Plus 8) in 70s Road Sports, Paul Tooms (Lotus Elan) in Historic Road Sports and Jamie Brashaw (March 793) in the combined Derek Bell Trophy/Classic F3 race. James Dodd had to work hard in his Ginetta G16 to fend off the Chevron B8 of Steve Hodges in the sports-racing element of the Guards Trophy.

Six weeks later, the Club was back at Donington Park to organise the racing element of the second Donington Historic Festival. The Club also had races for Historic Formula 2 and E-types, with a feisty Jaguar battle

Historic F3 cars line up at Silverstone

between Alex Buncombe and Martin O'Connell ending with O'Connell in the gravel at McLeans. Buncombe also won the second race while F2 victories went to Matthew Watts (March 772P) and a surprised Philip Gladman (Chevron B34) after Watts, David Gathercole and David Methley all retired from the lead.

The eighth running of Tour Britannia took place in early June as a field of 50 cars competed across two and a half days in Britain's only race and rally tour. Once again, the Club managed the racing element of the unique event, which took in races at Croft and Cadwell Park.

When the tour ended in Harrogate, the major winners were confirmed as Phil Hindley/Andy Bull (Competition), Richard Meaden/Nathan Blewer (Targa) and Melissa Raven/Jeremy Haylock (Regularity). The battles were close across all three elements of the event as Tour Britannia took crews to 10 venues, seven of them new to the tour and a first race at Croft.

In the competition category, Hindley and Bull took victory in their Porsche 911SC over the Ford Escort Mk1 of Roger Kilty and Lynette Banks with the Chevrolet Camaro of Stuart Scott and Steve Wood completing the overall podium. The result marked the fifth win in a row for Porsche, while Kilty's drive to second was a highlight of the event.

The competition started on Wednesday evening with a short special stage in the grounds of the base hotel, the Rudding Park Hotel in Harrogate. Although only half a mile long, the new asphalt surface was very loose in places and a pair of runs caught out

Mark Clubb battles in the E-type Challenge at Silverstone

Stuart Scott and Steve Wood in the ex-Richard Lloyd Camaro at Raby Castle on Tour Britannia

Roger Kilty slides his Escort Mk1 on Tour Britannia, June 2012

several crews. Most notably, the Porsche 911 of John Spiers/Susanne Niedrum slid wide and swiped a tree, inflicting considerable damage and unfortunately ending their event.

As Tour Britannia finished, the Club's Snetterton race meeting was about to begin and an innovative single-

Richard Plant leads the Barters in 70s Road Sports at Snetterton

Nick Fleming heads the 2012 Autosport three-hour at Snetterton

John Delane brought his ex-Jackie Stewart Tyrrell to race in the Derek Bell Trophy at the Brands Hatch Historic Super Prix

Max Blees (March 752) leads an F2 pack at Brands Hatch in July

driver strategy, inspired fuel calculations and a split-second decision enabled Nick Fleming (Chevron B8) to win the sixth HSCC Autosport 3-Hours. Caterham ace Luke Stevens, who partnered Fleming a year earlier, helped George Douglas' Ginetta G16 team to second place – repeating its 2010 result - ahead of James and Graeme Dodd's sister car, which effectively lost a lap due to its track position when one of four full-course cautions was launched.

In early July, the wrangles over the future of the FIA Historic Formula One Championship cost the cancellation of the planned race at the HSCC Historic Super Prix at Brands Hatch. Instead, five Historic F1 cars joined the Derek Bell Trophy grid and the ever-growing success of Historic F2 and Martini Trophy more than filled the gap. A decent crowd enjoyed lots of good racing and only a nasty Historic Formula Ford shunt cast anything of a shadow over the weekend. Elden racer John Crowell sustained significant injuries but later planned to return to racing.

Winners included David Methley who did a Lurani Trophy double in Formula Junior, double F2 victor Matthew Watts and Martini Trophy wins were shared by Silvio Kalb (March 76S) and David Gathercole (Lola

Michael Lyons starred at the Super Prix in his Hesketh 308E

The F5000/F2 pack at the Silverstone Classic

T212). Both John Burton (Chevron B26) and Nick Fleming (Chevron B36) featured, only to suffer car problems. Michael Lyons won both Derek Bell Trophy races in his Hesketh 308E to follow up an impressive Monaco victory.

Of particular HSCC interest in the 2012 Silverstone Classic were double-headers for Formula Junior, Formula 5000/Formula 2, E-type Challenge and Touring Cars from 1970 to 2000. The combined F5000/F2 grid, competing for the Peter Gethin Memorial Trophy, was a new addition for 2012 and the spectacle of F5000 grunt taking on F2 nimbleness was a real highlight of the racing.

With both races decided by a fraction of a second, the Peter Gethin races were two of the very best. But with Simon Hadfield and Michael Lyons in 5000s taking on Martin Stretton from the F2 camp, the racing was always like to be very special. Lyons, driving with tremendous assurance, grabbed the early lead with his Lola T400 in Saturday's race as Stretton made a sluggish getaway in his F2 March 742. While Stretton set about making up lost ground, Hadfield fired the Trojan T101 into second and led the chase of his young rival. This was a contest of Formula 5000s as

they were meant to be driven: with Lyons enjoying better downforce in the later Lola, but Hadfield tromping down the straights in the sleeker Trojan.

The contest was only settled when Hadfield had a quick spin at Stowe. But any thoughts that Lyons had of easing off were quickly dispelled as Stretton's dogged pursuit took him up to the gearbox of the Lola. Lyons used the grunt of the Lola to see off the flying March, but little more than a tenth of a second split them at the flag after a breathtaking trace. Hadfield recovered for this before young Lee Dwyer (March 782) and Autosport's Ben Anderson (Chevron B37) arrived.

Stretton made a much better start on Sunday but fans were denied a three-way fight when Lyons had the Lola's engine expire early on. Now it was Hadfield versus Stretton and Martin harried the Trojan constantly, and even stole ahead briefly, but Hadfield was back in front when it really mattered after another glorious contest. With Anderson and Dwyer both hitting trouble, Neil Fowler grabbed third after a debut run in David Wild's March 75B.

Alex Buncombe was the class of the Jaguar E-type Challenge aboard the car entered by series sponsor JD Classics. The GT star dealt with a first lap challenge from former BTCC ace Anthony Reid to be four seconds ahead by the end of the lap and then paced himself for victory. Buncombe made it a double on Sunday with another resounding victory, with Gregor Fisken and John Pearson completing the podium party at a respectful distance.

Jon Milicevic bagged the opening Formula Junior race, but had to fend off a typically determined challenge from David Methley. Matters were only resolved on the final lap when the chasing Methley pushed just too hard and spun into Brooklands. Methley made amends on Sunday morning after another typically fine contest. Sadly, Milicevic accidently knocked the fuel pump switch on the Cooper and pulled off, leaving Methley's Brabham BT6 clear of the chasing Sam Wilson (Cooper T59).

As the season headed for the closing stages, Callum Grant sealed the Historic FF1600 title at 17-years-old to join Michael Lyons as the youngest champions is the Club history.

James Nairn at Oulton Park's Shell Corner in 70s Road Sports; 2012 Gold Cup

Grant won the Grandstand Motor Sport title in his first season of racing, with three rounds still to run. Up until the Oulton Park Gold Cup race Grant, who only turned 17 in May, could have been caught by Lola T200 racer Simon Toyne, but with Toyne expected to miss the Brands Hatch race in September while racing at Spa, Grant was effectively champion before his home race. "It's been fantastic," said the Bolton racer. "I've only been off the podium once. Winning the first race at Donington was a surprise and after that I've just been trying to get points."

Forty-two years after it was last held, the HSCC and the 1000cc F3 Historic Racing Association revived the Nations' Cup. The event was held at the Circuit Dijon-Prenois (France) over the weekend of 6/7 October.

Run five times from 1966 to 1970, the annual Nations' Cup for 1000cc F3 'screamers' featured national teams of three drivers from across Europe. The event was a highlight of the F3 calendar and period race winners included Chris Irwin (GB), Clay Regazzoni (Switzerland) and Ronnie Peterson (Sweden). The Nations' Cup was motor racing's closest equivalent to the Olympic Games. In 1970, the GB (A) team comprised James Hunt, Bev Bond and Mike Beuttler and Bond was at

Dijon to see the event revived. He had returned to racing over the previous two seasons and was now Membership Secretary for the 1000cc F3 Historic Racing Association.

Grahame White was involved in the Nations Cup more than 40 years ago. "I was Clerk of the Course for the 1970 event at Thruxton and well remember Gerry Birrell winning the race followed by three Swedish drivers," said White. "Sweden took the team prize. The team element made it much more exciting for the drivers and that is what we wanted to recreate at Dijon."

Apart from Grant, other champions for 2012 included Formula Junior winner Robert Barrie (Lotus 18) who was only confirmed after a dramatic Silverstone final when Jon Milicevic was eliminated in a dramatic accident with David Methley. Nick Fleming won the Guards Trophy in his Lotus Elan and Ian Jones topped Classic Racing Cars in his Lotus 59 after an exemplary campaign. Tim Barrington was a worthy Historic F2 champion in his Lola T240 and more single-seater titles went to Jamie Brashaw (Classic Formula 3), Dean Forward (Historic Formula 3) and Nelson Rowe (Historic FF2000). Paul Tooms (Lotus Elan) and John Thomason (Triumph GT6) took the Road Sports titles.

David Gathercole won the 2012 Martini Trophy

2012 Guards Trophy presentations (left to right): James Dodd, Nick Fleming, Jack Sears and Al Fleming

Just before Christmas, Grahame White unveiled the Club's 2013 race calendar. New on the schedule was a two-day meeting at Thruxton over the Easter weekend (30/31 March), while the Silverstone International Trophy would again run on the Grand Prix circuit in mid-May. The Oulton Park Gold Cup would celebrate 60 years of the Cheshire track, while the season was to open with a one-day meeting at Donington Park in mid-March.

As had become customary, the Club was represented at three major shows over the winter. In November at the Classic Motor Show at the NEC the Club stand centred on Road Sports, while at Autosport International in January the theme was the history of saloon and touring car racing. A range of cars from across the Club's portfolio was on display at Race Retro at the end of February.

More news about the Thruxton Easter Revival Meeting was that the Jochen Rindt Trophy would be presented for the Historic Formula 2 races over the weekend. The Club's race meeting would mark the 45th anniversary of the first Formula 2 event at the Hampshire track in 1968, won by Rindt in his Brabham BT23C. The following season he won again at Thruxton in a Lotus 59 and then completed the hat-trick in 1970 in a Lotus 69. However, six month later, Rindt was killed in qualifying for the Italian Grand Prix at Monza. He duly became the sport's only posthumous Formula One World Champion.

Following Rindt's death, the British Automobile Racing Club commissioned the Jochen Rindt Memorial Trophy in time for the Thruxton Formula 2 race at Easter 1971 when Graham Hill took victory in his Brabham BT36.

THE 2012 HSCC RACING CHAMPIONS

Guards Trophy
Nick Fleming (Lotus Elan 26R)
Martini Trophy with Supersports
Silvio Kalb (March 76S) and David Gathercole (Lola T212/C)
Classic Racing Car Championship
Ian Jones (Lotus 59)
Historic Road Sports Championship
Paul Tooms (Lotus Elan)
70s Road Sports Championship
John Thomason (Triumph GT6)
Historic Formula 2
Tim Barrington (Lola T240)
Derek Bell Trophy
Frank Lyons (Gurney Eagle FA74)
Historic FF1600 Championship
Callum Grant (Merlyn Mk20)
Historic Formula Junior Championship
Robert Barrie (Lotus 18)
Classic Formula 3 Championship
Jamie Brashaw (March 793)
Historic Formula 3 Championship
Dean Forward (Brabham BT21)
Historic FF2000 Championship
Nelson Rowe (Reynard SF79)
Historic Touring Car Championship
Dan Cox (Ford Lotus Cortina)
E-type Challenge
Alex Buncombe, Mark Clubb and Roger Cope

The Club's stand at Race Retro, February 2013

Grahame White was involved in the creation of the trophy and had fond memories of the Austrian racer. "I had the pleasure of knowing Jochen both socially and through racing," said White. "I found him to be such a genuine person who was not fully aware of the huge amount of natural talent he had. He was sometimes surprised at the amount of attention he received in his early years, but he was always very appreciative of the friendliness of Formula 2 teams and drivers, and always enjoyed racing at Thruxton."

The Club's new-for-2013 Super Touring Trophy was confirmed to run at four high-profile historic race meetings, headlined by a return date at the Silverstone Classic (26-28 July). The season would start at the Thruxton Easter Revival (30/31 March), followed by rounds at the Historic Super Prix at Brands Hatch (13/14 July) and the Oulton Park Gold Cup (25/26 August).

The classes were to mirror those used at the 2012 Silverstone Classic, when 40 cars lined up to deliver two superb races. Classes would cover Group 2 (1970-73), Group 1 (1974-83), Group A (1983-90) and Super Touring Cars (1991-2000) and there was to be an invitation class for historically significant cars, including those from the World and German Touring Car Championships of the period.

Cars would run exactly as they did in period and comply with relevant period FIA regulations. The series was restricted to genuine cars with a period history and the planned four-event schedule, with some double-headers, was the perfect platform for car owners.

Good news for the Historic Formula Ford drivers was that the category would have the highest profile event in the history of the category with a double-header

Luke Clark-Bagnall on the limit at Donington Park

Craig Davies heads the Guards Trophy field into Redgate at Donington

Drama between Martin O'Connell and Nick Fleming at Thruxton

slot at the Silverstone Classic (26-28 July). The news was another boost for the Club's category for pre '72 FF1600s, which was already riding a wave of popularity with bumper grids of immaculate cars and fierce competition from a tremendous diversity of drivers. Typically, more than a dozen marques were represented on the grid with a 50-year span of drivers' ages.

The cars from the first five seasons of Formula Ford racing would have qualifying on Friday followed by 20-minute races on both Saturday and Sunday at one of the biggest events in European historic racing. A grid of more than 40 cars was expected for the races on the Silverstone Grand Prix circuit. "This is excellent news for Historic Formula Ford, which consistently delivers close and exciting racing," said Grahame White. "We are very grateful to Nick Wigley and his team at Goose Communications for making this possible."

A swift and very positive response from the competitors pointed to a strong grid for the pair of non-championship races. Championship Chairman Andrew Mansell said the chance to race at the Silverstone Classic was a massive boost for Historic Formula Ford and urged drivers to take the opportunity to race at the high-profile event. "It is 12 years since Historic FF was last invited to the Silverstone Classic, and it may be another 12 years before we get the privilege of being included again," said Mansell.

The racing season started at a wet and greasy Donington Park on a day when conditions steadily improved. The star of the day was young Luke Clark-

Tiff Needell guides his Lotus 69 through the Thruxton chicane, March 2013

Mark Charteris (Mallock Mk20/21) flies over the Mountain at Cadwell Park

Bagnall in the 70s Road Sports race that kicked off the HSCC season.

Julian Barter was the class of the field in his TVR 3000M and while poleman Richard Plant slithered his Morgan Plus 8 home in second, Clark-Bagnall fired his Triumph GT6 from 36th and last on the grid to third place. As first reserve, Clark-Bagnall had started from the back of the grid after a last-minute clearance to race. He had posted sixth best time in qualifying in his Triumph GT6, but went into the race as 36th and last car on the grid.

Clark-Bagnall was up to seventh with a magnificent opening lap and was soon into fourth and chasing down the Ferrari of David Tomlin. Third was as far as he was going to get, but it was a mighty performance. "I wasn't expecting that at all: I wasn't even expecting to race," said Clark-Bagnall. "I was told at the last minute that I was racing and the conditions were perfect for the car."

There was a May date for the 2012 edition of Tour Britannia as Phil Hindley and Andy Bull turned in a faultless performance when they took their Porsche 911SC to a commanding victory with two and a half minutes in hand over the rest of the field. Races at Mallory Park and Silverstone, managed by the HSCC, and 18 asphalt special stages made the ninth running of the tour a busy and rewarding event for the crews. "It's a fantastic event," said Hindley. "It's a lot of things rolled into one and it's a real test to build a car to win this event."

THE 2013 HSCC RACING CHAMPIONS

Guards Trophy
Chris Scragg (Jaguar E-type)
Martini Trophy with Supersports
James Dodd (Chevron B23) and
Andrew Schryver (Chevron B21/23)
Classic Racing Car Championship
Ian Jones (Lotus 59)
Historic Road Sports Championship
John Shaw (Porsche 911)
70s Road Sports Championship
Oliver Ford (Lotus Europa)
Historic Formula 2
Robert Simac (March 712M)
Derek Bell Trophy
Neil Glover (Lola T330/332)
Historic FF1600 Championship
Sam Mitchell (Merlyn Mk20)
Historic Formula Junior Championship
Mark Woodhouse (Elva 100)
Classic Formula 3 Championship
Graham Fennymore (Ralt RT3)
Historic Formula 3 Championship
Dean Forward (Tecno)
Super Touring Trophy
Stewart Whyte (Honda Accord)
Historic FF2000 Championship
Nelson Rowe (Reynard SF79)
Historic Touring Car Championship
Tim Davies (Ford Lotus Cortina)
E-type Challenge
John Pearson, Graham Bull and
John Truslove

The Formula 5000 Lola T142 of Adam Simmonds at the Gold Cup

Dean Forward, here at Croft, won the 2013 Historic F3 title

Jeremy Smith gave the March 2-4-0 a first win at Silverstone

Daryl Taylor (Chevron B8) heads a Guards Trophy pack at Silverstone, May 2013

Graham Fennymore in the ex-Brundle Ralt RT3

Touring Car variety at Snetterton, June 2013

Rachel Watts (Lotus Elan) and John Shaw (Porsche 911) in Historic Road Sports at Snetterton

The Super Touring pack at Brands Hatch in July

Martin O'Connell (left) and Nick Fleming top the Martini Trophy grid at Brands Hatch in July

The Guards Trophy field pours out of Druids at Brands Hatch

Hindley cemented his advantage in the two races, winning by half a minute at Mallory Park on Friday and by a minute on the Silverstone International circuit on Saturday. The second day also took on special stages at Arncott, Stoneleigh and Packington Hall. Once again, Porsches were the car to have on Britain's classic race and rally tour and Hindley was in control on Friday after 11 special stages at Mallory Park, Arbury Hall and the Porsche track at Silverstone as well as the race at Mallory Park.

At the Silverstone International Trophy in May history was made in the opening Derek Bell Trophy race when Jeremy Smith took the six-wheeled March 2-4-0 to its first ever race win. Mark Dwyer's F2 March led the chase of the increasingly effective DFV-powered car. However, in race two, Michael Lyons borrowed his dad's Lola T400 and stormed ahead after his intended McLaren M26 cracked a cylinder liner in qualifying. "That's the culmination of two years of my father's life: it has taken a long time to get here," said Smith after victory in race one. "It was the first clear run for the car and a first win. We're over the moon."

The Chevron B8s of Nick Fleming and Neil Burroughs scraped wheel-arches at the first corner of the seventh HSCC Autosport Three-Hour race at Snetterton in early June, and were separated by just 13.568s at the chequered flag when an overjoyed Fleming claimed his third successive victory after the most exciting battle in the race's recent history. Burroughs tackled the annual enduro with relish in Loaded Gunn Racing's car, setting off as if in a sprint. "Neil was a bit robust at Riches, but I had to pull out all the stops to beat him," said Fleming. "It was a fantastic race, but our experience won the day."

By the time the season closed at Silverstone in October, the Club's 15 championships and series were resolved after some tremendous on-track battling and off-track sporting rivalry. Kent-based hotelier Chris Scragg had a fine season to win the Guards Trophy in his Jaguar E-type, while Road Sports titles went to the consistent John Shaw (Porsche 911) and Oliver Ford who really got his Lotus Europa working well in the 70s division.

After some epic battles in the Historic FF1600 Championship, Sam Mitchell (Merlyn Mk20) emulated his father Westie's 2009 title success. Nelson Rowe retained his Historic FF2000 title and Dean Forward

(Tecno) took a second Historic Formula 3 crown, while Frenchman Robert Simac started an impressive run of Historic Formula 2 titles in his ex-Jean-Pierre Jaussaud March 712M. Neil Glover (Lola T330/332) secured the Derek Bell Trophy for the third time in five seasons while Stewart Whyte (Honda Accord) was the inaugural winner of the Super Touring Trophy. A famous car won the Classic F3 title as former Caterham racer Graham Fennymore raced the ex-Martin Brundle Ralt RT3.

Unfortunately, a fine season for Club ended on a sad note with news that Bob Owen had died and Terry Harrison penned a tribute for the Club magazine. "Bob Owen died at the beginning of November 2013 at the age of 82. In the early years of the HSCC Bob was a very important person in the formation of the Club. He was the Competition Secretary for a number of years and at the time the HSCC had to negotiate with other race organising clubs to get a race for our type of cars included in their race programme.

"In 1973 Bob agreed to be the Chairman for one year as well as being Competition Secretary. During this year new rules for eligibilty were brought in clearly defining what was or was not permissable. At the end of 1973 he reported that the Club was financially healthy and that membership had risen to over 260.

"Bob's competition career started in 1963 with a Lotus Seven, but before the end of the year he had acquired his first Aston Martin DB3S. This was the first production DB3S and was originally owned by Ken

49 Historic FF1600s leave the Silverstone Classic grid

Greg Thornton leads Michael Lyons, Neil Glover and Mark Dwyer in a stunning Derek Bell Trophy race at Oulton Park

Chris Scragg (left) receives the Jaguar Trophy from Gordon Spice

*2013 marshals of the year
Peter Talling (left) and
Ian Chalmers (right) with
Richard Attwood*

*The Club display at Race
Retro, February 2014*

Wharton. After a few races and an engine rebuild this car was sold to Brian Joscelyne at the end of 1964. It was replaced by another Aston Martin, the ex-works car DB3S/10, which was badly damaged by another driver in a big accident at Silverstone. There followed a lengthy rebuild and Bob had a few races in it in 1966.

"Bob then moved onto Maseratis, the first being a 2-litre T61 'Birdcage' which was followed by a 3-litre car. In 1971 he entered both cars in the prestigious JCB Championship and raced the 2-litre car while Brian Joscelyne raced the 3-litre. At the end of the year he was equal first in the championship sharing the honours with Bill Wilks in a Lotus 16: Brian Joscelyne won his class as well. The 2-litre was again raced in 1972 but by 1973 he had acquired the 5-litre rear-engined Maserati 151/65.

"This car was originally raced at Le Mans by Jo Siffert and Jochen Neerspach but without success. A lot of work was required to make this car useable after which is was raced mainly at Oulton Park by Bob and on occasion by Craig Dent. Bob's last race was a one off drive at Oulton Park in Hugh Clifford's Tojeiro Climax.

"A couple of years ago Grahame White invited Bob to be a guest at the HSCC Gold Cup Meeting at Oulton Park. He enjoyed the occasion and gave out some of the awards. He spent a couple of days taking in all the changes and was happy with the direction in which the Club was going."

Notable changes as the 2014 calendar was unveiled were championship status for the Super Touring Trophy and a new format for the Autosport three-hour following a new arrangement with the GT and Sports Car Cup.

With four dates at major UK historic racing festivals, the Super Touring Trophy would also appear on the BTCC support programme at Oulton Park in June. Stewart Whyte, winner of the 2013 Super Touring Trophy said the news was excellent for everyone with a passion for the cars. "It's a good time to be involved in Super Touring and the championship is getting more and more recognition," said Whyte. "I think 2014 will be the year for it to really take off and it will be great to be on the BTCC programme at Oulton Park."

Grahame White was equally pleased with the developments. "We are delighted to be running a full championship for the Super Touring cars in 2014 and we've arranged an exceptional calendar," said White. "The signs are that the championship is going to be very popular indeed, both with the competitors and the fans."

Having been firstly a Guards Trophy race and more recently a championship round, for the 2014 Autosport 3-Hour Race the HSCC teamed up with the GT & Sports Car Cup for the race to be for Pre '66 GT and Pre '61 sports-racing cars. All cars would run on Dunlop L-section tyres, with AC Cobras, Jaguar E-types and TVR Griffiths all running to a minimum weight of 1000 kgs.

Qualifying for the race would be on the Friday evening with the 3-hour race taking place on the Saturday morning, finishing in time for lunch. There was a mandatory two-driver entry with an option for a third driver, with no driver being able to do more than 70 minutes in a continous period. As part of the package an exclusive Friday test session was included in with the entry fee.

Competitors with a sports-racing car were not being forgotten. With qualifying on Friday, the sports-racing cars would have a 40-minute pit stop race with an optional driver change and a choice of L or M-section Dunlop tyres. This was the second of the races where the bigger-engined sports-racing cars were invited as part of the McLaren Trophy.

There was a big boost for Classic Formula 3 when it was announced as one of the grids for the 2014 Silverstone Classic, a move designed to mark the category's 50th anniversary season. The HSCC's Classic Formula 3 category was one of the new races at the world's biggest classic and historic racing festival (25-27 July) with a pair of races for the 1600cc and 2-litre F3 cars of the 1971-1984 era. The event also marked 50 years since the creation of the modern Formula 3 category for the 1964 season.

Event director Nick Wigley said that the Classic F3 race was an important addition to the weekend's stellar race line-up. "This leads on from the fantastic Formula Ford race we had last year: we like to celebrate the feeder series for Formula 1," said Wigley. "It's a fantastic era to celebrate and we're hoping to get a grid of 50 cars, which would be amazing," said Wigley. "We've got many of the cars driven by drivers who went on to F1 fame like Nelson Piquet, Derek Warwick and Nigel Mansell."

Another golden anniversary would be celebrated a week later at Croft. Exactly 50 years after the first race meeting at the North Yorkshire track, the Croft Nostalgia Weekend would celebrate the circuit's half century with a full programme of HSCC racing.

Croft Autodrome hosted its first race meeting on August 3 1964 with the *Daily Mirror* Trophy Meeting for touring cars, GTs, sportscars, single-seaters and motorbikes. On August 2/3 2014, the fifth Nostalgia Weekend would bring a busy weekend of racing from the HSCC, featuring Historic Touring Cars, Historic Formula Ford, Historic Formula 3, Historic Road Sports, 70s Road Sports, Guards Trophy, Formula Junior, Historic FF2000 and Classic Clubmans. Live music, fashion displays, World War Two encampments and air shows would all feature in the weekend, which had become a very popular date for many racing members.

The 2014 racing season got underway at Donington Park in early April and prolific single-seater racer Benn Simms scored a unique double at his home track, winning both Historic FF1600 and Historic FF2000 races in his Jomo and a Reynard SF79 borrowed from Stuart Boyer. Two weeks later at Thruxton, category veterans John Cleland and Patrick Watts shared the Super Touring wins and Neil Fowler (in the March 782 of Peter Williams) won the Jochen Rindt Trophy as the leading Formula 2 runner in the Derek Bell Trophy. However, Sunday's rain delivered a giant-killing win for Mark Charteris in his Classic Clubmans Mallock.

Benn Simms heads the Historic FF field at Donington Park

Ian Bankhurst (Alexis HF802) leads the Historic F3 pack at the Donington Historic Festival, May 2014

BRIAN COCKS

Former Chairman and Chief Executive

By 1976 the HSCC had come some way from its mid-sixties roots of D-types and Listers and was providing a home for more modern cars: Lotus 23s, Elva Mk 7s and so on in sports-racers and Porsches 356, Speedsters, XK Jaguars, Lancia B20s and so on in the field of production racing cars.

However for its racing the club was still a customer of the AMOC, Jaguar Drivers' Club and other race organisers in providing separate races for its members, whilst Lloyds and Scottish was by now actively running races for the 50s sports cars along with 50s single-seaters whose remit was the VSCC. Plainly there was a need to provide a club which was a race organiser.

The 1978 HSCC AGM was a fairly fraught affair. The previous Chairman had died and most of the committee were desperately overworked and a major change was needed. In the end there were four candidates for Chairman, Brian Cocks, Bert Young, John Harper and Brewster Righter. There was a run-off to decide the final two and after that vote Brian Cocks was elected by 30 votes to 23.

He was duly elected Chairman of the HSCC and the next 13 years until he left at the end of 1989 were arguably the most important formative period of the club. His 'Recent History' Chairman's newsletter in April 1978 showed that his organisational talent was well up to the job.

Brian had recently firstly acquired a Lotus 23B and had ceased his involvement with the 750 MC where he had been an organiser, Clerk of Course and promoter of the 6-Hour Relay race and was living with wife Kay in Minsterworth in Gloucestershire, running his Briokay sportswear clothing business.

Brian was a Londoner who had eventually ended up in Scotland as regional manager for Parker pens. He held an international race and an international rally licence and in those days any individual holding these two licences was entitled to a permanent race number which they could, and did, require race organises to accept. Brian's permanent race number was 61 and that number reflected his great success in selling the Parker 61 fountain pen. Whilst in Scotland he had become very involved with the 750 MC and that experience was to become very important when he became HSCC Chairman.

Brian as Chairman had two or three principal objectives. Firstly to turn the HSCC into a race organising club, secondly to extend the range of cars which the

Racing the Crossle at Brands

HSCC catered for and thirdly to turn the club into a professional organisation.

He achieved those objectives comprehensively with major input from John Foulston of Atlantic Computers. John appeared on the scene in 1978/9 and Brian was very quick to encourage John in his motor sport ambitions; he had been running with the AMOC in their Porsche/Ferrari/Aston races in his 512 BB road car.

With Brian's encouragement John quickly acquired a range of cars and became the club treasurer. John's money, or access to it through Atlantic Computers Ltd, and Brian's ambition were a marriage made in heaven and during the next five or six years the club moved to become a major player in UK historic motor sport.

The first major meeting was at Donington Park in partnership with Classic Cars magazine who had their first historic race day. In those days a circuit could be rented bare and the HSCC committee provided most of the staff. I was on the gate at Coppice Corner and I shall never forget the piles of cash in the press room at the end of the day with Pat and David Dawson counting it.

By 1986, when JGF bought Brands Hatch, the HSCC was the major player in organising historic racing in the UK. Atlantic Computers sponsorship had brought meetings all over Great Britain, FIA Historic Championship rounds, several UK championships and even one year a hillclimb at Wiscombe Park. By now the club had purchased a building in Wiltshire where Brian ran the office, ably assisted by his new wife Tina when she was not travelling for her work.

However, John Foulston's death at Silverstone in 1987 slowed things a little. Jem Marsh had in the meantime become HSCC Chairman as the joint role, Chairman and CEO of the HSCC, had become very difficult to maintain for Brian. His final two years at the helm pushed the club onward but when his contract came up for renewal for 1990 Brian and the club were unable to find common ground and a parting of the ways came about.

Brian had his own style which was not always to everyone's taste, his oft-quoted assertion was that too much democracy was anarchy, but come the hour come the man is the old saying. Brian Cocks was the man of the hour for the HSCC.

Jeremy Hall wrote this appreciation of Brian Cocks following Cocks' death in 2014

In his Lotus 30

Lawrence Denne heads an
FF2000 pack

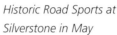
Historic Road Sports at
Silverstone in May

Al Fleming: a racer and a
gentleman

A week after the Thruxton meeting came tragedy
when Al Fleming lost his life at the wheel of his Lotus
Elan during qualifying at Hockenheim. Over previous
seasons Al, his wife Val and racing son Nick has
become popular members of the HSCC fraternity in a
pair of Elans, a Chevron B8 and more recently a Ralt
RT1 and Chevron B36. His death, at the age of 69,
was a terrible blow to historic racing. In a dark period
when the Club also lost Formula Ford 2000 prime-
mover John Taylor and former F3 racer Barrie Maskell,
the death of Brian Cocks was another loss to the story
of the HSCC.

In June, a big grid lined up for the new-look Autosport
three-hours at Snetterton. Driving the only Jaguar
E-type of four to last more than six laps in conditions
made treacherous by rain and oil, Chris Ward and Alex
Buncombe earned praise from 1964 winner Jack Sears
when they triumphed in the 50th Anniversary edition
of the endurance race.

"They did a fantastic job on a day which reminded
me very much of '64, with heavy rain and the sun
glinting off the waterlogged track," said 84-year-old
'Gentleman Jack,' who watched the JD Classics pair

Ian Flux in the Osella PA3 of Sean Walker in the Martini
Trophy at Donington

Robin Pearce chases Richard Plant at Silverstone

build a two-lap advantage over Jeremy and Denis Welch (Austin-Healey 3000).

At Snetterton, Denis Welch was his usual self: driving superbly and loving every minute of his sport. Tragically, he died less than two months later when his Lotus 18 Grand Prix car flipped over after a clash of wheels during the HGPCA race at the Silverstone Classic.

In early August, Tour Britannia ran in the north-west and North Wales. After one of the closest lead battles in the event's 10-year history, Phil Hindley and Andy Bull claimed a hard-earned victory to maintain their unbeaten record on Britain's only classic race and rally tour.

The 10th edition of Britain's only classic race and rally tour featured scrutineering and documentation at Tarporley, Cheshire on Wednesday morning before the competition opened in the afternoon with two special stages and then a race at nearby Oulton Park. Once again, the HSCC was responsible for the organisation and management of the races. Thursday and Friday took in two full days of competition across North Wales and included two visits to the spectacular Anglesey for races on both the international and

coastal tracks. Other headline venues included the sensational toll road around the Great Orme near Llandudno as well as stately homes, an airfield and several stretches of private road.

The result completed a hat-trick of Tour Britannia wins for Hindley's Porsche 911 SCR, but it took a mighty attack on the final day before Hindley could

GT cars in the Snetterton three-hours in 2014

James Dodd leads the Super Touring field at Oulton Park, June 2014

THE 2014 HSCC RACING CHAMPIONS

Guards Trophy
Mike Whitaker (TVR Griffith)
Martini Trophy with Supersports
Jonathan Loader (Chevron B19)
Classic Racing Car Championship
Jonathan Baines (Merlyn Mk20)
Historic Road Sports Championship
John Shaw (Porsche 911)
70s Road Sports Championship
Peter Shaw (TVR Tuscan)
Historic Formula 2
Robert Simac (March 712M)
Derek Bell Trophy
Jon Finch (Chevron B34)
Historic FF1600 Championship
Benn Simms (Jomo JMR7 and Alexis Mk14)
Historic Formula Junior Championship
Jon Milicevic (Cooper T59)
Classic Formula 3 Championship
David Shaw (Ralt RT1 and March 803B)
Historic Formula 3 Championship
Jim Blockley (Brabham BT21)
Classic Clubmans Championship
Mark Charteris (Mallock Mk20/21) and Adam Paterson (Mallock Mk18)
Super Touring Trophy
James Dodd (Honda Accord)
Historic FF2000 Championship
Benn Simms (Reynard SF77 and Royale RP30)
Historic Touring Car Championship
Tim Davies (Ford Lotus Cortina)

The field assembles before the start of the Autosport three-hours

Julian Barter and Peter Shaw head the 70s Road Sports field at Croft

Post-race celebrations for Denis and Jeremy Welch

DENIS WELCH

Club supporter and champion

The tragic death of Denis Welch at Silverstone in July 2014 robbed the historic racing community of one of its most popular characters and the HSCC of one of its most loyal advocates.

The Staffordshire racer was renowned for his skill at the wheel of Austin Healeys but in 2014 he was realising a lifetime ambition by racing a 1960s Formula 1 car: the Lotus 18 owned by Malcolm Ricketts. Tragically, he was killed while racing this car at the Silverstone Classic.

After some hillclimbing from as early as 1959, Denis started racing in the early 1960s in a Mini and then enjoyed great success with a 1650cc Lotus twin-cam engined Ford Anglia in Special Saloons. He later dabbled with single-seaters before the arrival of sons Jeremy and Tim curtailed his racing for a few years.

From his own website, Denis recalled those early days. "I met Tina in 1963 while she was rallying her Mini and I was mad enough in those days not only to be a navigator but also to be driven by a female. Together we both realised that my heart was in the motor industry or more so motorsport and we got married in 1969. For many years I worked at various garages gaining as much experience as possible and whilst working for Reginald Tildesley of Walsall as the Rallye Sport Manager I met two people who remained long time friends: Mike Freeman and Phil Marks."

A long-time love affair with Austin Healeys led him to building an old road car into a racer in the early 1980s and prompted the start of a business specialising in Healey parts. His exuberant driving style thrilled spectators as he slid the Healey to countless wins.

He explained his return to racing. "In 1977 Tina and I brought our own garage business in the small village of Yoxall in the Staffordshire countryside. For a few years this remained just a straightforward routine garage, but like any drug the craving never leaves and it was not long before my feet were getting itchy to get back into some

form of racing. Ever since I was a lad I had always had a love affair with the Big Healey and by this time I had bought a standard road going 3000.

"In 1982 we returned to the circuits at Snetterton, racing with our now legendary '6200 NO' affectionately known as the 'The Bulldog'. We soon found that it was almost impossible to buy race parts for the big Healeys as the BMC competition department no longer existed. So we started to manufacture high quality competition parts for the full range of big Healeys and after 30 years we had become the largest manufacturer of competition parts for these models throughout the world."

Into the new millennium he branched out into other forms of racing and won many races with a Lotus 23B and then his beloved Formula Junior Merlyn Mk5/7 'Mr Poo', which he took to three victories at Monaco. In 2014 he arranged to borrow the Lotus 18 Grand Prix car for a season with the HGPCA.

"We competed in so many races that I lost count and raced 'The Bulldog' all over Europe and as far afield as Bathurst in Australia where I won both races. Also a very thrilling race was the street circuit in Macau where I came third in my Lotus 23B 'Miss Betty'."

In 2007 he sold Denis Welch Motorsport Limited to his eldest son Jeremy. Tina and Denis retired to a small farm in the Staffordshire Moorlands with some fabulous outbuildings which they converted into storage facilities and a workshop for his own race cars. Denis was hugely popular across the sport and his enthusiasm for racing was boundless. Out-going and with a fine sense of humour, he was deeply missed.

In the Merlyn Formula Junior at Cadwell Park

Michael Lyons and Andrew Smith head the Derek Bell Trophy grid at Brands Hatch

Steve Perez slides in the Oulton Park rain during Tour Britannia

get ahead of the Ford Escort Mk2 of Steve Perez and Paul Spooner.

Both the Oulton Park Gold Cup and the Silverstone Finals meeting were beset by rain, but good racing abounded. In Cheshire, Richard Evans and Michael Lyons thrilled the fans to share Derek Bell Trophy victories, while the ex-Chris Craft Crowne Racing Lola T292 emerged from a rebuild to take a Martini Trophy win with Tony Sinclair at the wheel. Michael Mallock took Historic Formula Ford victory in his father Ray's Mallock Mk9, the car's first win since 1969 while Ben Tusting topped the Historic FF2000 contest. Mark Woodhouse (Elva 100) and Jon Milicevic (Cooper T59) shared the Formula Junior spoils.

Milicevic went to the Silverstone Finals Meeting and settled the Formula Junior title with second place to his good friend Sam Wilson, while an epic Historic Formula Ford race fell to former champion Neil Fowler after a glorious contest with Callum Grant. Warren Briggs (Ford Mustang) topped the Historic Touring Cars, but second place was enough for Welshman Tim Davies to retain the overall title with his Lotus Cortina.

Other wins at Silverstone, as conditions steadily improved, went to Charles Barter (Datsun 240Z) in 70s Road Sports and Will Schryver (Chevron B6) in the Guards Trophy. David Shaw (March 803B) took a clear Classic F3 win to settle the title, having damaged his ex-Piquet Ralt RT1 at Monaco in May.

Andy Wallace was guest of honour as 279 members and their guests celebrated the season at the

Whittlebury Hall in late November. Other champions for the year included Jonathan Loader (Martini Trophy), TVR enthusiast Mike Whitaker (Guards Trophy), James Dodd (Super Touring Trophy), Peter Shaw (70s Road Sports) and Benn Simms who used a total of four cars on his way to taking an FF1600 and FF2000 double.

Heading into 2015, there were three significant changes within the Club's portfolio of championships. The E-type Challenge concluded a three-year run at the close of 2013, but new for 2015 was a race series for all models of pre '66 Jaguars. The Jaguar Heritage Challenge would be open to the XK series, C and D-types, MK I and MK II saloons and pre-1966 E-types.

"Jaguar has established a strong presence in celebrations including the Mille Miglia and Goodwood Revival in recent times. A single-marque race series will be an exciting addition to our plans for next year," said Derek Weale of Jaguar Land Rover. The dates for the series were Donington Historic Festival (2-4 May), Silverstone International Trophy (16/17 May), Brands Hatch Super Prix (11/12 July), Oulton Park Gold Cup (29-31) August and the Nurburgring Oldtimer in mid-August. The race format was 40 minutes, with a mandatory pit stop and optional driver change.

Meanwhile, the Martini Trophy races were opened up to later and different types of cars and included pre-1980 Sports Racing GT and Touring Cars of a type that would have competed in the World Endurance Championship and or in an international competition in period. The series was re-branded as Pre '80 Endurance.

The joint Historic Road Sports/FISCAR field at Brands in July 2014

Sports 2000 would continue to be invited to compete and race distances were set at between 45 and 60 minutes with mandatory pit stops and optional driver changes. Five race dates were planned with four UK and one on the Continent. The organisation team for these races included Vanessa and Flavien Marçais from Automobiles Historiques who already organised the very successful GTSCC series.

At selected race meetings in 2015 the Classic Formula 3 Championship was to incorporate rounds for Universal Racing Services Classic Formula Ford 2000 Series. Combining the two series on the track, whilst they race for their individual trophies, opened up the number of venues the FF2000 series could race on and also made

The Historic Formula Ford drivers scale a tank at the Croft Nostalgia meeting

Jon Milicevic splashes through the rain at Croft, August 2014

Ray Mallock and John Harrison in Classic Clubmans at Brands Hatch, September 2014

Darwin Smith in the Historic F2 race at Zandvoort

Jonathan Baines, 2014 Classic Racing Car champion

for a more economical use of track time. The Universal Racing Services series made a natural pairing with CF3 as there was already provision for this type of car within the existing Classic Formula 3 regulations.

After 10 years of service as the Historic Road Sports Chairman, Mike Eagles decided in October it was time to hand over the leadership of the championship to someone else. In the 10 years of Mike's leadership HRS had grown to become one of the staple formulae of the Club. Mike himself a champion in 1998 and a class

winner in 2010, had striven to bring a little variety to the grid. Firstly with a Milano GT and latterly with the De Tomaso Mangusta; both cars requiring a lot of development and bravery to master.

Mike's knowledge of motor sport insurance had been invaluable to the Club over the years, and he remained a great supporter of the Club and the HRS especially as he assumed the role of Class A representative, taking over from Roddie Fielden. With Mike stepping down an election was held with current competitors having a vote. Two candidates stepped forward, Paul Tooms and Kevin Kivlochan. Kevin was voted in as Chairman and Paul retained his position as the Class C representative. Kevin was a driver returning to his racing roots having been a class winner in HRS in 1995 and 1998 he won his class again in 2014.

Shortly before the start of the 2015 racing season came news that Jeremy 'Jem' Marsh, co-founder of Marcos cars and former chairman of the HSCC, had died at the age of 84. He was an engineer, constructor and racer and left a legacy of hundreds of period sports cars.

The Marcos story started in 1959 with Marsh and Frank Costin and the first wooden-chassis car, which was soon being raced by Marsh and a young Jackie Stewart.In 1964 Marsh introduced the GT, which was to become the iconic Marcos design. The model had been winning races for half a century and continued to enjoy success in Guards Trophy races, usually with Volvo power.

A year later the Mini Marcos was unveiled and raced at Le Mans in 1966. Later, financial problems dogged the company, but in the 1990s Marcos was resurgent in GT racing and returned to Le Mans with the LM600. Marsh served as HSCC Chairman from 1986 to 1988 after a period as Vice-Chairman to Brian Cocks and David Duffy. He was a Club champion in both the Pre '60 and Classic Sports Car Championships.

In January, the Club celebrated Brabham racing cars with a special display at *Autosport* International. Eleven cars built by the late Sir Jack Brabham formed the display, and former Brabham drivers were on hand as the life and work of the Australian legend was honoured.

Through the 1960s, the company that Brabham led in partnership with designer Ron Tauranac built over 500 racing cars for most single-seater classes of the day as well as several sports-racing cars. Although a works Cooper driver when the company started in 1961, Brabham raced his own Grand Prix cars from mid-1962 onwards. Race car production took off in style, starting with the Formula Junior BT2 and covering cars for Formula 1, 2, 3, Formula Ford and Junior. Right through to 1970, when Brabham retired to Australia, the cars were renowned for strength, build quality, competitiveness and ease of operation. A remarkably high proportion of those 500 cars remained active in historic racing more than 40 years later.

The HSCC was also very prominent at Race Retro, the International Historic Motor Sport Show at the end of February. The Club had the biggest stand in the central Speed Street with more cars than ever as members old, new and prospective dropped by for a catch up.

Of particular note was the Sports 2000 Royale that was on hand to promote the Club's new involvement in the category, centred on a new race at the Croft Nostalgia Festival in August. Club vice-chairman Chris Alford raced in the category from the very first race in 1977 and continued to be a big fan of the class. He arranged for former Sports 2000 racers John Brindley and John Webb to come to the stand for a photograph. One of the real star cars on the Club stand was the stunning Lola T332 of racer and preparer Steve Farthing, who planned to make his Formula 5000 debut more than 30 years after he was a young gun in Formula Ford 2000.

The 1-litre Historic F3 Racing Association had its own stand and was showing one of the few Titan Mk3 1000cc Formula 3 cars. The car had recently come out of storage after 30 years and could race again once restored. Encouraged by the explosion of interest in 1-litre F3 as an historic class, current owner Bob Wilson got his Mk3 out of storage in Liverpool for the first time since the 1980s with a view to getting it restored.

At the Club's Annual General Meeting in March, a new Chairman was confirmed when Frank Lyons took over from Chris Sharples, while Chris Alford would continue in the role of Vice-Chairman. Lyons was well-known in historic racing circles as a racer and has been particularly involved in the promotion of racing for Formula 5000 cars. His racing stable also covers sports-racing cars, Historic Formula 1 cars and Historic Formula 3 cars. He had been regularly joined on track by his wife Judy and son Michael.

Lyons took over the position after Sharples stood down following nearly a decade in office. Under his chairmanship, the Club had grown and prospered with an ever-increasing portfolio of race championships and series as well as an expanding role in organising the racing element of high-profile race meetings including the Silverstone Classic, the Donington Historic Festival and the Walter Hayes Trophy.

Lyons said: "I consider it a great honour to become Chairman of the Club I joined in the early 1990s as

The Brabham BT49 F1 car of Joaquin Folch on the stand at the NEC

a novice in Historic Formula Ford. I've watched the HSCC grow and I've been involved in the Derek Bell Trophy and as a member of the Club's board. Chris has done a very good job as Chairman. I hope to be a good custodian and take the Club into its 50th anniversary season next year. We are a Club for the members and I'm looking forward to working with the rest of the team."

The Club's 2015 racing season started over Easter at Thruxton, Great Britain's fastest circuit with the rare spectacle of a boldly-driven three-litre Formula 1 car at full stretch.

Formula 1 cars raced in F5000's ShellSport International and Aurora AFX successors in period, but none lapped as quickly as Michael Lyons' stirring 1m07.648s (125.37mph average) in his Hesketh 308E during Saturday's race. Pursuers Richard Evans (March 79B) and Mark Charteris (Mallock Mk20/21) drove brilliantly too, beating the Lola T300 of 1974 Thruxton F5000 winner Ian Ashley both days. Hot on the heels of his last-corner 1000cc F3 victory at Goodwood, American James King (March 712) was honoured to receive the Jochen Rindt Trophy as best F2 finisher, the great Austrian having dominated Thruxton's first three Easter Monday Internationals from 1968 to 1970.

Single-seaters on display with the Club at Race Retro

Tony Robinson and Phil Clarke won Tour Ireland after a nail-biting final day for the Irish edition of Tour Britannia in mid-May. After three days of competition over some of the most spectacular and scenic terrain in Ireland and North Wales, Porsche 911s took a clean sweep of the overall podium as just 10 seconds covered Robinson/Clarke, John Spiers/Susanne Niedrum and Stephen Radcliffe/Peter Gunson.

"It's been superb," said Robinson. "I've always enjoyed Tour Britannia and this year the Irish stages made it doubly good fun." Event newcomers Tony and Aston Blake took their Porsche 911 to fourth while Mike Smith and Peter Thomas were first non-Porsche home with their Ford Escort Mk2 in fifth. In the concurrent regularity rally, the Austin Allegro of rallying veterans Doug Dawe and Ernie Waldron took a dominant victory, leading from the start to finish half a minute ahead of the Porsche of Harry and Lorraine Sherrard.

From the sunshine and scenery of the Great Orme at Llandudno to the closed public roads in the Wicklow Mountains south of Dublin, day one was full of variety and challenge as Robinson and Clarke set the early pace to take a narrow lead in the competition event. The day started on the spectacular road around the Great Orme with two special stages before the crews headed to Holyhead for the ferry to Ireland. After a short trip out of Dublin, four closed-road special stages awaited near the famous Sally Gap.

Day two was all about racing with two races at Mondello Park followed by a race Anglesey and a ferry crossing in between. It proved to be another good day for Robinson and Clarke as they increased their overnight lead to 27 seconds. Day three was based in North Wales with another race at Anglesey and then five asphalt special stages including the incredible hillclimb at Nant Gwrtheyrn. Radcliffe later set the pace on the fast runways at Llanbedr airfield, but Robinson kept his nerve to score a narrow but deserved victory as the survivors arrived back in Llandudno late on Friday afternoon.

At Snetterton in early June, Martin O'Connell mastered very wet conditions in Sandy Watson's Jaguar E-type to score a solo victory in the Autosport Three-Hours, while the Formula Ford fraternity was rocked by the death of Rob Fowler overnight. The racers paid suitable tribute to the popular preparer in Sunday's race and delivered a spectacle of which he would have approved. Across the pair of races, the cumulative winning margin for Rob Wainwright over Callum Grant was one-hundredth of a second.

In early July, the 26th running of the Club's annual Historic Super Prix on the Brands Hatch Grand Prix circuit was a huge success, with big grids, exciting racing and a fabulous atmosphere. The weekend had a strong single-seater flavour with cars from F1, F2, F3, Formula 5000, Formula Atlantic, Formula Junior, FF2000 and FF1600 all in action. Other headline races

Michael Lyons (Hesketh 308E) at speed at Thruxton

Tony Robinson tackles the Great Orme stage on Tour Ireland

Nick and Harry Whale in the Wicklow Hills on Tour Ireland

included the Jaguar Heritage Challenge and Pre '80 Endurance Series, while the Club's regular roster of championships all added to a weekend of big grids and superb racing.

Two rounds of the HSCC Historic Formula 2 FIA International Series wowed the spectators as the unrelated Darwin Smith and Andrew Smith showed just how good historic racing can be. Although Darwin won twice in his F2 March 722 against Andrew's Formula Atlantic March 79B, they raced wheel-to-wheel across two races and put on a stunning display of flat out racing. It was close on Saturday but even closer on Sunday when just a quarter of a second split them after 20 minutes of racing. "That was a great race with Andrew," said Darwin. "I enjoyed every second of that," added Andrew.

By the end of September, eight overall champions had been confirmed for the 2015 season, with six more titles to be decided during the second half of October.

Pre '80 Endurance at
Silverstone, May 2015

Race start at Anglesey on
Tour Ireland

After a thrilling pair of races at Brands Hatch in late September, Richard Mitchell was confirmed as Historic Formula Ford 1600 champion after a remarkable debut season of racing. The Devon-based youngster started the season as a novice but was immediately on the pace with the Speedsport team. Despite a troubled weekend at Croft, he clinched the title with one round remaining.

Kevin Kivlochan secured the ONI PLC HSCC Historic Road Sports Championship with a commanding race win at Brands Hatch in his Morgan Plus 8. It had been a fine campaign for Kivlochan who returned to his racing roots this season in the car prepared by RW Racing Services. Meanwhile, the 70s Road Sports Championship had already been settled in favour of Lotus Europa racer Jim Dean following the Oulton Park race at end of August.

As expected, Mark Charteris settled the HSCC Classic Clubmans Championship after two more race wins in his Mallock Mk20/21. However, there was a late

Danny Stanzl (Elden Mk8) heads an FF1600 pack
at Cadwell Park

THE 2015 HSCC RACING CHAMPIONS

Guards Trophy	**Mike Gardiner (TVR Griffith)**
Pre '80 Endurance Series	**John Burton (Chevron B26)**
Classic Racing Car Championship	**Ian Jones (Lotus 59)**
Historic Road Sports Championship	**Kevin Kivlochan (Morgan Plus 8)**
70s Road Sports Championship	**Jim Dean (Lotus Europa)**
Historic Formula 2	**Robert Simac (March 712M)**
Derek Bell Trophy	**Richard Evans (March 79B)**
Historic FF1600 Championship	**Richard Mitchell (Merlyn Mk20)**
Historic Formula Junior Championship	**Andrew Tart (Bond)**
Classic Formula 3 Championship	**Max Bartell (Chevron B34)**
Historic Formula 3 Championship	**Leif Bosson (Brabham BT28)**
Classic Clubmans Championship	**Mark Charteris (Mallock Mk20/21)**
	and Clive Wood (Mallock Mk20B)
Super Touring Trophy	**Stewart Whyte (Honda Accord)**
Historic FF2000 Championship	**Tom Smith (Royale RP27)**
Historic Touring Car Championship	**Simon Benoy (Hillman Imp)**
Jaguar Classic Challenge	**Andy Wallace (Jaguar Mk2)**

Martin O'Connell on his way to winning at Snetterton

Sam Wilson heads the Formula Juniors at the Silverstone Classic

Andy Wallace demonstrated the Le Mans-winning Jaguar XJR9 at the Gold Cup, August 2015

Neil Smith (Alfa Romeo 156) heads a Super Touring pack at Silverstone

Neil Fowler and Ben Mitchell go wheel-to-wheel at the Silverstone Finals

Simon Armer (March 703) takes Historic F3 victory at Castle Combe, October 2015

Darren McWhirter slides his Jaguar XK120 at Oulton Park

French visitors packed out the Classic F3 field at Brands Hatch

change in Class B as Clive Wood (Mallock Mk20B) nipped ahead with two wins at Brands Hatch. Simon Benoy sealed the ByBox Historic Touring Car Championship title after a mighty season in his Hillman Imp, while Ian Jones had already added another Classic Racing Car Championship crown to his impressive tally with his Lotus 59. The Super Touring Trophy winner Stewart Whyte sealed the crown during a weekend as a support race to the modern BTCC at Rockingham. It was the Scot's second title in three seasons in his Honda Accord.

A few days later, Frenchman Robert Simac secured the Historic Formula 2 FIA International Series for a third year running at the Motors Cup meeting at Dijon-Prenois in early October. Simac sealed the title in the penultimate race of the season at his home track of Dijon and then won the 1600cc class again on Sunday to make it 10 class wins from 10 rounds in his March 712M.

The remaining titles were resolved at another highly successful Finals Meeting at Silverstone in October, when more championships were won by Max Bartell (Classic F3), Mike Gardiner (Guards Trophy) and Leif Bosson (Historic F3). Earlier, Andy Wallace won the Jaguar Heritage Challenge and John Burton was the Pre '80 Endurance Series winner. The Historic FF2000 Championship went down to the wire at the Walter Hayes Trophy meeting when Tom Smith (Royale RP27) narrowly claimed the title.

The end of season awards were presented by guest of honour Howden Ganley at Whittlebury Hall in late November as 220 members and guests shared in the celebrations of the HSCC's 49th year. However, as the year concluded, plans were already being finalised to make 2016, the Club's golden anniversary season, even more special.

11 Historic Sporting Trials

Martyn and Daphne Halliday

Back in the spring of 2012, the HSCC was involved in the formation of the Historic Sporting Trials Association. Over five seasons, this branch of the sport enjoyed remarkable expansion and much of that growth was from HSCC racing members finding a cheap, fun form of motor sport for the winter months.

Club member and regular racer Martyn Halliday was a founder member of the Historic Sporting Trials Association and was the driving force in the development of the movement.

Sporting trials had been around for more than 50 years and provided great fun for competitors as

Simon Hadfield having a taste of trialling

purpose-built specials tackle demanding climbs on private land. "Historic sporting trials is something that a lot of trials people have been talking about for years but a group of us think now is the time to actually do something rather than talk," said Halliday in September 2011.

Halliday had arranged for Michael Schrvyer, Simon Hadfield and Marcus Pye to try sporting trials. Michael had just bought a Cannon and they spent a day with trials guru Ian Wright at his base in Kent. From that day came the suggestion to organise historic sporting trials.

"We aim to provide suitable trials during the winter after the racing season has finished. The emphasis is

on having a good time with friends," said Halliday at the time. "These are very early days and we are open to suggestions for taking this forward. After all, if the great Stirling Moss, Graham Hill, Colin Chapman and Grahame White competed in trials I would have thought the members of the HSCC would like to follow in their footsteps."

The inaugural Historic Sporting Trial was judged a great success after 25 entries and 22 starters gathered in Warwickshire in 2012. The event at Long Compton in Warwickshire enjoyed fine weather, a good crowd of spectators and excellent competition.

"Well, we did it," said Halliday after a year of planning for the first event. "From my point of view I thought our inaugural Historic Sporting Trial went off rather well and gives us a base to develop historic sporting trials in the future." Grahame White represented the Club and was tempted to have a go in his 1960s Canon: a restoration project was instigated with Historic F2 racer Tim Barrington.

"I was amazed at the number of spectators: it was lovely to see many old trials friends meeting up for the first time in years which helped generate a very relaxed atmosphere. The standard of period dress was superb and the weather could not have been better. For our first event we had 13 Ford 1172 engined cars entered and I have been told of more that will come out in the future," said Halliday.

The line-up for the first trial at Long Compton, May 2012

Rachel and Roger Arnold

Grahame White and Breda Keane

Success! Jim Chapman cleans a hill

In the late summer of 2013, the Club organised its first trial at Ware in Hertfordshire. The venue was owned by Frank Lyons and it was planned to hold a barbecue as well to make it a very social day with some motor sport thrown in.

By the end of 2013, there had been six well-supported historic sporting trials. Entries varied between 15 and 27. "Considering our inaugural trial was in May 2012, that was nothing short of amazing; well beyond our wildest dreams," said Halliday.

Ahead of 2014, the HSTA arranged a meeting of organisers to discuss ways of improving trials. For 2014 there would be only two classes, Historic and Post Historic. Classes A1 and B1 (cars without fiddle brakes) were discontinued as there appeared to be little support from competitors and some of the cars that had competed regularly in this class were being returned to their original specification with fiddle brakes.

The 2014 season started badly with the cancellation of the first event in January when the farmer withdrew permission to use his waterlogged land. In March, Southsea Motor Club held its Ron Faulkner Trial in a wooded valley near Petersfield. HSCC competitors included Grahame White, Frank Lyons, David Methley, Geoff Richardson and Martyn Halliday but the racers were having difficulty finding grip on the slippery chalk and did not trouble the established trialers in the results.

In April 2014 the historic sporting trial competitors took part in the Derbyshire Trial. This was a joint venture with the modern sporting trial movement which, while being an enjoyable event, did highlight the difference in approach between the two disciplines. Historic sporting trials are more relaxed

The Gordon Jackson Trial in Gloucestershire, June 2014

with competitors watching each other and lots of banter, rather than the more formal proceedings of modern trials. HSCC racers Jim Chapman and Stuart Tizzard had their first outing in Jim's IRIS trials car.

In June, 26 competitors contested the Saturday afternoon Gordon Jackson Trial at Horsley in Gloucestershire. The organising club had a few problems but it was an enjoyable event culminating in a meal in an excellent Cotswold pub. HSCC racers Neil Davis and Stuart Tizzard had their new cars out for the first time.

In August everyone who was not on holiday was at Frank Lyons' farm for the HSCC trial. By now interest among HSCC members was really starting to grow

and Chris Atkinson and Peter St Barbe came to have a look. Formula Ford racer Dick Dixon was one of the officials.

The final trial in the Cotswolds in November was the first really wet event. Despite the weather everyone enjoyed themselves in a record-breaking entry of 40 drivers. From the HSCC was Formula 5000 racer Chris Atkinson entered in his ex-Michael Schryver Cannon and he asked Formula Junior racer Westie Mitchell to join him. Lotus Cortina racer Peter Hore had his first outing in his Concorde.

The progress continued through 2015 and included the HSCC Historic Sporting Trial at Plashes Farm, which took place on one of the hottest days of the year in late August. With the temperature over 30 degrees and high humidity everyone was very glad they did not have to don racing suites and helmets for the day's sport at Frank Lyons' Farm.

Among the 34 starters were a number of first-timers including Colin Cheffey and racer Grant Tromans while Formula Ford racers Andrew Mansell and Dick Dixon were having their first serious drives in borrowed cars. Westie and Ben Mitchell came out in Ian Wright's first car while Michael Lyons and motocrosser Tom Pearmain shared one of Frank Lyon's Cannons.

The new Sywell Historic Sporting Trial on Sunday 31 January, 2016 proved to be a real test of man and machine and was the wettest historic trial to date. Taking place in an old stone pit a few hundred yards from Sywell Aerodrome, 44 hardy souls gathered

Frank Lyons and Trevor Wood

Chris and Carol Fox in the TMS

The line-up for the fifth anniversary trial at Long Compton, May 2016

in the rain to do battle on a new site which offered scope for further really good events. The landowner, Historic F2 racer Mike Bletsoe-Brown, had cleared the pit of undergrowth to allow access to steep climbs and drops in a relatively compact area. Six sections had been laid out on the dry and windy Saturday but half an inch of rain fell overnight turning the gullies and troughs into places totally devoid of grip.

Chris Atkinson and Westie Mitchell at Sywell, January 2016

Scrutineering and signing-on were completed in the rain and then the fun and games really started. Some sections started on level grass but this rapidly deteriorated in to a grip-less morass leaving many struggling to reach even the 10 marker. Engines started to misfire under the constant strain of being revved to the limits and soon the retirements started to mount.

Although the rain stopped in time for the second lap the damage had been done. The experienced trials men came to the fore, showing how to drive under the conditions by using a combination of high revs and momentum to maintain progress. Conditions were so bad it was decided that two laps were enough and the trial was halted at what should have been the lunch break.

Ground conditions were a whole lot better for the HSTA 5th Anniversary Trial back at Long Compton in May 2016. An incredible entry of 57 gathered at this scenic location on a sunny spring day to show just how far the movement had progressed in five years.

In addition to all the regulars a few new names appeared, all driving historic Cannons. Dean Tromans and John Beale were sharing theirs

Father and son Tim and Leo Kary in the Imhof

while Grant Tromans had restoration guru Paul Lanzante sharing another. Nigel Bennett from the Isle of Wight christened his newly-built car and a contingent from the Stroud club comprised Ian Moss, Ryan Eamer and Nigel Moss in post-historic Cannons and father and son Eric and Dave Wall in their historic Canhi. Making guest appearances were BTRDA Sporting Trials champion, Ian Veale sharing the ex-Rex Chappell Cannon with Monty Peters while historic racer and motoring scribe Mark Hales was having his second outing sharing the Post Historic Cannon of Geoff Richardson. Sadly, Monty Peters, a great advocate and supporter of the HSTA, died shortly after the trial.

Ian Wright produced a dominant performance in the Historic Class whilst it was a close run contest between Steve Courts and Mark Howse in the Post Historic class and at the end they were separated by one point in Mark's favour.

It's been amazing," said Halliday, reflecting on the growth of the HSTA during the autumn of 2016. "It wouldn't have happened without the support of the HSCC and the racers and the main new converts are practically all racers. The support is unbelievable and it has grown faster than anyone expected.

Peter Hore at Long Compton in 2016

"We aim to run six events from the autumn to the spring and avoid all the historic race dates. The priority is to have fun and we have lots of double-drive cars. We run to period regulations and the car values are not depreciating. Running costs are negligible: petrol to and from events and a £45 entry fee. One set of tyres will last a season and it is a day's motor sport for not much more than £100."

2016
The golden
anniversary year

The 1966 Castle Combe-winning Jaguar D-type

The 2016 season was all about celebrating the Club's golden anniversary and the focal point of the season was to be a two-day race meeting at Castle Combe on 16/17 April.

The main celebration for the April weekend, which marked the start of the Club's 2016 racing season, was to be a re-creation of the first grid. Wherever possible, the original cars from the 1966 race were being tracked down and for those that were not available a car of the same make and model would feature.

Once the grid had been formed at lunchtime on both Saturday and Sunday, members of the public would be invited to take part in a grid walk and get a closer look at the cars. Later, the cars were to complete a parade lap of the track. When not on-track, the 50th anniversary cars would be on display in the paddock and several drivers from the 1966 race were expected to attend.

Half a century earlier, renowned historic racer Neil Corner had won the inaugural Griffiths Formula race in his Jaguar D-type from the Lotus Mk10 of Chris Warwick-Drake and the Aston Martin DB3S of John Le Sage. In total 25 cars entered the race but there were some non-starters and 14 cars finished the race.

"We're very pleased to be starting our 2016 season with a celebration event at Castle Combe," said Grahame White. "The response to re-creating the first grid has been very encouraging and it is wonderful to discover that some of the cars are still in the same ownership."

However, the golden anniversary year was not just about Castle Combe and the Club would also mark its 50th anniversary with celebrations on the Brands Hatch Grand Prix circuit (1-3 July) and the traditional Oulton Park Gold Cup (27-29 August).

The Brands Hatch Grand Prix circuit had been a highlight of the HSCC calendar for 26 years and was an opportunity for Club members to tackle the wonderful layout which remained relatively unchanged since it opened in 1964. The event was to expand to three days in 2016 with support from circuit owner Jonathan Palmer in celebration of the club's Golden Jubilee, which allowed for an expanded race programme. The Race of Champions title was to be brought back into use for the Derek Bell Trophy and MotorSport Vision planned a programme of on and off-track attractions to make the event a flagship historic festival.

In addition to a full range of HSCC domestic championships, the Brands Hatch event featured two races for the HSCC Historic Formula 2 FIA International Series, a round of the HSCC Pre '80 Endurance Series and the HSCC Super Touring Trophy. A very welcome guest grid would be the HGPCA with races for pre-1966 rear-engined Grand Prix cars.

The Oulton Park Gold Cup would be another feature event of the club's 50th anniversary season, with its traditional August Bank Holiday date at the charismatic Cheshire track. The 2016 programme was to include a full range of domestic championships as well as feature races for the HSCC Super Touring Trophy and the Jaguar Classic Challenge along with a return for the HGPCA with races for pre-1966 rear-engined Grand Prix cars.

The Club launched its 2016 season in style at *Autosport* International at the NEC in January with a stand representing the history of the HSCC. The centrepiece featured two of the cars that took part in the Griffiths Trophy Race of 14 May 1966.

On display was the race-winning Jaguar D-type of Neil Corner, alongside the second-placed Lotus X raced in period by Chris Warwick-Drake. The Jaguar had been restored to its previous Ecurie Ecosse livery by Gary Pearson who arranged the loan of the car with current owner Christian Glasel. The Lotus, owned by Malcolm Paul and raced originally by Mike Anthony, was sporting the replica silver hare on the bonnet, as carried by all of Mike's race cars.

Other cars featured on the stand were a Cooper-Bristol loaned by Paul Grant and prepared by IN Racing, representing the HSCC's first single-seater championship. Ian Nuthall's IN Racing also delivered Chris Helliwell's Jamun T2 raced by multiple Historic Formula Ford champion Paul Sleeman.

Commemorating the days of Atlantic Computers and the club's Historic GT Championship was the McLaren M8C of Stephen Minoprio. Jonathan Loader kindly reproduced some RJB Logos to go on his Chevron B19, which was owned by Richard Budge, prepared by Vin Malkie and taken to successive RJB Mining Championship victories by Mike Wilds.

The class of 1966: (L-R) Chris Drewett, Geoff Thomas, Bernard Worth, Penny Woodley, Michael Ward, Philip Martino, Ivan Sharrock and Steven Gibson

Phil Hall's stunning March 752 at Race Retro

Club Chairman Frank Lyons supported the stand with two cars, his ex-James Hunt McLaren M26 Formula 1 car and the Gurney Eagle FA74 F5000 which also had James Hunt connections. Tony Steele loaned his Lola MkII Formula Junior, which he had raced for over 40 years. Tony was the first competitor to win in Formula Junior with the HSCC back in 1976 when the category had a class in the Pre '60 Single-Seater Championship. The line up was brought up to date by the Super Touring Honda Accord loaned by Graeme Dodd.

On Friday Grahame White organised a gathering of current and former racers, which focussed on the Griffith Trophy of 1966 and previous Chairmen and champions. Amongst those attending were current and former Chairmen and Vice-Chairmen Frank Lyons, Chris Sharples, Nick Overall, Stephen Minoprio, Chris Alford and Don Hands and the first FIA Thoroughbred Grand Prix champion Martin Stretton. On hand was the winner of the first race at the first race meeting organised by the HSCC John Brindley, multiple race winner Willie Green, multiple Historic Formula Ford Champion Paul Sleeman, RJB Mining Champion Mike Wilds and multiple race winner and former committee member John Harper.

A little over a month after *Autosport* International, the Club had an eight-car stand at Race Retro, which was held over three days at the end of February at Stoneleigh near Coventry. Once again the Club was partnered by Formula Junior Historic Racing Association, who persuaded John Sykes to loan his recently completed restoration of a Lola Mk2.

Also on display was the Classic Formula 3 Championship-winning Chevron B34 of Maxim Bartell, the F2 March 752 of Phil Hall, James Lovett's FF1600 Lola T200 loaned by Neil Fowler, Richard Perry's Merlyn Mk4A, Iain Daniels' Lotus Elan and Richard Dutton's Ford Lotus Cortina. Daryl Taylor loaned his Lola T390 and arranged for a range of Berazzi wheels to be on display. The Lola attracted a lot of interest including a visit by Nick Faure who had raced the car in period at Le Mans.

The 50th anniversary of the Club would also be marked in style at the Silverstone Classic (July 29-31) with a very special parade. On the Sunday of the event, a 50-car parade would show the breadth of the Club's race programme with at least three cars representing each of the HSCC's 16 championships and series.

The parade would span single-seaters from Formula 5000 cars from the Derek Bell Trophy and Historic Formula 2 to Formula Junior, Classic Racing Cars, Classic and Historic Formula Ford 2000 and Historic Formula Ford. Sports and GT cars would come from the Guards Trophy, Pre '80 Endurance Series and Jaguar Classic Challenge. Touring Cars from the Super Touring Trophy and Historic Touring Car Championship will span four decades, and two generations of Formula 3 cars would be on show from the Historic and Classic categories. Meanwhile, entry-level historic racing was to be represented by Historic and 70s Road Sports and Classic Clubmans.

FRANK LYONS

Chairman in 2016

"I came into the HSCC as a novice in Formula Ford in around 1996. I'd been racing motorbikes for a number of years and when I started my business I could no longer compete at the level at which I had been competing.

"So I stood back for a while and I had a friend doing Formula Ford. I went along with him to help and back in period I would have loved a Formula Ford, but I couldn't afford one. I joined the Club and was very, very pleased with the camaraderie in the Formula Ford paddock. Then my wife Judy got fed up watching me roaring round and decided she would have a go as well.

"Over the years I have watched the Club growing and growing and it's a credit to the board, the previous Chairmen and to Grahame White that the Club is in a good place. It is strong financially and we've got good championship Chairmen and we seem to be growing it. But this is still a Club and what makes it unique is the fact that we are able to run as many championships as we do, with the amount of track time we have.

"We want the Club to move forwards with the times, giving the members what they want. We are starting to look at other venues but track time costs and there is very little you can do about that.

"People used to say to me at modern meetings: 'I want to get my son into racing, do I put them in a Formula Renault?' My reply would be: 'Go and put them into Historic Formula Ford. It will cost you £20,000, you'll run for a season for £10,000 and you'll find out whether your youngster is any good or not, as opposed to spending £30,000 for one weekend.'

"It's maybe time for us to invest in the future of the various series we've got going. The weak ones need to be analysed and the strong ones need to be supported. My job as chairman has been easier than I thought as the team in the office run a very, very slick operation.

"In the 50th anniversary year I'm very proud to be Chairman. I also feel that you can stay too long in one job and we should have fresh eyes on a fairly regular rotation."

Part of the 50th anniversary parade at the Silverstone Classic

The 50-car parade was planned to include cars from five decades and cover everything from a Formula 5000 Lola to a Lotus Elan.

More news for 2016 was that the Universal Racing Services Classic Formula Ford 2000 Series would move to the HSCC for 2016 with an eight-event schedule at some of the high-profile historic race meetings. Contenders in the category for FF2000 cars built up to 1983 would race alongside three existing HSCC classes during the season. The Classic FF2000s would share four races with Classic F3 cars, two with Classic Racing Cars and two with Historic Formula Ford 2000.

"It is good news that we've found a home for these cars and I think they'll fit in very well with the HSCC," said Ken Thorogood from Universal Racing Services. "There are as many as 40 cars out there and I hope this move will attract more of them out."

The 50th anniversary event at Castle Combe in April proved a great success and notable cars included two that are still owned by the same person, half a century later. Bernard Worth (Ferrari 166 Mille Miglia) and Ian Dussek (HRG 1500) were back on the Castle Combe circuit after a 50-year gap while Fred Damodaran travelled from Scotland to be re-united with the Allard J2X he owned and raced from the 1960s to the late 1980s.

A Jaguar D-type from Jaguar Heritage commemorated the model's success in the 1966 race, while the Lotus-Bristol MkX raced to second place in 1966 by Chris Warwick

The ex-Betty Haig Frazer Nash back at Castle Combe in 2016

Bernard Worth and his Ferrari at the 50th anniversary celebration

The Healey Silverstone raced by Brian Dermott in 1966

The ex-Mockridge Jowett Jupiter

The 1966 grid re-creation in April 2016

The ex-Martin Morris Frazer Nash

The grid walk-about at Castle Combe

Frank Lyons (right) talks to TV presenter Paul Woodford

Drake was there with current owner Malcolm Paul. The late Betty Haig was one of the prime movers behind the Griffiths Formula and her Frazer Nash was there.

Stephen Curtis, Mike Ward, Chris Drewett and Ivan Sharrock all took part in the original race and were back at Castle Combe to join in the celebrations. Many old friendships were re-kindled as the drivers recalled the 1966 race and the parade laps were flagged away by Penny Woodley, daughter of Guy Griffiths, who started the 1966 race.

"We were very pleased with how the weekend went," said Grahame White. "There was a very special atmosphere and I'd like to thank all the car owners and drivers for making such an effort to come and be part of our celebrations." Many of the drivers from the 1966 race enjoyed the event so much that they returned to HSCC race meetings over the balance of the season to present the race winners and see more of just how much historic racing had developed since that fledgling race in 1966.

The Castle Combe weekend's racing, held in spring sunshine, got the 50th anniversary season off to a flying start. Some of the weekend's best racing came in the opening rounds of the Historic Formula Ford 1600 Championship, which ran as two points-scoring races due to the size of the entry. In the first race, a mighty contest between Mark Shaw and Dan Eagling raged race-long as former F3000 racer Shaw claimed his first race win since moving over to historic racing.

Shaw was starting his title campaign with Mike O'Brien's squad while Eagling, in only his second FF1600 race, was giving the Lotus 61 of Andy Langridge a shake-down run after a restoration. Eagling battled into the lead before a brief safety car

Ian Pearson won in Classic FF2000 at Castle Combe

period. From the green flag, Eagling and Shaw went wheel-to-wheel as James Buckton and Benn Tilley making it a four-way battle.

However, as the race developed the lead contest was between Shaw and Eagling and it was Shaw who just got the verdict. "There was a lot of pressure on," said the Scot. Tilley belied his limited experience to take a fine third and fastest race lap with Buckton fourth as Will Nuthall fended off Danny Stanzl and category newcomer Neil Shinner for fifth.

The second Historic FF1600 race was for the other half of the over-subscribed grid. Callum Grant set the pace in this one but had to deal with a determined challenge from Ben Tusting, who could not win as he'd picked up a jump start penalty. However, by disputing the lead with Grant, Tusting was able to get far enough clear of Benn Simms to keep second place once the penalty was applied.

The 70s Road Sports grid at Castle Combe

Mervyn Selwyn (Lotus Elan) in Historic Road Sports

Historic Touring Cars head out of Quarry

Malcolm Jackson (Mallock Mk20) leads the Classic Clubmans battle

The Guards Trophy field heads for Avon Rise

Michael Schryver and Simon Hadfield blitzed the 40-minute Guards Trophy race in Schryver's Chevron B6. At the head of the fantastic 38-car grid was James Schrvyer (Chevron B8) but he jumped the start and then had to race hard to negate the time penalty and retain second. Charles Allison made it an all-Chevron podium, while the GT division was all-TVR Griffiths as the Mike Gardiner/Dan Cox car led home Peter Thompson and John Spiers.

Ray Mallock took his U2 Mk2 to victory in the front-engined Formula Junior race. However, as Mallock struggled later in the race with gearbox issues, Andrew Tart chased hard in the front-wheel drive Bond and the gap was down to a second at the flag. "I was very happy to keep up with someone like Ray," said Tart.

Stuart Roach was on course to win the rear-engined Formula Junior race until he parked his Alexis Mk4 after battery failure. Cameron Jackson, battling with clutch problems, took over in his Brabham BT2 while Greg Thornton, fresh from racing his Ford Mustang in the previous race, led the chase in his Lotus 20/22.

The pair of HSCC Road Sports Championships started their seasons with bumper grids, excellent racing and two wins for Lotus Elans. In the 70s division, Julian Barter was the class of the field but Peter Shaw (TVR Tuscan) was always a contender after leading the early laps.

On Sunday, Shaw switched to his Historic Road Sports Lotus Elan and saw off the Morgan Plus 8 squadron for victory. Reigning champion Kevin Kivlochan quickly made up ground from a lowly grid position until struck by a misfire and the car later stopped completely. Tim Pearce had a quick spin at Quarry but fought back to grab second from Richard Plant in their Plus 8s.

Cumbrian Andrew Park took the opening Historic Formula Ford 2000 Championship round but had to defend hard in the early laps as Nelson Rowe mounted a stern attack. However, Rowe was having gear selection woes and that led to a quick spin, which promoted Benn Simms to second but Park was away and clear. Andy Jarvis topped the Classic Racing Car section in his Palliser.

Peter Thompson took victory in the opening round of the HSCC Historic Formula 3 Championship. Andrew Hibberd set the pace in the race until sidelined with

Ian Flux leads David Shaw in Classic F3 at Silverstone, May 2016

The Harris/Wilmoth Austin Healey 3000 in the Silverstone Guards Trophy race

fuel pump issues and so Simon Armer and Ewen Sergison completed the podium. In Classic F3, Richard Trott went clear from the similar Chevron B43 of Simon Jackson as Ian Pearce topped the URS Classic FF2000 division.

Warren Briggs won a typically entertaining Historic Racing Saloons opener as his Ford Mustang enjoyed a dry track after a wet and slippery qualifying session. Chris Sanders chased valiantly in his Lotus Cortina.

Concern over his gearbox forced Mark Charteris to make a cautious start in the Classic Clubmans race

Michael Lyons (McLaren M26) heads the Derek Bell Trophy pack at Silverstone

The GT and Sports Car Cup field on Hangar Straight

and prompted an excellent early dice as Malcolm Jackson led. Spencer McCarthy joined in as well, but Charteris was soon able to take control as McCarthy moved through to second from Jackson.

A month later, the racing focus moved to the Silverstone Grand Prix circuit for the International Trophy. Despite difficult weather conditions during Saturday, over 430 competitors took part in 14 races with close finishes and excellent across two very full days.

Highlights included a double win for Michael Lyons in the McLaren M26 with which James Hunt won the 1977 British Grand Prix, three wins for Leo Voyazides and an epic Jaguar Classic Challenge victory for Julian Thomas and Calum Lockie.

Lyons was racing in a double-header season-opener for the Derek Bell Trophy, which included the Classic F3 Championship, and a fabulous field of rapid single-seaters gathered for the weekend. Andrew Smith's Formula Atlantic March 79B was the closest challenger to the F1 car and in the rain of Saturday Smith was able to keep Lyons in sight. However, in the dry on Sunday Lyons romped clear in the famous car. In the concurrent Classic F3 contests, father and son Simon and Dominik Jackson took a win apiece, with Dominik winning on Saturday in his March 803 after his long break from racing.

There was also family rivalry in the 70s Road Sports Championship, run in Saturday's rain. Julian Barter guested in Jim Dean's Lotus Europa and was able to keep the Datsun 240Z of his father Charles at arm's length as he found the Europa superbly balanced in the conditions.

Later, the Historic Road Sports Championship delivered a close finish as Peter Shaw just held off the fast-closing John Davison in a battle of the Lotus Elans. There was only a quarter of a second in it at the flag as Robin Pearce took his Morgan to third and Kevin Kivlochan battled up from the back of the grid to fourth place after qualifying problems.

George Tizzard had his dad Stuart's Lenham Spyder all to himself for the Guards Trophy race and he made good use of it to overhaul the Martin O'Connell/Sandy Watson Chevron B8 and win the 40-minute race. "The car was amazing; I'm just lucky to drive it," said Tizzard. Watson, meanwhile, had to nurse a B8 that

was short on tyres and brakes. Best of the GT pack was Mike Whitaker and his task was eased when the similar TVR Griffith of Mike Gardiner/Dan Cox lost its front bodywork in a clash in traffic.

Sam Wilson (Lotus 20/22) was the class of the Formula Junior field and took a double win, although Cameron Jackson was unfortunate to lose out on Saturday when a suspension problem halted his Brabham BT2. Jack Woodhouse, on his Brabham debut in the BT6 of John Truslove, and Andrew Hibberd (Lotus 22) led the chase, though Hibberd was down the order a little on Saturday after a spin.

Historic Formula 3 Championship debutant Jon Milicevic took a commanding Historic F3 win in his just-finished Brabham BT21B and dedicated the win to his mate Sam Wilson who got an engine together for the Brabham in just 48 hours in the run up to the race. Simon Armer (March 703) was strong on a briefly slippery track and edged ahead of Peter Thompson (Brabham BT21) for second.

Ian Pearson and Andrew Park took the spoils in the combined Classic and Historic FF2000 contest that wrapped up a busy weekend. Pearson was able to ease clear of a big battle for second as Park and Nelson Rowe contested the Historic division with Classic racer Mark Mercer watching from close quarters. Park eventually got the nod to make it two Historic wins from two rounds but it had taken a mighty effort from many people to get his car fixed after it was damaged in testing on Friday.

The Historic FF1600 Championship field had a very slippery track on Saturday but some exemplary driving delivered a remarkably clean race. It all finally came down to the last couple of corners as Benn Simms was reeled in by Rob Wainwright as they threaded through backmarkers. Wainwright saved his best for the end and managed to run side-by-side with Simms towards Luffield and drive ahead. "Over the last two laps it seemed to be wetter but the car felt better," said Wainwright after a fine performance. Teenager Benn Tilley was impressive once more as he raced his Merlyn in the wet for the first time to head Mark Shaw and take the final podium position while Sam Binfield drove a blinder for his best result to date in fifth in his Titan Mk6.

Leo Voyazides won both the ByBox Historic Touring Car Championship round and the Pre '80 Endurance

Sam Mitchell, Rob Wainwright and Callum Grant in an FF thriller at Snetterton

race, albeit in very different cars. In the touring car race, he took his Ford Falcon clear of a fine field of cars and edged away as Warren Briggs (Ford Mustang) and Andy Wolfe (Lotus Cortina) battled hard for second and Briggs had to push to repel the Cortina. Endaf Owens (Mini Cooper) and Simon Benoy (Hillman Imp) headed the smaller cars.

The Pre '80 Endurance race was all about the gorgeous Lola T280 that Voyazides shared with Andy Wolfe. From a strong and varied grid, Martin O'Connell led away in his Chevron B19, but even O'Connell's talents could not keep the DFV-powered Lola at bay for too long. Voyazides did the first stint before hopping out and handing the car over to Wolfe to finish the job.

O'Connell ran second from John Burton with Donington winner Michele Liguori back in fourth, this time running his 2-litre Lola T296. Hans Huebner topped the GT cars in his glorious Porsche 911RSR while the David Axisa/Gary Pearson Tiga SC79 headed the Sports 2000 class after some good battling.

Julian Thomas and Calum Lockie scored a tremendous victory in the Jaguar Classic Challenge and were unlucky not to back it up with a GT and Sports Car Cup win. Lockie did the opening stint in the 40-minute Jaguar race before Thomas took over during a mid-race safety car period to battle to the finish with fellow E-type racers Martin Stretton and John Pearson. On the penultimate lap Thomas briefly dropped to third

but got back into the lead with a move down inside of Stretton under braking for Brooklands. They were almost side-by-side through Woodcote and Thomas got the win by a quarter of a second with Pearson close behind in third.

On Sunday, Lockie and Thomas were on target to add GTSCC spoils as Lockie had just taken the lead from the AC Cobra of Leo Voyazides and Andy Wolfe when the race was red-flagged after Brian Lambert rolled his MGB at Club, fortunately without injury. The results were taken back a lap and handed victory to Voyazides and Wolfe. Right in contention from a magnificent 50-car grid when the race was halted was the Lister Jaguar of Tony Wood and Will Nuthall, while Jeremy Welch and Martyn Corfield were the best of the smaller-engined cars in their Austin Healey 3000.

Close finishes were a major feature at Snetterton in early June for a 15-race programme included a celebration of the life of Archie Scott Brown. The second running of the Historic Archie Scott Brown Trophy race was a 30-minute invitation race for pre-1959 sports-racing cars, run in association with FISCAR. The race delivered a grandstand finish as the Lister Knobblies of Mark Lewis and Roberto Giordanelli battled mightily to the flag and the verdict went to Lewis by just a third of a second.

There was also a close finish to the hour-long round of the Guards Trophy as less than five seconds covered the top three cars. The race was shortened due to a smaller

Charles Barter celebrates victory at Cadwell Park, June 2016

Glenn Eagling's F3 Ensign LNF3 at Cadwell Park

than expected entry and victory went to the Chevron B8 of Steve Brooks and Robert Beebee, while second overall and leading GT car, the TVR Griffith of Mike Gardiner and Dan Cox was only 3.8s behind. Less than a second down on the TVR to complete the overall podium was the Chevron B6 of Nick Thompson and Sean McLurg. Beebee completed a very successful weekend by taking two more wins in the Allcomers races.

The Historic FF1600 Championship racers once again delivered some epic action across three races and there was a blanket finish in the opening race as Callum Grant headed Rob Wainwright and Sam Mitchell over the line with less than four-tenths of a second covering three cars. Wainwright won the second race from Mitchell by the comfortable margin of 1.6s as Grant failed to finish. Wainwright then elected to miss the third race, which was not for championship points, and Mitchell won as Grant fought through to second from the back of the grid.

Not to outdone, the first Historic FF2000 Championship finish was even closer as Andrew Park beat Benn Simms by a coat of Reynard paint in a nail-biting dash to the flag. Sunday's race was very much a repeat as Park and Simms raced wheel to wheel until Park was caught out by a backmarker at the last corner and had a quick spin. He still finished second to Simms as Andrew Storer completed the podium.

Formula Junior Championship wins went to Nicholas Fennell (Lotus 27) and Greg Thornton (Lotus 20/22), with Thornton just beating Alex Morton (Lightning Envoyette) by a third of a second.

Graham Pattle (Lotus Cortina) took a double win in the ByBox Historic Touring Car Championship races and

Mark Charteris (Mallock Mk20/21) was unstoppable in the pair of Classic Clubmans races. Simon Jackson (Classic F3 Chevron B43) and Ian Pearson (URS FF2000 Van Diemen RF83) were also weekend double winners.

Two weeks after Snetterton was the annual Wolds Trophy meeting at Cadwell Park (18/19 June). There was no Father's Day gift for Charles Barter in the 70s Road Sports Championship as his son Julian pushed him hard in an absorbing race-long contest on Sunday. Julian won the opening race in his Lotus Elan, but Charles was inspired on Father's Day and earned his present the hard way in his Datsun 240Z to win by three-quarters of a second.

Maintaining the Father's Day theme, Stuart Roach and his father Keith raced in the HSCC/FJRHA Silverline Historic Formula Junior Championship and Stuart won three of the weekend's races in his front-engined Alexis Mk2 and his rear-engined Condor S111. However, in the second rear-engined race the Condor lost third gear and then oil pressure, so Roach was denied a clean sweep of four wins. Instead, there was a memorable result for John Sykes (Merlyn Mk5/7) who took his first overall race win.

Nearly 40 cars arrived in Lincolnshire for the Historic Formula Ford 1600 Championship and delivered some fantastic racing across four races. The big winner was Callum Grant, who won both races, in his Merlyn Mk20. However, neither win was easy as Benn Simms pushed him hard in the first race and Rob Wainwright was only a third of a second behind on Sunday as impressive teenager Benn Tilley completed the podium.

Jon Milicevic (Brabham BT21B) was another double winner as two races for the Historic Formula 3

The Formula Ford pack blasts off at Cadwell Park

Martin Dyson leads Simon Holmesmith in 70s Road Sports

Championship remembered racing journalist Justin Haler. On Sunday, an inspired Ewen Sergison led the early laps in his Brabham BT21 and was still well in touch at the flag despite a strong challenge from Simon Armer (March 703).

Andrew Park maintained his early season form in the Historic Formula Ford 2000 Championship with two more wins in his Reynard SF81. He had taken five wins and a second from the opening six races, although a tangle with Benn Simms in the opening race ended a fierce lead contest.

The URS Classic FF2000 and Classic Racing Cars fields shared a grid and delivered double wins for Ian Pearson (Van Diemen RF83) and Andy Jarvis (Palliser WDB2), although Brian Cullen (Crossle 19F) headed Jarvis in the opening laps of the first race.

Peter Shaw (Lotus Elan) and Kevin Kivlochan (Morgan Plus 8) shared the wins in the Historic Road Sports Championship, with Kivlochan moving ahead on Sunday when the Elan retired with ignition dramas. Dave Boland (Ginetta G4) chased the Morgan home.

The ByBox Historic Touring Car Championship allowed John Avill (Lotus Cortina) a weekend double despite considerable pressure from Graham Pattle (Lotus Cortina) in race one and Simon Benoy (Hillman Imp) on Sunday. Pattle was chasing hard on Sunday when his car suffered a spectacular transmission failure as it crested the Mountain. Completing a very full weekend were rounds of the Classic Clubmans Championship, where Mark Charteris (Mallock Mk20/21) was in stunning form and two rounds of the Lackford Engineering Sprite and Midget Challenge won by David Weston.

The Club's 50th anniversary race meeting at Brands Hatch (1-3 July) was a runaway success with big grids and close racing across three very full days of action on the Grand Prix circuit. The specially extended three-day meeting, The Legends of Brands Hatch Super Prix, was one of the biggest in the Club's 50-year history.

It was a weekend for multiple wins and the most successful driver was Michael Lyons who won four races in two very different cars. On his debut in the category, Lyons won both races for the Super Touring Trophy in a Volvo S40 and backed it up with a double Derek Bell Trophy victory in his Formula 1 Surtees TS9. The pair of Derek Bell Trophy races ran for the Historic Race of Champions award.

Andrew Hibberd was on top form to win three races with a double in the Historic Formula 3 Championship in his ex-Chris Irwin Brabham BT18. Hibberd then added another win in the Formula Junior race for disc-braked, rear-engined cars in his Lotus 22 against a very strong field. As the Formula Junior category continued its Diamond Jubilee celebrations, just on 100 cars competed across three races with other wins going to Stuart Roach (Alexis Mk2) and Chris Drake (Elva 300).

Also double winners were Leo Voyazides and Simon Hadfield who took a commanding win in the GT and Sports Car Cup (AC Cobra) and then won the Pre '80 Endurance race in their Lola T282. They nearly added a third win in the Guards Trophy with their Daytona Cobra Coupe, but were beaten home by less than four-tenths of a second by the Elva Mk7 of Max Bartell and Callum Grant. Voyazides later made it three wins by taking the ByBox Historic Touring Car Championship spoils in his Ford Falcon.

Formula Junior drivers past and present at Brands Hatch

Cameron Jackson (Brabham BT2) heads a Formula Junior pack

Ross Hyett in his Ford Mustang at Brands

Historic Road Sports head for Paddock Hill Bend at Brands Hatch, July 2016

Saturday's closest finish came in the first race for the HSCC Historic Formula 2 FIA International Series, supported by Berazzi Wheels. A delighted Mark Dwyer (March 742) beat Richard Evans (Chevron B42) by just 0.119s on a damp track. In the dry on Sunday, Evans pulled clear for victory.

Other drivers to take double wins across the weekend were Valerio Leone in his March 783 from a superb field for the Classic Formula 3 Championship and Jon Fairley (Brabham BT11) in the pair of HGPCA races for Pre '66 Grand Prix cars. HSCC Road Sports wins, from strong grids, went to Charles Barter (Datsun 240Z) and John Davison (Lotus Elan).

Andrew Park topped the Historic Formula Ford 2000s by less than a second from URS Classic FF2000 runner Marc Mercer but it was even closer in the Classic

Andrew Park on his way to FF2000 victory at Croft

Mark Jones tops a Touring Car battle at Croft, August 2016

Racing Car section of the race as Dan Pyett (Tecno) beat Andy Jarvis (Palliser) by a fifth of a second! Finally, after sharing a dramatic Guards Trophy win on Saturday, Callum Grant and Max Bartell headed the Historic FF1600 race that closed the weekend.

Star drivers from the history of the Formula Junior category along with over 100 cars in action made the 'Legends of Brands Hatch Super Prix' (1-3 July) a milestone event in the Formula Junior Diamond Jubilee celebrations. The event was part of the three-year Formula Junior Diamond Jubilee World Tour and a category record entry of more than 100 cars was confirmed.

The F2 Tecno of Julian Stokes in Classic Racing Cars at Croft

As well as the three races on Saturday, category prime-mover Duncan Rabagliati invited a raft of drivers and constructors from the Formula Junior story and many of them were at Brands Hatch. Period drivers on hand included Kurt Ahrens, Sir John Whitmore, David Piper, Peter Procter, Hugh Dibley, Roger Nathan, Bill Bradley and Mike Anthony. Meanwhile, former Grand Prix driver Howden Ganley, patron of the Diamond Jubilee, was re-united with the futuristic Gemini MkIVA he raced at Brands Hatch in 1963.

"We've never had this many cars running at one event before," said Rabagliati. "We had over 90 cars at Brands Hatch in 2008 for our Golden Jubilee. I'm very pleased that we had some famous names from the Formula

Dick Coffey's Turner on the attack at the Croft hairpin

217

Junior story joining us at Brands Hatch to make it a truly special event in our Diamond Jubilee celebrations."

The annual Croft Nostalgia Festival (6/7 August) was another successful event in the 50th anniversary season with some great competition across 19 races. Notable successes in a superb weekend of action included a double win in Formula Ford 1600 for Callum Grant, a 70s Road Sports double for Jim Dean and another step towards the Historic FF2000 Championship title for Andrew Park.

The Croft weekend marked round five of seven for the Guards Trophy with a race on Saturday delivering overall victory for Hugh Colman in his Chevron B8 from the similar car of Charles Allison and Peter Thompson. The mighty TVR Griffith of Mike Gardiner and Dan Cox again topped the GT cars and took a fine third overall from a strong field.

A fabulous entry of Historic Formula Ford 1600s demanded four races to ensure everyone got to race at least twice and it was 2012 champion Callum Grant who was the class of the pack with two wins in the points' scoring races. Rob Wainwright twice led the chase of the winning Merlyn Mk20 in his Elden Mk8 and then switched cars to score a double victory in the combined Classic Racing Cars/Historic Formula 3 races. Wainwright was at the wheel of a rare 1970 Crossle 18F Formula 2 car recently restored at the race preparation business he runs with his father Gerry.

Andrew Park took a win and a second in the Historic Formula Ford 2000 Championship to move closer to the title. With key rival Benn Simms absent following recent engine problems, Park was once more on top form in his Reynard SF81, although in the second race he was headed by the flying Andrew Smith (Royale RP27).

The Historic Touring Car Championship delivered more crowd-pleasing action and a double win for Mark Jones (Lotus Cortina) despite a major challenge from the Ford Mustang of Warren Briggs. In the second race Briggs lost a lot of time off the start and had to fight back up to second, dealing with impressive teenager James Clarke (Lotus Cortina) in the process.

Out-going champion James Dean won both rounds of the 70s Road Sports Championship in his Lotus Europa and kept Julian Barter (Lotus Elan) at bay in the process, while Kevin Kivlochan (Morgan +8) twice topped the Historic Road Sports element despite a stern chase by the Ginetta G4 of David Boland.

Simon Armer's March 703 headed the Historic Formula 3 Championship contenders to boost his title hopes with two maximum scores, while Jonathan Hughes (Brabham BT6) scored a weekend double win in the Silverline UK Formula Junior Championship. However, it was very close on Sunday as he beat Cameron Jackson (Brabham BT2) by less than a fifth of a second. John Sykes made a piece of Formula Junior history by racing the rare Merlyn Mk2 for the first time and twice finishing as leading front-engined car.

Mark Charteris and John Harrison had two good battles in the Classic Clubmans Championship for the rapid front-engined sports racers, before Charteris was able to pull clear. Finally, James Dunkley took an impressive pair of wins in the Lackford Engineering Midget and Sprite Challenge from an excellent field.

The Oulton Park Gold Cup meeting (27-29 August) was dedicated to the memory of the two people who were central to the creation of the Club, Guy Griffiths and Betty Haig. On-track, some demonstration laps by Andy Middlehurst in his incredible ex-Jim Clark Lotus H16-engined 43 evoked memories of the 1966 Gold Cup.

In honour of Oulton Park's racing heritage, the famous Gold Cup title was revived with a new Historic Gold Cup which was presented to Peter Horsman (Lotus 18/21) after a double win in the races for pre '66 Grand Prix Cars from the Historic Grand Prix Cars Association. The trophy was presented by period Lotus Grand Prix mechanic Bob Dance.

Whitaker, Gardiner and Spiers in a TVR contest at Oulton Park

Andy Middlehurst in the ex-Jim Clark Lotus 43 at Oulton Park

Ric Wood's Ford Capri in the Super Touring Trophy at the Gold Cup

Jim Dean leads the 70s Road Sports at Oulton Park

There was also a Lotus victory in one of the weekend's most exciting races as Europa racer Jim Dean won the 70s Road Sports Championship round. Charles Barter forged his Datsun 240Z into an early lead but Dean's Lotus Europa went with him while Russell Paterson (Morgan Plus 8) and Julian Barter (in Dean's other Europa) watched the fun from close quarters.

Barter managed to knock off his master switch momentarily with his elbow and Paterson edged ahead of Barter into the final lap before Dean charged past the Datsun on the exit of Cascades. Dean then nipped ahead of the Morgan to score a memorable win.

Two sensational Historic Formula Ford 1600 races thrilled the fans on Monday as Sam Mitchell and Benn Simms shared the wins after lead battles featuring as many as six cars. The opening race was only settled on the final lap when Callum Grant hit brake trouble and ran wide over the grass at Knickerbrook and Benn Tilley flipped over after an inadvertent clash of wheels with Simms. Through the drama, Mitchell emerged to win from Rob Wainwright and Max Bartell.

The later race seemed set for a second Mitchell win until he spun at Old Hall. Grant took over, but his car hit trouble and he was pushed down the order as Simms came through to beat Bartell by a fraction of a second.

The Historic Road Sports race was a thriller as Kevin Kivlochan got his Morgan Plus 8 to the flag by a fifth of a second from the Lotus Elan of John Davison. The Elan eroded Kivlochan's lead despite a spin at Druids and Davison's recovery drive was a highlight.

Mark Dwyer dominated the Derek Bell Trophy with two resounding wins in his Formula 2 March 742. Neil Glover gave chase in his Formula 5000 Chevron B37, but had to concentrate on fending off Paul Campfield's Chevron B24. Mark Woodhouse was the cream of the Historic Formula Junior front-engined division in his Elva despite the best efforts of Mike Walker in the Bond, while Andrew Hibberd duly took both rear-engined races.

A bumper Historic Touring Car field had no answer to the pace of Warren Briggs in his Ford Mustang as John Avill headed the Lotus Cortina pack in the opening race. In the second race, Briggs was again unstoppable but this time 16-year-old James Clarke raced very well to beat Avill for second.

Stewart Whyte bagged a Super Touring Trophy double with two pretty untroubled wins in his Honda Accord. John Cleland, racing his Vauxhall Vectra for the first time in a year, took second in the first race. Local ace Mark Jones ran third on Sunday but went one better to take second on Monday in his Renault Laguna.

Andrew Park was top of the Historic Formula Ford 2000 pack to win twice and clinch the championship title by making it nine wins from 11 rounds to date. Tom White pushed his older Osella to second in both races. The final wins of a very full weekend went to John Murphy's Crossle 22F (Classic Racing Cars/Classic FF2000) and Mark Charteris in Classic Clubmans.

The Historic Formula Ford pack delivered two stunning races at Brands Hatch on Saturday 17 September), with the top three covered by four-tenths of a second in both contests. It was Rob Wainwright from Benn Tilley and Callum Grant in the first race, but later on it was Grant, Tilley and Wainwright after two fantastically close and fair races as Grant and Wainwright continue their battle for the overall title.

Although he had already won the 2016 title, Andrew Park added two more wins to his remarkable run of victories in the Historic Formula Ford 2000 Championship. However, this was not always easy for

Park as his throttle stuck open part way through the first race and he had to drive his Reynard SF81 on the ignition switch. Things were easier in the second race as Tom White (Osella FAF) again finished second.

A strong field contested a double-header for the HSCC Classic Formula 3 Championship and URS Classic Formula Ford 2000 Series. Simon Jackson (Chevron B43) and Ian Pearson (Van Diemen RF83) were the double winners, with Pat Gormley (Safir RJF3) splitting them on the overall podium as he kept up a determined chase of Jackson. Adrian Langridge (Dastle Mk10) headed the 1600cc F3 cars.

Mark Charteris set the standard in the Classic Clubmans Championship for rapid front-engined sports-racing cars and won twice in his Mallock Mk20/21 as Spencer McCarthy (Mallock Mk20B/21) headed the pursuit. In the battle for the Class B title Clive Wood won twice but only by three-tenths of a second in the later race as arch rival Barry Webb ran him very close. An eclectic mix of cars contested two Allcomers races, with Ian Burford (Ginetta G4) and James Claridge (Lotus Elan) finishing as the leading contenders from the HSCC ranks.

For the first time, the annual Finals Meeting on the Silverstone National Circuit grew to a full weekend on 15/16 October. It delivered some tremendous racing as titles were won and lost and, apart from a soaking wet start to Sunday, ran in bright autumn sunshine.

Robert Simac, Historic F2 champion for the fourth time in 2016

The Historic Formula Ford Championship went down to a straight fight between Callum Grant (Merlyn Mk20) and Rob Wainwright (Elden Mk8) and victory in the first of two championship races was the perfect way for Grant to clinch the title for a second time. Grant also won the Chris Mudge Memorial Trophy as aggregate winner across the two championship races.

The racing provided in four races by a 50-car Formula Ford entry was outstanding and the second championship race was one of the best of the season as up to 12 cars formed a lead pack. Eventually Sam Mitchell and Grant edged clear and former champion Mitchell took victory by a quarter of a second. Up into an incredible third went teenager Benn Tilley after starting 22nd on the grid for the qualification race, while fellow teenager Ed Thurston also starred as he took third in the opening championship race.

In the Historic Touring Car Championship, Simon Benoy managed to get his Hillman Imp repaired after a first-lap accident at Oulton Park at the end of August and raced the un-tried car to a brace of class wins to make sure of the title. In the opening race, run on a damp but drying track, Mark Jones just worked his Lotus Cortina ahead of the Mini Cooper of Jon Milicevic in the closing stages. Later in the day, on a fully dry track, Mike Gardiner (Ford Falcon) swept ahead.

Callum Grant celebrates winning the Historic Formula Ford title

Richard Piper (Chevron B43) heads a Classic F3/Classic FF2000 pack

The Merlyn Mk6 of Neil and George Daws in the Guards Trophy

THE 2016 HSCC RACING CHAMPIONS

Guards Trophy
**Martin Richardson (MGB) and
John Davison (Lotus Elan 26R)**

Pre '80 Endurance Series
Leo Voyazides (Lola T280)

Classic Racing Car Series
Andy Jarvis (Palliser WDB2)

Historic Road Sports Championship
Dick Coffey (Turner Mk1)

70s Road Sports Championship
**Julian Barter (Lotus Elan and Lotus
Europa)**

Historic Formula 2
Robert Simac (March 712M)

Derek Bell Trophy
Martyn Donn (Lola T760)

Historic FF1600 Championship
Callum Grant (Merlyn Mk20A)

Historic Formula Junior Championship
Jonathan Fyda (U2 Mk3)

Classic Formula 3 Championship
Simon Jackson (Chevron B43)

Historic Formula 3 Championship
**Simon Armer (March 703/Brabham
BT21B)**

Classic Clubmans Championship
**Mark Charteris (Mallock Mk20/21)
and Barry Webb (Mallock
Mk16BW)**

Super Touring Trophy
Darren Fielding (BMW 320i)

Historic FF2000 Championship
Andrew Park (Reynard SF81)

Historic Touring Car Championship
Simon Benoy (Hillman Imp)

Jaguar Classic Challenge
Julian Thomas (Jaguar E-type)

*Jamie Brashaw (March 73A) won in the Derek Bell Trophy
at Silverstone*

Julian Barter and Richard Plant in 70s Road Sports

Julian Barter settled the 70s Road Sports
Championship title after splitting his season between
a Lotus Elan and a Lotus Europa. Racing the Elan at
Silverstone he enjoyed a tremendous battle with the
Morgan Plus 8 of Richard Plant and on Sunday Plant
was central to the Historic Road Sports race that
closed the weekend as he led the chase of race winner
Kevin Kivlochan in another Morgan.

The Derek Bell Trophy was settled in favour of Martyn
Donn (Lola T760) after two tremendous races. The
opener ran on a damp track and tyre choice was critical
as Mark Dwyer swept to victory in his Formula 2 March
742. On a dry track, Jamie Brashaw thundered ahead in
his Formula 5000 March 73A as Dwyer beat Neil Glover
(Chevron B37) for second place.

Andrew Hibberd (Lotus 22) and Will Mitcham (U2
Mk2) shared victories in the HSCC/FJHRA Silverline
Historic Formula Junior Championship rounds, while
Mark Woodhouse (Elva 100) sealed the front-engined
title. The Historic Formula Ford 2000 Championship
delivered two winners as category newcomer Charlie

Jon Milicevic at the front of a Touring Car battle

Peter Shaw's Lotus Elan heads a Guards Trophy group

Kemp (Reynard SF79) and Tom White (Osella FAF) took a win each after two excellent races.

The battle for the Guards Trophy was an absorbing contest as Martin Stretton (Elva Mk7S) took the fight to the Chevrons of Mark Colman and father and son pairing Michael and Will Schryver. Unfortunately, brake issues struck Stretton who eventually had to pull off with a seized rear caliper as Colman took a fine solo win.

The Guards title race ended in a tie when John Davison (Lotus Elan) and Martin Richardson (MGB) could not be split. Davison only needed to finish to be crowned champion, but suffered an electrical fire on the grid and finally retired after only nine laps. Mike Gardiner

and Dan Cox (TVR Griffith) could have taken the title but a lack of class starters meant reduced points and left them short of Davison's tally. Meanwhile 2007 champion Richardson won his class to equal Davison's score and they remained inseparable even when the tie-break regulations were considered.

Sharing a grid were the resurgent Classic Racing Car Series and a non-championship race for Historic Formula 3 cars. From a much improved grid of Classic Racing Cars, John Murphy (Crossle 22F) was victorious while Julian Stokes (Tecno) starred after a stirring recovery drive to second after spinning out of the lead at Becketts on lap one. Behind Stokes, Mark Goodyear (Lotus 59) drove a fine race to see off the Pallisers

The final championship race of the 50th anniversary season: Kevin Kivlochan on his way to Historic Road Sports victory in his Morgan Plus 8

Mike Painter (Brabham BT16) in a Classic Racing Car contest

The rising star of 2016 in Formula Ford was Benn Tilley

of Andy Jarvis and Steve Worrad. Andrew Hibberd topped the Historic F3 cars in his Brabham BT18.

Mark Charteris (Mallock Mk20/21) added another victory in the final of the Classic Clubmans Championship, but had to find a way around John Harrison (Mallock Mk21) after a good battle over the opening stages. Barry Webb (Mallock Mk16BW) was confirmed as Class B champion after a steady run to a finish. Only Clive Wood (Mallock Mk20B) could have beaten Webb to the title, but he lost the class lead to Adam Wheeler with a spin. Peter Needham (Tiga SC82) topped the invitation class for period Sports 2000s, which drew five cars as the initiative quietly gathered momentum.

The combined Classic Formula 3 Championship and URS Classic Formula Ford 2000 Series double-header provided a strong grid and battles all the way down the field. In the damp opener, tyre choice was critical and Ian Pearson (Van Diemen RF82) moved ahead as his slicks came good. Later, on a dry track, David Shaw (Ralt RT1) put the F3 cars back on top with a narrow victory over Simon Jackson (Chevron B43) and Keith White (Ralt RT1).

The weekend was a fitting conclusion to the major race programme for the 50th anniversary season of the Historic Sports Car Club. As the Historic Road Sports field toured into the pit lane after the final race, the sun was low in the sky and quickly set on half a century for the Club. It had been quite a journey.

Appendix 1
The champions

Jem Marsh, 1978 Classic Sports champion

HSCC Racing Championship for the Goodwood Trophy (1971 to 1977)

1971	Barry Bird (AC Le Mans)
1972	John Lucas (Porsche 356 Coupe)
1973	Eric Studer (Porsche Carrera Speedster)
1974	Simon Phillips (Frazer Nash)
1975	John Beasley (Lister Chevrolet)
1976	John Beasley (Lister Chevrolet)
1977	Bobby Bell (Lister Jaguar)

Pre '60 Historic Sports Car Championship (1983 to 1993)

1983	Chris Smith (Lotus 17)
1984	Jem Marsh (Marcos GT)
1985	Peter Walker (Lola Mk1)
1986	Denis Welch (Austin-Healey 100/6)
1987	Denis Welch (Austin-Healey 100/6)
1988	David Beckett (Lister Chevrolet)
1989	Not held
1990	Not held
1991	David Beckett (Lister Chevrolet)
1992	Not held
1993	Andrew Wilkinson (Lotus XI)

* run in conjunction with the Aston Martin Owners' Club from 1988

Classic Sports Car Championship (1974 to 2006)

1974   Mike Salmon (Aston Martin DP212)
1975   Richard Thwaites (Elva Mk7S)
1976   Richard Thwaites (Brabham BT8)
1977   David Dawson (Lotus 23)
1978   Jem Marsh (Marcos GT)
1979   John Corfield (Diva GT)
1980   John Brindley (Lotus 23B)
1981   Roger Ealand (Marcos 1800GT)
1982   John Brindley (Lotus 23B)
1983   John Corfield (Diva GT)
1984   Roger Ealand (Marcos 1800GT)
1985   Tony Thompson (Lotus Elan 26R)
1986   Tony Thompson (Lotus Elan 26R)
1987   Tony Thompson (Lotus Elan 26R)
1988   Denis Welch (Austin-Healey 100/6)
1989   Tony Thompson (Lotus Elan 26R)
1990   Simon Hadfield (Lotus Elan)
1991   Denis Welch (Austin Healey 3000)
1992   Denis Welch (Austin Healey 3000)
1993   John Jarvis (Lotus Elan)
1994   David Methley (Marcos GT)
1995   David Methley (Marcos GT)
1996   Richard Hayhow (Lotus Elan)
1997   David Methley (Marcos GT)
1998   Sid Marler (Lotus Elan)
1999   Sid Marler (Lotus Elan)
2000   David Methley (Marcos GT)
2001   Mark Ashworth (MGB)
2002   Chris Reece (Lotus Elan)
2003   Brendan Roberts (Lotus Elite)
2004   Simon Ashworth (MGB)
2005   Simon Ashworth (MGB)
2006   Les Ely (Jaguar E-type)

Guards Trophy (2007 to date)

2007   Martin Richardson (MGB)
2008   Robert Barrie (Porsche 911)
2009   Robert Barrie (Porsche 911)
2010   Clive Wilson (Elva Mk7)
2011   Tom Smith (MGB)
2012   Nick Fleming (Lotus Elan 26R)

2013   Chris Scragg (Jaguar E-type)
2014   Mike Whitaker (TVR Griffith)
2015   Mike Gardiner (TVR Griffith)
2016   Martin Richardson (MGB) and John Davison
        (Lotus Elan 26R)

Group 4 Historic Special GT Championship (1977 to 1981)

1977   Willie Green (Ford GT40)
1978   Rodney Bloor (Chevron B8)
1979   Mike Wheatley (Lola T70 Mk3B)
1980   Reg Skeels (Mercury GT)
1981   John Foulston (McLaren M1B)

Atlantic Computers Historic GT Championship (1982 to 1990)

1982   Richard Thwaites (Chevron B6)
1983   Keith Ashby (Chevron B6)
1984   John Brindley (McLaren M1C)
1985   Nigel Hulme (Lola T70 Mk3B)
1986   David Franklin (McLaren M6B)
1987   John Foulston (McLaren M8D)
1988   Colin Pool (Chevron B19)
1989   Colin Pool (Chevron B19)
1990   Richard Arnold (Chevron B19)

HSCC 2-Litre GT Championship (1986 to 1992)

1986   Simon Hadfield (Chevron B6)
1987   Michael Schryver (Chevron B6)
1988   Michael Schryver (Chevron B6)
1989   Michael Schryver (Chevron B6)
1990   Michael Schryver (Chevron B6)
1991   Phil Buck (Chevron B8)
1992   James Watt (Royale RP4)

RJB Mining Group 6/Thundersports Championship (1992 to 2001)

1992   Mike Wilds (Chevron B31/36)
1993   Ian McCullough (Crossle C9S)
1994   George Douglas (Ginetta G12)
1995   Peter Lee (Chevron B8)
1996   Mike Wilds (Chevron B31/36)

Robert Barrie, 2008 Guards Trophy champion

Tom Smith, 2011 Guards Trophy champion

Mike Gardiner, 2015 Guards Trophy champion

John Foulston, 1987 Historic GT champion

1997   David Hudson (Sturdgess SL1)
1998   Mike Wilds (Chevron B31/36)
1999   Nicholas Pearce (Tiga SC79)
2000   Steve Mills (Tiga SC80)
2001   Lawrence Benson (Chevron B8)

Martini Trophy with Supersports (2011 to 2014)

2011   Doug Hart (March 75S) and Charlie Kemp
        (Lola T210)
2012   Silvio Kalb (March 76S) and David
        Gathercole (Lola T212/C)
2013   James Dodd (Chevron B23) and Andrew
        Schryver (Chevron B21/23)
2014   Jonathan Loader (Chevron B19)

Pre '80 Endurance Series (2015 to date)

2015   John Burton (Chevron B26)
2016   Leo Voyazides (Lola T280)

Pre '65 Single Seater Championship (1982 to 1995)

1982   Mike Littlewood (BRM P261/Brabham BT2/
        Cooper T56)
1983   John Narcisi (Brabham BT6)
1984   Tony Steele (Lola Mk5)
1985   John Narcisi (Brabham BT6)
1986   John Jarvis (Brabham BT14)
1987   Chris Smith (Chevron B17)
1988   Steve Hitchins (Lotus 23B) *included a sports
        car class
1989   Martyn Smith (Brabham BT15)
1990   John Narcisi (Brabham BT6)
1991   Not held
1992   Not held
1993   Not held
1994   Mark Gillies (Lotus 22)
1995   Tony Steele (Lola Mk2)

Classic Racing Car Championship (1996 to date)

1996   Series of races; no winner announced
1997   Tim Barrington (Brabham BT21C)
1998   Alan Baillie (Jovis)
1999   Geoff Farmer (Brabham BT18B)

Ian Jones, 2015 Classic Racing Car champion   *Andy Jarvis, 2016 Classic Racing Car winner*

2000   Richard Urwin (Brabham BT28)
2001   Ed Mercer (Palliser WDB2)
2002   James Long (Brabham BT15)
2003   Matthew Watts (Brabham BT16)
2004   John Bladon (Merlyn Mk9)
2005   Matthew Watts (Brabham BT16)
2006   Cliff Giddens (Brabham BT16)
2007   Anthony Goddard (Merlyn Mk9)
2008   Ian Gray (Brabham BT16)
2009   Chris Holland (Brabham BT21)
2010   Ian Gray (Brabham BT16)
2011   Ian Gray (Brabham BT16)
2012   Ian Jones (Lotus 59)
2013   Ian Jones (Lotus 59)
2014   Jonathan Baines (Merlyn Mk20)
2015   Ian Jones (Lotus 59)
2016*   Andy Jarvis (Palliser WDB2)

* series of races in 2016

Post-Historic Road Sports Championship (1981 to 1987)

1981   Michael Schryver (Lotus Elan)
1982   John Atkins (AC Cobra)
1983   John Gray (Triumph TR5)
1984   John Ward (Honda S800)
1985   John Atkins (AC Cobra)
1986   Roger Connell (TVR Griffith)
1987   Kevin Irons (Datsun 240Z)

John Atkins, 1982 Post-Historic Road Sports champion

James Dodd, 2013 Martini Trophy winner

Jonathan Loader, 2014 Martini Trophy winner

Ian Gray, 2010 Classic Racing Car champion

Jonathan Baines, 2014 Classic Racing Car champion

Road Sports Championship (1988 only)

1988   Kevin Irons (Datsun 240Z)

Standard Road Sports Championship (1989 to 1994)

1989   Bodo Linhoff (Datsun 240Z)
1990   Simon Park (Lancia Fulvia)
1991   Kevin Irons (Datsun 240Z)
1992   Guy Evans (Lotus Elan)
1993   Guy Evans (Lotus Elan)
1994   Paul Stafford (Datsun 240Z)

Improved Road Sports Championship (1989 to 1994)

1989   Julian Dodd (Fairthorpe Electron)
1990   Aidan Mills-Thomas (AC Cobra)
1991   Aidan Mills-Thomas (AC Cobra)
1992   Aidan Mills-Thomas (AC Cobra)
1993   Antony Ross (Alfa Romeo Spider)
1994   Vernon Taylor (Datsun 240Z)

Rory Stockbridge 2007 70s Road Sports champion

John Thomason, 2011 70s Road Sports champion

James Dean, 2015 70s Road Sports champion

Oliver Ford, 2013 70s Road Sports champion

70s Road Sports Championship (1994 to date)

1994   Series of races
1995   Richard Thorne (Alfa Romeo GTV)
1996   Andy Shepherd (Lotus 7)
1997   Peter Gregory (Datsun 240Z)
1998   Jason Kennedy (Lancia Beta Coupe)
1999   Des Fitzgerald (Lotus Elan)
2000   Adam Bagnall (Triumph GT6)
2001   Charles Barter (Datsun 240Z)
2002   Adam Bagnall (Triumph GT6)
2003   Adam Bagnall (Triumph GT6)
2004   Richard Thorne (Morgan Plus 8)
2005   John Thomason (Triumph Spitfire)
2006   John Thomason (Triumph Spitfire)
2007   Rory Stockbridge (Lotus Europa)
2008   Ian Jacobs (Jensen Healey)
2009   Julian Barter (TVR 3000M)
2010   Peter Shaw (TVR Tuscan)
2011   John Thomason (Triumph GT6)
2012   John Thomason (Triumph GT6)
2013   Oliver Ford (Lotus Europa)
2014   Peter Shaw (TVR Tuscan)
2015   Jim Dean (Lotus Europa)
2016   Julian Barter (Lotus Elan and Lotus Europa)

Historic Road Sports Championship (1995 to date)

1995   Paul Howarth (Lancia Fulvia)
1996   Chris Horner (Turner Mk1)
1997   Mike Eagles (Turner Mk1)
1998   Mike Eagles (Turner Mk1)
1999   Kevin Kivlochan (TVR Griffith)
2000   Justin Murphy (Alfa Romeo Giulia)
2001   Mike Eagles (Milano GT)
2002   Nick Adams (Lotus Elan)
2003   Dick Coffey (Turner Mk1)
2004   Robert Barrie (Porsche 911S)
2005   Andy Shepherd (Lotus 7)
2006   David Randall (Ginetta G4)
2007   Josh Sadler (Ginetta G4)
2008   Colin Sharp (Triumph TR5) and Dick Coffey (Turner Mk1)

Chris Horner, 1996 Historic Road Sports champion

Justin Murphy, 2000 Historic Road Sports champion

John Shaw, 2014 Historic Road Sports champion

Kevin Kivlochan, 2015 Historic Road Sports champion

Neil Glover, 2013 Derek Bell Trophy winner

Richard Evans, 2015 Derek Bell Trophy winner

Dick Coffey, 2016 Historic Road Sports champion

2009	Jonathan Rushton (Morgan Plus 4)
2010	David Randall (Ginetta G4)
2011	Paul Tooms (Lotus Elan)
2012	Paul Tooms (Lotus Elan)
2013	John Shaw (Porsche 911)
2014	John Shaw (Porsche 911)
2015	Kevin Kivlochan (Morgan Plus 8)
2016	Dick Coffey (Turner Mk1)

Classic and Sportscar Novice Championship (1987 to 1991)

1987	Ronnie Farmer (TVR Griffith)
1988	Bodo Linhoff (Lotus Elan)
1989	Martin Cliffe (TVR Tuscan)
1990	Guy Evans (Lotus Elan)
1991	Steve McKechnie (Lotus Elan)

Pre '71 Single Seater Championship (1984 to 1990)

1984	Jim Wallis (Brabham BT30)
1985	John Foulston (McLaren M19A)
1986	John Foulston (McLaren M19A)
1987	Mike Pendlebury (Lotus 69)
1988	John Beasley (Lola T300)
1989	Rick Hall (McLaren M10B)
1990	Rick Hall (Surtees TS8)

Historic Formula Racing Car Championship (1991 to 1996)

1991	Paul Gardener (March 712)
1992	Michael Schryver (Lotus 69)

1993	Arnie Black (Crossle 19F)
1994	Michael Schryver (Lotus 72)
1995	Arnie Black (Crossle 19F)
1996	John Narcisi (Trojan T101)

Derek Bell Trophy (1997 to date)

1997	Nicholas Pearce (Delta T78/79)
1998	Nick Shrigley-Feigl (Chevron B28)
1999	John Robinson (Reynard SF78)
2000	John Bladon (Surtees TS11)
2001	John Crowson (Chevron B40)
2002	Nick Crossley (March 73A)
2003	Paul Smith (Reynard SF79)
2004	Stuart Tilley (Modus M1)
2005	Frank Lyons (Lola T332)
2006	Mark Dwyer (March 742)
2007	Frank Lyons (Lola T400)
2008	Greg Thornton (Surtees TS11)
2009	Neil Glover (Lola T330/332)
2010	Neil Glover (Lola T330/332)
2011	Michael Lyons (Lola T400)
2012	Frank Lyons (Gurney Eagle FA74)
2013	Neil Glover (Lola T330/332)
2014	Jon Finch (Chevron B34)
2015	Richard Evans (March 79B)
2016	Martyn Donn (Lola T760)

Historic Formula 1 Championship (1987 to 1994)

1987	Series of races
1988	Don Wood (Arrows A3)
1989	Richard Peacock (Tyrrell 010)
1990	Alan Baillie (Penske PC3)
1991	Series of races
1992	Series of races
1993	Series of races
1994	Series of races

FIA Cup for Thoroughbred Grand Prix Cars (1995 to 1999)

1995	Martin Stretton (Tyrrell 005)
1996	Michael Schryver (Lotus 72)
1997	Bob Berridge (RAM 01)

Martin Stretton, 2009 Historic Formula 2 champion

Robert Simac, Historic Formula 2 champion 2013, 2014, 2015 and 2016

Andrew Tart, 2015 Formula Junior champion

Nelson Rowe, 2007 Historic Formula Ford champion

Michael Lyons, 2008 Historic Formula Ford champion

Sam Mitchell, 2013 Historic Formula Ford champion

1998   Bob Berridge (Williams FW08)
1999   Bob Berridge (Williams FW08)

Historic Formula 2 (2007 to date)
2007   Martin Stretton (March 712M)
2008   Bo Warmenius (March 772)
2009   Martin Stretton (March 712)
2010   Katsu Kubota (March 712M)
2011   Diogo Ferrao (March 712M)
2012   Tim Barrington (Lola T240)
2013   Robert Simac (March 712M)
2014   Robert Simac (March 712M)
2015   Robert Simac (March 712M)
2016   Robert Simac (March 712M)

*Historic Formula 2 ran with other promoters before 2007

Sir John Chisholm, 2007 Formula Junior champion

Historic Formula Junior Championship (2007 to date)
2007   Sir John Chisholm (Gemini Mk3A)
2008   Jon Milicevic (Lotus 18)
2009   Chris Drake (Elva 300)
2010   Jon Milicevic (Cooper T59)
2011   Jon Milicevic (Cooper T59)
2012   Robert Barrie (Lotus 18)
2013   Mark Woodhouse (Elva 100)
2014   Jon Milicevic (Cooper T59)
2015   Andrew Tart (Bond)
2016   Jonathan Fyda (U2 Mk3)

*Historic Formula Junior ran with other clubs before 2007

Historic Formula Ford 1600 Championship (1992 to date)
1992   Series of races
1993   Series of races
1994   Series of races
1995   Bryan Hayward (Lotus 61)
1996   Paul Sleeman (Jamun T2)
1997   Paul Sleeman (Jamun T2)
1998   Benn Simms (Merlyn Mk20)

1999   Paul Sleeman (Macon MR8)
2000   Paul Sleeman (Macon MR8)
2001   Neil Fowler (Lola T200)
2002   Neil Fowler (Lola T200)
2003   Neil Fowler (Lola T200)
2004   Neil Fowler (Merlyn Mk20)
2005   Neil Fowler (Lola T200)
2006   Nelson Rowe (Crossle 20F)
2007   Nelson Rowe (Crossle 20F)
2008   Michael Lyons (Merlyn Mk11)
2009   Westie Mitchell (Merlyn Mk20)
2010   Darren Burke (Macon MR8)
2011   Benn Simms (Alexis Mk14)
2012   Callum Grant (Merlyn Mk20)
2013   Sam Mitchell (Merlyn Mk20)
2014   Benn Simms (Jomo JMR7 and Alexis Mk14)
2015   Richard Mitchell (Merlyn Mk20)
2016   Callum Grant (Merlyn Mk20A)

Classic Formula 3 Championship (1995 to date)
1995   Series of races
1996   Series of races
1997   Terry Nightingale (Mallock Mk11B)
1998   Winston Bunn (Ensign LNF3)

Benn Simms, 2008 Classic Formula 3 champion

Jamie Brashaw, 2012 Classic Formula 3 champion

1999	Mike Campbell-Cole (Brabham BT41)
2000	Peter Williams (Argo JM6)
2001	Peter Williams (Argo JM6)
2002	Neil Dunkel (Argo JM3)
2003	Chris Levy (March 713M)
2004	Steve Maxted (Argo JM6)
2005	Steve Maxted (Argo JM6)
2006	Keith White (Ralt RT1)
2007	Benn Simms (March 803B)
2008	Benn Simms (March 803B)
2009	Bill Coombs (Argo JM6)
2010	Benn Simms (March 803B)
2011	Jamie Brashaw (March 793)
2012	Jamie Brashaw (March 793)
2013	Graham Fennymore (Ralt RT3)
2014	David Shaw (Ralt RT1 and March 803B)
2015	Max Bartell (Chevron B34)
2016	Simon Jackson (Chevron B43)

Max Bartell, 2015 Classic Formula 3 champion

*Formerly known as Toyota F3, the class ran with other clubs before 1995

Historic Formula 3 Championship (2012 to date)

2012	Dean Forward (Brabham BT21)
2013	Dean Forward (Tecno)
2014	Jim Blockley (Brabham BT21)
2015	Leif Bosson (Brabham BT28)
2016	Simon Armer (March 703/Brabham BT21B)

Super Touring Trophy (2013 to date)

2013	Stewart Whyte (Honda Accord)
2014	James Dodd (Honda Accord)
2015	Stewart Whyte (Honda Accord)
2016	Darren Fielding (BMW 320i)

Classic Clubmans Championship (2014 to date)

2014	Mark Charteris (Mallock Mk20/21) and Adam Paterson (Mallock Mk18)
2015	Mark Charteris (Mallock Mk20/21) and Clive Wood (Mallock Mk20B)
2016	Mark Charteris (Mallock Mk20/21) and Barry Webb (Mallock Mk16BW)

Historic Racing Saloon/Historic Touring Car Championship (1994 to date)

1994	Series of races
1995	Series of races
1996	Series of races
1997	Nevil Smith (Ford Lotus Cortina)
1998	Peter Wray (Ford Lotus Cortina)
1999	Graeme Dodd (Jaguar Mk2)
2000	Paul Haywood-Halfpenny (Ford Lotus Cortina)
2001	Simon Garrad (BMW 2000Ti) and Graeme Dodd (Jaguar Mk2)
2002	Adrian Oliver (Hillman Imp)
2003	Adrian Oliver (Hillman Imp)
2004	Adrian Oliver (Hillman Imp)
2005	Dan Cox (Ford Anglia)
2006	Mike Hanna (Hillman Imp)
2007	Simon Benoy (Hillman Imp)
2008	Dan Cox (Ford Lotus Cortina)
2009	Dan Cox (Ford Lotus Cortina)
2010	Roger Godfrey (Austin Cooper S)
2011	Roger Godfrey (Austin Cooper S)
2012	Dan Cox (Ford Lotus Cortina)
2013	Tim Davies (Ford Lotus Cortina)
2014	Tim Davies (Ford Lotus Cortina)
2015	Simon Benoy (Hillman Imp)
2016	Simon Benoy (Hillman Imp)

Simon Benoy, 2007 Historic Saloon champion

*The class ran with the BRSCC before 1994

Mark Charteris, 2015 Classic Clubmans champion

Simon Garrad leads Graeme Dodd, joint Historic Saloon champions in 2001

Leif Bosson, 2015 Historic Formula 3 champion

Stewart Whyte, 2013 Super Touring Trophy winner

Roger Godfrey, 2011 Historic Touring Car champion

Dan Cox, 2012 Historic Touring Car champion

Nelson Rowe, 2013 Historic Formula Ford 2000 champion

Tom Smith, 2015 Historic Formula Ford 2000 champion

Andrew Park, 2016 Historic Formula Ford 2000 champion

Andy Wallace, 2015 Jaguar Classic champion

Historic Formula Ford 2000 Championship (2008 to date)

2008	Colin Wright (Reynard SF77) series winner
2009	Neil Fowler (Reynard SF79) series winner
2010	Oliver Thorpe (Royale RP27) series winner
2011	Russell Love (Reynard SF79)
2012	Nelson Rowe (Reynard SF79)
2013	Nelson Rowe (Reynard SF79)
2014	Benn Simms (Reynard SF77 and Royale RP30)
2015	Tom Smith (Royale RP27)
2016	Andrew Park (Reynard SF81)

JEC XK Series Sports Car Challenge (1999 2000)

1999	Chris Jaques (XK120)
2000	Chris Jaques (XK120)

Jaguar XK Championship (2003 and 2006)

2003	Graeme Dodd (XK120)
2006	Nigel Webb (XK120)

E-type Challenge (2011 to 2013)

2011	Jon Minshaw and John Burton
2012	Alex Buncombe, Mark Clubb and Roger Cope
2013	John Pearson, Graham Bull and John Truslove

Jaguar Classic Challenge (2015 to date)

2015	Andy Wallace (Jaguar Mk2)
2016	John Burton (Jaguar E-type)

The following championships were not organised by the HSCC, but had clear links to the club. These details are included for the sake of completeness.

JCB Historic Car Championship

1971	Bob Owen (Maserati Tipo 61) and Bill Wilks (Lotus 16)
1972	Willie Green
1973	Neil Corner
1974	Neil Corner
1975	Willie Green

B.A.T. Historic Championship

1977	Willie Green (Ford GT40)

Historic Car Championship

1978	Roddy MacPherson (Cooper Bristol)

Lloyds and Scottish Historic Car Championship

1979	Willie Green (Ferrari Dino)
1980	Willie Green (Ferrari Dino and Maserati 250F)
1981	Michael Bowler (Lister Jaguar)
1982	Mike Salmon (Aston Martin DBR2)

Appendix 2
The annual awards

Please note that these records are not complete

The John Foulston Memorial Award for the highest number of outright wins

1988	Steve Hitchins
1990	Aidan Mills-Thomas
1991	Aidan Mills-Thomas
1992	Aidan Mills-Thomas
1993	Mike Whatley
1994	John Henderson
1995	Mike Whatley
1996	Mike Wilds
1997	Paul Sleeman
1998	Mike Wilds
1999	Paul Sleeman
2000	Paul Sleeman
2001	Neil Fowler
2002	Simon Garrad
2003	Graeme Dodd
2004	Edwin Jowsey
2005	Steve Maxted
2006	Matthew Watts
2007	Matthew Watts
2008	Benn Simms
2009	Jon Milicevic
2010	Darren Burke
2011	Benn Simms
2012	Paul Tooms
2013	Nelson Rowe
2014	Mark Charteris
2015	Max Bartell
2016	Andrew Park

The David Barraclough Trophy; the spirit of the series in Historic Road Sports

1975	John Lucas
1976	Robert Mansfield
1977	Mel Clarke
1978	Tony Standen
1988	Kevin Irons
1991	Chris Horner
1992	Bernie Chodosh
1994	Chris Burbury
1995	Mike Adams
1997	Chris Horner
1998	Kevin Kivlochan
1999	Robin Stainer
2000	Chris Camp
2001	Chris Horner
2002	James Bilderbeck
2003	Stuart Downward
2004	James Owen
2005	Matthew Newman
2006	James Owen
2007	Chris Gawne
2008	John Fitzgerald
2009	Martyn Halliday
2010	Adam Simmonds
2011	Richard Owen
2012	Dick Coffey
2013	Nick Savage
2014	Patrick Ward-Booth
2015	Ian Burford
2016	Tony Davis

Julian Barter (right) receives the Spirit of the 70s Award from Richard Attwood in 2009

The spirit of the series in 70s Road Sports

1998	John Gadbury
1999	Mark Bennett
2000	Paul Stafford
2001	Andy Shepherd
2004	Mark Oldfield
2005	Julian Barter
2006	Bevi Harwood-Penn
2007	James Nairn
2008	Graham Hall
2009	Julian Barter
2010	Howard Bentham
2011	Mark Bennett
2012	Jan Trotter
2013	James Nairn
2014	James Dean
2015	Alex Page
2016	James Nairn

The Forward Enterprise Trophy for the best performance in a GT car

1974	Mike Salmon and Lord Downe
1975	Richard Thwaites
1976	Richard Thwaites
1977	David Dawson
1978	Jem Marsh
1979	John Corfield
1980	Jim Gathercole
1981	Roger Ealand
1982	Anthony Griffin
1983	John Corfield
1984	Roger Ealand
1985	Tony Thompson
1986	Tony Thompson
1987	Tony Thompson
1988	Tony Thompson
1989	Tony Thompson
1990	Simon Hadfield
1991	Denis Welch
1992	Denis Welch
1993	John Jarvis
1994	David Methley
1995	David Methley
1996	Richard Hayhow
1997	David Methley
1998	Peter Aylett
1999	Stephen Minoprio
2000	David Methley
2001	Stephen Minoprio
2002	Jon Minshaw/Jason Minshaw
2005	Simon Hadfield/David Clark
2007	Shaun Lynn/David Clark
2008	John Pearson/Gary Pearson

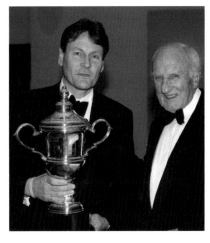

Simon Hadfield (left) receives the Forward Enterprise Trophy from Jack Sears in 2012

2010	Jon Minshaw/Martin Stretton
2011	Chris Scragg/Dave Coyne
2012	Simon Hadfield/Leo Voyazides
2013	John Pearson/Gary Pearson
2014	Simon Hadfield/Leo Voyazides
2016	Mike Whitaker

The best prepared car in Novices

1989	Nick Robinson
1991	Adam Richardson

The Touring Trophy

1972	Donald Hill
1975	Norman Shave
1976	Rod Leach
1977	Rod Leach

The Forward Enterprise Trophy

The Opposite Lock Trophy

Edwin Jowsey won the Opposite Lock Trophy in 2002

The Opposite Lock Trophy for the best novice

1976	Richard Bond
1977	Rodney Bloor
1978	Rodney Bloor
1979	John Heath
1981	Simon Hadfield
1983	Colin Cooper
1984	Amanda Langton
1985	David McLaughlin
1986	Stephen Davis
1987	Jon Reakes
1988	Kelvin Lambeth
1989	Sean Mooney
1990	Roger Murray
1991	Michael Abbott
1992	John Pearson
1993	Michael Murray
1994	Bob Norton
1995	Roger Waite
1996	Benn Simms
1997	John Bladon
1998	James Murray
1999	Chris Sharples
2000	Paul Wyeth
2001	John Goldsmith
2002	Edwin Jowsey
2003	John Sykes
2004	Paul Drayson
2005	Dean Bower
2006	Tom Bradshaw
2007	Michael Lyons
2008	Jamie Brashaw
2009	Robert Wainwright
2010	Jeremy Taylor
2011	Neil Brown

The Alan Brownlee Trophy for the best novice in a sports car

1972	Robert Mansfield
1973	Simon Phillips
1974	Brewster Righter
1975	Hon Amschel Rothschild
1976	John Jarvis
1977	David Grant
1978	Dave Lewis
1979	Paul Grist
1987	Nick Blunsden
1988	Christopher Pearce
1989	Martin Cliffe
1991	John Catt
1992	Paul Dobson
1994	Robert Boughton
1995	Roddie Fielden

The Alan Brownlee Trophy Coupe des Dames

1998	Louise Kennedy
1999	Josephine Sebastian
2000	Vivien Ayers
2001	Jenny Baker-Carr
2002	Lucy Hammond
2003	Janet Sherry
2004	Janet Sherry
2005	Janet Sherry
2006	Christina Totty
2007	Lorraine Gathercole
2008	Amanda Whitaker
2009	Amanda Whitaker
2010	Rachel Watts
2011	Vicky Brooks
2012	Vicky Brooks
2013	Vicky Brooks
2014	Vicky Brooks/Kirsty Brooks
2015	Trish Hunter

The Full Bore Trophy for committee work

1973	Peter Dixon
1974	Philip Rambaut
1975	Jim Pitt
1976	Philip Edbrook
1977	Michael Bowler
1978	Peter Dixon
1979	Jack Rance/George Rance
1987	Peter Walker
1988	Jem Marsh
1989	Ted Walker

The Full Bore Trophy

1991	Mike Freeman
1992	Don Cressy
1994	Simon Park
1995	Hal Danby
1996	John Narcisi
1997	Don Hands
1998	Robin Stainer
1999	Grahame White
2000	Derek Downing
2001	Andrew Schryver
2003	Mike Southin
2004	Stephen Minoprio

The Bill Phillips Trophy for the best Pre '60 car

1975	Simon Phillips
1976	Robert Mansfield
1977	Mel Clarke
1978	Tony Standen
1979	Paul Howarth
1983	Pete McManus
1988	Michael Schryver
1989	Tim Burrett
1991	Martin Coleman
1992	Geoff Ottley
1994	Philip Walker
1998	Geoff Williams
1999	Tim Burrett
2000	Duncan Rabagliati
2002	Richard Hackett
2004	Trevor Groom
2005	Chris Gawne
2006	John Truslove
2007	Tim Bishop
2008	Paul Dixon
2009	Crispian Besley
2010	Richard Owen

2011	Michael Ashley-Brown
2012	Peter Chappell
2013	Will Mitcham
2015	Andrew Tart

The Single-Seater Trophy

1977	Tony Steele
1978	Mike Harrison
1979	Gerry Walton (front-engined)
1979	Phil Bowler (rear-engined)
1983	Nick Lees
1987	David Jordan
1988	Gerry Marshall (front-engined)
1988	Tony Goodwin (rear-engined)
1989	Fredy Kumschick
1991	Willie Green
1992	John Fenning
1994	Ray Harper
1995	Bill Gowdy
1996	Winston Bunn
1997	James Wigmore

The best non-winged car in the Pre '71 Single-Seater Championship

1989	Sean Mooney
1991	Bill Gowdy
1992	Malcolm Carter
1994	Phoebe Rolt
1995	David Coplowe
1996	John Pearson

Autosport/Grove Air Endurance Trophy

1982	Stirling Moss/Tony Goodwin
1983	Martin Colvill/John Atkins
1984	Roger Ealand/David Methley
1985	John Atkins/Gordon Bruce
1986	Tony Thompson/David Chaney
1987	Roger Ealand/David Methley
1988	Tony Thompson/David Chaney
1989	Tony Thompson/David Chaney

The Autosport/Grove Air Trophy

1994	Aidan Mills-Thomas/ Bill Shepherd
1995	Gary Pearson/ Richard Attwood
2007	Michael Schryver/ Simon Hadfield
2008	Michael Schryver/ Simon Hadfield
2009	James Cottingham/ Jeremy Cottingham
2010	Gareth Burnett/Alex Ames
2011	Nick Fleming/Luke Stevens
2012	Nick Fleming
2013	Nick Fleming
2014	Chris Ward/Alex Buncombe
2015	Martin O'Connell

Air Hanson Three-Hour Team Challenge

1990	Gerry Marshall/ Ronnie Farmer
1991	Tony Thompson/ David Chaney
1992	Aidan Mills-Thomas/ Bill Shepherd
1993	Tony Thompson/ Robin Longdon
1994	David Bennett/ Philip Nelson
1995	Paul Stafford/David Shutter/John McIntosh/ Chris Taggart
1996	Michael Schryver/ Simon Hadfield

The John Bull Shipping Trophy for the best novice in Classics

1983	Charles Lees
1987	Ray Harper
1988	Chas Windridge
1989	Jeremy Welch
1991	Chris Reece
1992	David Gathercole

Gibbs Trophy for Post-Historic Road Sports champion

1987	Kevin Irons
1988	Kevin Irons

The Cool Air Trophy for the best-prepared car in Classics

1983	Robin Longdon
1987	Reg Skeels
1988	David Abbott
1989	John Jarvis
1990	David Summerson
1991	Peter Korner
1992	Roger Fountain
1993	Allen Lloyd
1994	Christopher Ross
1995	Charles Fripp
1998	Richard Hayhow
1999	Richard Tovey
2002	Paul Busby
2008	Tony Howard

Seven Seas Challenge for the greatest number of outright wins in Classics

1971	Martin Morris
1976	Bill Friend
1977	David Dawson
1978	Jeffray Johnstone
1979	John Brindley
1980	Alex Seldon
1981	Stephen Mitchell
1982	Alan Minshaw
1983	Tony Thompson
1984	Steve Hitchins
1985	Steve Hitchins
1986	Steve Hitchins
1987	Mike Littlewood
1988	Tony Thompson
1989	Tony Thompson
1991	Tony Thompson
1992	Roy Eaton
1995	Chris Reece

Roger Joice Memorial Award

1983	Jem Marsh

Dion Peters Award for Preparation

1983	Pete McManus

The Special Committee Award

1991	Mike Freeman

Trane Air Conditioning Trophy for the greatest number of lap records

1987	Tony Thompson
1988	Tony Thompson/ Denis Welch
1989	Tony Thompson/ Roger Ealand

Sprint Trophy

1975	Philip Rambaut
1976	Jeremy Broad
1977	Roy Waldron
1978	Dave Price
1979	Richard Downs
1980	Anthony Taylor
1981	Anthony Taylor
1982	Patrick Phelan
1983	Don Cressy

Hillclimb Trophy

1970	Michael Bowler
1971	Sandy Gibb
1972	Sandy Gibb
1973	Mike Smailes
1975	Chris Stewart
1976	Chris Stewart
1978	Robin Rew
1979	Robin Rew
1988	John Harper

The Hillclimb Trophy

Hillclimb Trophy for Road Sports

1972	Sandy Gibb
1973	John Lucas
1983	Graham Bayley

Spirit of competition for 2-litre cars

1994	Mike Scott
1995	David Hudson
1996	David Hudson
1997	David Beckett
1998	Lawrence Benson
1999	David Beckett
2000	Jeff Wilson
2006	Jim Chapman
2007	Sean McLurg/ Nick Thompson
2008	Ted Williams
2009	Stuart Tizzard
2010	Sean McLurg/Nick Thompson
2011	Doug Hart
2012	James Dodd
2013	James Dodd
2014	Hugh Colman
2015	George Douglas
2016	Brian Casey

The Graham Eccles Memorial Trophy for Historic F1

1992	Kelvin Lambeth
1994	Graham North
1995	Bob Berridge
1996	Martin Stretton
1997	Helen Bashford-Malkie

The Frazer Nash Shield

1969	David Muirhead
1972	Robert Mansfield
1973	Simon Phillips
1974	Simon Phillips
1975	Simon Phillips

The Lancia Trophy for the best performance in a Lancia

1987	John Grist
1988	Simon Park
1989	Simon Park
1991	Mike Silverleaf
1992	Simon Park
1994	Dave Edwards

1995	Richard Thorne
1997	Tim Burrett
1998	Tim Burrett
1999	Louise Kennedy
2000	Cliff Brindley
2001	Louise Kennedy
2002	Mark Oldfield
2003	Jon Smart
2004	Jai Sharma
2005	Tim Burrett
2006	Chris Gawne
2007	David Marshall
2008	Tim Burrett
2009	Alex Childs
2010	Ken Rorrison
2011	Charles Aram

The Bellini Trophy for the best performance in a Chevron

1983	Ray Bellm
1987	Richard Dodkins
1988	Phil Buck
1989	Michael Schryver
1991	Phil Buck
1992	Mike Wilds
1994	Richard Evans
1995	Helen Bashford-Malkie
1996	Mike Wilds
1997	Richard Evans
1998	Mike Wilds
1999	Mike Wilds
2000	Nick Crossley
2001	Martyn Porter
2002	Mike Southin
2003	Alan Parker
2004	Simon Hadfield
2005	Simon Hadfield
2006	Richard Trott
2007	Michael Schryver
2008	Paul Smith
2009	Michael Schryver
2010	Nick Fleming
2011	Nick Fleming

2012	Stuart Tizzard
2013	Andrew Schryver
2014	Jonathan Loader
2015	Max Bartell
2016	Simon Jackson

The Lotus Trophy for the best performance in a Lotus

1983	John Brindley
1984	Malcolm Ricketts
1985	Tony Thompson
1987	Judy Freeman
1988	Ian Giles
1989	Simon Hadfield
1990	Phil Cooper
1991	Michael Schryver
1992	Tim Wright
1993	Michael Schryver
1994	Simon Hadfield
1995	Sean Walker
1996	Andrew Marler
1997	Adam Crowton
1998	Andrew Marler
1999	Sid Marler
2000	Nick Adams
2002	Chris Reece
2003	Brendan Roberts
2004	Andy Shepherd
2006	Albert Clements
2007	Michael Hibberd/ Andrew Hibberd
2008	Jon Milicevic
2009	Steve Cooke
2010	Jeremy Taylor
2011	Paul Tooms
2012	Ian Jones
2013	Oliver Ford
2014	Andrew Hibberd
2015	Jim Dean
2016	John Davison

The Bellini Trophy

Paul Tooms (right) receives the Lotus Trophy from Jonathan Palmer in 2011

The McLaren Trophy

The Jaguar Trophy

The McLaren Trophy for the best performance in a McLaren

1987	John Foulston
1988	John Brindley
1989	Rick Hall
1990	Simon Hadfield
2004	Frank Lyons
2005	Richard Piper
2014	Marcus Mussa

The Denis Welch Trophy for the best performance in a Healey

1969	Peter Woodley
1970	Peter Woodley
1973	Dick Tindell
1974	Roy Drudge
1976	Simon Short
1977	Simon Short
1979	Eric Hall
1987	Denis Welch
1988	Denis Welch
1989	Allan Cameron
1991	Robert Mills
1992	Roly Nix
1994	Dave Hardy
1995	Tim Hassall
1997	Paul Klinkby-Silver
2008	Denis Welch
2009	Denis Welch
2012	Andrew Hayden

The Jaguar Trophy for the best performance in a Jaguar-engined car

1969	David Beckett
1970	Neil Corner
1972	Paul Skilleter
1973	John Harper
1974	John Harper
1975	David Ham
1976	Peter Van Rossem
1977	David Ham
1978	Martin Morris
1979	Roger Joice
1983	David Duffy
1987	Michael Scott
1988	Geoffrey Ottley
1989	Bruce Goddard
1991	Phil Stott
1992	Rob Schirle
1994	David Pennell/John Pearson
1995	Harvey Cooke
1997	Peter Trent
1998	David Ottley/Geoffrey Ottley
1999	Graeme Dodd
2000	Graeme Dodd
2001	Graeme Dodd
2002	Trevor Groom
2003	Graeme Dodd
2004	Les Ely
2005	Les Ely
2006	Les Ely
2007	Paul Castaldini
2008	Steve Tandy
2009	Steve Tandy

2010	Colin McKay
2011	Jon Minshaw
2012	Paul Castaldini
2013	Chris Scragg
2014	Colin McKay
2015	Robert Gate
2016	John Burton

The Porsche Trophy for the best performance in a Porsche

1972	John Lucas
1973	Eric Studer
1974	John Lucas
1975	John Lucas
1976	John Lucas
1977	John Lucas/Chris Stewart
1978	Tony Standen
1979	John Lucas
1987	Richard Corey-Smith
1991	Adam Richardson
1992	David Piper

The Dragon Trophy for the best performance in a March

1987	Trevor Needham
1988	David McLaughlin
1991	Pat Blakeney
1992	Steve Hartley
1994	Paul Bason
1995	Dave Abbott
1997	Simon Ford
1998	David Abbott
1999	Michael Scott
2000	Daniel Goodman
2001	Paul Wyeth
2002	Nick Crossley
2003	Chris Levy

Chris Scragg (left) receives the Jaguar Trophy from Gordon Spice in 2013

Jamie Brashaw (Left) receives the Dragon Trophy from Jack Sears in 2012

2004	Chris Levy	2014	Jim Blockley	1983	Graham Bayley
2005	Ian Jacobs	2015	Leif Bosson	1989	Adrian Hall
2006	Paul Campfield	2016	Leif Bosson	1991	Bill Croxson
2007	Benn Simms			1992	Antony Ross
2008	Benn Simms			1998	Stuart Passey
2009	Benn Simms			1999	Jim Evans
2010	Katsu Kubota			2000	Justin Murphy
2011	Diogo Ferrao			2001	Andrew Colley
2012	Jamie Brashaw			2002	Rollo Beale
2013	Robert Simac			2003	Rollo Beale
2014	Robert Simac			2004	James Dodd
2015	Richard Evans			2005	James Dodd
2016	Robert Simac			2006	James Nairn

The Merlyn Trophy for the best performance in a Merlyn

1996	Chris Alford
1997	Kevin Stanzl
1998	Benn Simms
1999	Kevin Stanzl
2000	Kevin Stanzl
2002	Adrian Rush
2003	Ollie Smith
2004	Jason Minshaw
2005	Westie Mitchell
2006	Westie Mitchell
2007	Michael Lyons
2008	Michael Lyons
2009	Westie Mitchell
2010	Ben Mitchell
2011	Ben Mitchell
2012	Callum Grant
2013	Sam Mitchell
2014	Max Bartell
2015	Richard Mitchell
2016	Callum Grant

The Brabham Trophy for the best performance in a Brabham

1988	Hon Andrew Fellowes
1989	Nick Overall
1994	Geoff Farmer
1995	Ermanno Ronchi
1996	Geoff Farmer
1997	Tim Barrington
1998	Tim Barrington
1999	Geoff Farmer
2000	Steve Worrad
2001	Rodger Newman
2004	Matthew Watts
2005	Ian Gray
2006	Cliff Giddens
2007	Matthew Watts
2008	Ian Gray
2009	Chris Holland
2010	Ian Gray
2011	Ian Gray
2012	Tim Kary
2013	Chris Holland

2007	Matthew Newman
2008	James Fuller
2009	Paul Hopkinson
2010	Will Morton
2012	David Erwin
2013	Bob Trotter
2015	Jon Wagstaff
2016	Jon Wagstaff

The Peter Gerrish Lancia Award for the highest points scored in a Lancia

1991	Mike Silverleaf/ Richard Thorne

The AC Trophy for the best performance in an AC

1972	Sandy Gibb
1974	Philip Rambaut
1975	Philip Rambaut
1976	Brewster Righter
1977	Brewster Righter
1978	Hon Amschel Rothschild

The Samuels Trophy for the best performance in an Alfa Romeo

1972	Philip Stokeley
1974	Philip Stokeley
1975	Philip Stokeley
1976	Peter Cabrol
1977	Jon Dooley
1978	Chris Mann

Matthew Watts (right) receives the Brabham Trophy from Chris Sharples in 2008

Richard Mitchell (left) receives the Merlyn Trophy from Howden Ganley in 2015

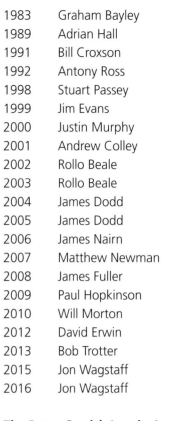

The AC Trophy

1978	Martin Colvill	2012	John Thomason	2015	Ian Jones
1980	Martin Colvill	2013	Oliver Ford	2016	Andy Jarvis
1981	Alex Boswell	2014	Peter Shaw		
1982	John Atkins	2015	Jim Dean		
1983	John Atkins	2016	Julian Barter		
1984	John Atkins				

1978 Martin Colvill
1980 Martin Colvill
1981 Alex Boswell
1982 John Atkins
1983 John Atkins
1984 John Atkins
1985 John Atkins
1986 Aidan Mills-Thomas
1987 Aidan Mills-Thomas
1988 Paul Stafford
1990 Aidan Mills-Thomas
1991 Emma Hire
1992 Robin Stainer
1993 Adrian Hall
1997 Peter Lanfranchi
1998 Peter Lanfranchi
2000 Peter Lanfranchi
2001 Peter Lanfranchi
2002 Robin Stainer
2003 Robin Stainer
2004 Tony Hill
2006 Tony Hill
2013 Robert Bremner

Classic and Sportscar award for the best-driven car in 70s Road Sports
1994 Paul Allen
1995 Peter Gregory
1996 John Moon
1997 Jason Kennedy
1998 Bruce Stapleton

Classic and Sportscar award for the best performance in 70s Road Sports
1994 Andrew Stanford
1995 Colin Jasper
1998 Bruce Stapleton
1999 Dave Edwards
2000 Richard Thorne
2001 Andy Reeves
2002 James Calvert
2004 Richard Thorne
2005 John Thomason
2006 John Thomason
2007 Rory Stockbridge
2008 Ian Jacobs
2009 Julian Barter
2010 Peter Shaw
2011 John Thomason

2012 John Thomason
2013 Oliver Ford
2014 Peter Shaw
2015 Jim Dean
2016 Julian Barter

The Reg Skeels Trophy
1994 Michael Schryver
1995 Arnie Black

The John Brown Engineering Trophy for Formula Ford
1995 Peter Gillam
1996 Barry Hargreaves
1997 Roger Waite

Barrington Trophy for the best performance in Classic Racing Cars
1999 Geoff Farmer
2000 Richard Urwin
2001 Ed Mercer
2003 Matthew Watts
2004 John Bladon
2005 Matthew Watts
2006 Cliff Giddens
2007 Anthony Goddard
2008 Ian Gray
2009 Chris Holland
2010 Ian Gray
2011 Ian Gray
2012 Ian Jones
2013 Ian Jones
2014 Jonathan Baines

2015 Ian Jones
2016 Andy Jarvis

Goodwood Challenge Trophy
1969 Peter Woodley
1970 Michael Bowler
1971 Barry Bird
1972 John Lucas
1973 Eric Studer
1974 JF Phillips
1975 John Beasley
1976 John Beasley
1977 Bobbie Bell
1978 Roddie McPherson
1979 Roddie McPherson
1983 Rob Grant
1984 Frank Lockhart
1986 Gerry Walton
1987 Frank Lockhart
1988 Frank Lockhart
1989 Frank Lockhart
1990 David Gilmour
1994 Philip Walker
2000 Brendon Roberts
2001 Les Goble
2002 Simon Hadfield
2003 Simon Hadfield
2004 Michael Steele
2005 Gary Pearson
2006 Derek Bell
2007 John Chisholm
2008 Michael Hibberd

Chris Holland (right) receives the Barrington Trophy from Richard Attwood in 2009

The Goodwood Challenge Trophy

Gary Pearson (left) receives the Goodwood Challenge Trophy from Chris Craft in 2010

Dan Cox (right) receives the Lola Trophy from Chris Alford in 2007

Julian Barter (right) receives the Spirit of the 70s Award from Richard Attwood in 2009

2009	Ian Bankhurst
2010	Gary Pearson
2011	Jon Minshaw/ Martin Stretton
2012	Gary Pearson
2013	Simon Hadfield
2014	Gary Pearson
2015	James King

Neil Fowler (left) receives the Lola Trophy from Chris Craft in 2010

Fergus Whatling (left) receives the Terence Smith Award from Andy Wallace in 2014

Ron Tauranac Spirit of Classic Formula 3

2003	Frank Gomm
2004	Alan Parker
2005	Alan Goodman
2006	John Bradshaw
2007	Bill Coombs
2008	Marcus Mussa
2009	Paul Dibden
2010	Tom Thornton
2014	Greg Caton

Lola Trophy for the Clubman of the Year

2005	David Wild
2006	Iain Rowley
2007	Dan Cox
2008	Frank Lyons
2009	Dallas Smith
2010	Neil Fowler
2011	Dick Dixon
2012	Frank Lyons
2013	Andrew Mansell

Terence Smith Quiet Achiever Award

2006	Dick Dixon
2007	Bob Birrell
2008	Duncan Rabagliati
2009	Sue Smith
2010	Myra Whatling
2011	Peter Hore
2012	Julian Floyd
2013	Sarah Mitrike
2014	Fergus Whatling
2015	Martyn Halliday
2016	Andrew Mansell

Monson Trophy for best newcomer

2007	Michael Lyons
2008	Oliver Thorpe
2009	Jack Woodhouse
2010	Ben Mitchell
2011	Andy Jones

Ian Jones (left) receives the Premier Cru award from Gordon Spice in 2013

Jon Milicevic (right) receives the BMMC Award from Tony Brooks in 2008

Leif Bosson (left) receives the Peter Hanson Award from Howden Ganley in 2015

Chris Lawrence Award

1989	Julian Dodd
2008	Jonathan Ruston
2009	Jonathan Ruston
2010	Mark Hoble
2011	Mark Hoble

Moss Thorpe Memorial Award

1994	Simon Ford
1995	Rob Moores
1996	Rob Moores
1997	Rob Moores
1998	Rob Moores
1999	Simon Ford

The Stone Age Award

2008	David Wild
2009	David Wild

Mark Hoble (right) receives the Chris Lawrence Trophy from Jonathan Palmer in 2011

Quickshift Award

2007	Rodger Newman
2008	Tony Keele
2009	Alasdair Pike
2010	Chris Holland
2011	Rachel Arnold
2012	Peter Hamilton
2013	Andy Jarvis
2014	Leif Bosson

British Motorsport Marshals' Club 50th Anniversary Award

2007	Sir John Chisholm
2008	Jon Milicevic
2009	Chris Drake
2010	Jon Milicevic
2011	Jon Milicevic
2012	Robert Barrie
2013	Mark Woodhouse

Peter Hanson Award for Historic F3

2004	Vincent Rivett
2005	Richard Erwin
2006	Roland Fischer
2007	Keith Norman
2008	Francois Derossi
2009	Chris Holland
2010	David Methley
2011	Nigel Bancroft
2012	Dean Forward

2012	Callum Grant
2013	Sam Mitchell
2014	Michael O'Brien
2015	Richard Mitchell
2016	Benn Tilley

John Nichol Premier Cru Award

2007	Anthony Goddard
2008	Ian Gray
2009	Chris Holland
2010	Ian Gray
2011	Ian Gray
2012	Ian Jones
2013	Ian Jones
2014	Jonathan Baines
2015	Ian Jones
2016	Andy Jarvis

The Peter Hanson Award

The Lion Trophy

2013	Dean Forward
2014	Jim Blockley
2015	Leif Bosson
2016	Simon Armer

Special Achievement Award

2002	Alan Baillie
2003	Chris Alford and the Beale family
2011	Sam Wilson
2013	Nick Fleming

The Lion Trophy

| 2015 | Andrew Park |
| 2016 | Chris Alford |

Guards 1000 Trophy

| 2015 | Michael Hibberd |
| 2016 | Mike Gardiner and Dan Cox |

TOUR BRITANNIA RESULTS

5-8 September 2005
Overall winners: Ray Bellm/Paul Lanzante (Ford GT40)
Regularity winners: Jon Ruston/Jeremy Haylock (Talbot 105)

5-8 September 2006
Overall winners: Bruce Stapleton/ Alistair Cowin (Morgan +8)
Regularity winners: Jon Ruston/ Jeremy Haylock (Porsche 356)

3-6 September 2007
Overall winners: John Grant/Charles Elwell (Chevron B16)
Regularity winners: Michael Birch/ Jeremy Haylock (Porsche 911)

1-4 September 2008
Overall winners: Sean Lockyear/Roy Stephenson (Porsche 911)
Regularity winners: Emma Henchoz/Jeanne Taylor (Volvo PV544)

7-9 September 2009
Overall winners: Nick Whale/Harry Whale (Porsche 911RS)
Regularity winners: Bob Linwood/ Ann Linwood (Citroen SM)

7-9 September 2010
Overall winners: Sean Lockyear/Ian Reed (Porsche 911)
Regularity winners: Howard Warren/Guy Woodcock (Porsche 911)

17-19 June 2011
Overall winners: John Clark/Emma-Jane Gilbart-Smith (Porsche 911)
Regularity winners: Jon Ruston/ Jeremy Haylock (Talbot 105)

7-9 June 2012
Overall winners: Phil Hindley/Andy Bull (Porsche 911SC)
Regularity winners: Melissa Raven/ Jeremy Haylock (Porsche 911S)

10-11 May 2013
Overall winners: Phil Hindley/Andy Bull (Porsche 911SC)
Regularity winners: Melissa Raven/ Jeremy Haylock (Porsche 356)

8-9 August 2014
Overall winners: Phil Hindley/Andy Bull (Porsche 911SC)
Regularity winners: Max Taylor/ Mike Hickson (Aston Martin DB2/4)

13-15 May 2015*
Overall winners: Tony Robinson/Phil Clarke (Porsche 911)
Regularity winners: Doug Dawe/ Ernie Waldron (Austin Allegro)

*The 2015 event was titled Tour Ireland as it included special stages and races in the Republic of Ireland

Phil Hindley and Andy Bull won Tour Britannia in 2014

Alan Morgan

AndrewMansell

Bob Birrell

Charles Barter

Chris Alford

Dallas Smith

David Pullen

Duncan Rabagliati

Stuart Tizzard

Frank Lyons

Hugh Price

Keith Messer

Kevin Kivlochan

Marcus Pye

Peter Hore

Roger Bevan

Appendix 3
Club officials

Chairman

1969 to 1972	Clive Aston
1973	Bob Owen
1974 to 1977	David Muirhead
1978 to 1984	Brian Cocks
1985	David Duffy
1986 to 1988	Jem Marsh
1989 to 1992	Don Cressy
1993 and 1994	Richard Arnold
1995 to 2004	Nick Overall
2005 to 2014	Chris Sharples
2015 and 2016	Frank Lyons

Vice Chairman

1974 and 1975	Roger St John Hart
1976 and 1977	Roger Brierley-Jones
1978 to 1981	Bert Young
1982 to 1985	Jem Marsh
1986 to 1988	Alex Seldon

Carrie, Alan and Donna: the office team

Emma Jemmett

1989 to 1991	Mike Freeman
1992 to 1994	Nick Overall
1995 to 1997	Don Hands
1998 to 2004	Stephen Minoprio
2005 to 2015	Chris Alford
2016	Charles Barter

Chief Executive

1985 to 1989	Brian Cocks
1990 to 1995	Steve Lydon
1996	post vacant
1997 to 2016	Grahame White

Secretary and Competition Secretary

1966 to 1973	Betty Haig
1974	Graham and Enid Boston
1975	Pat Owen
1976 to 1978	Philip and Barbara Edbrook
1979	Tina Gue
1980	Anne Womack
1981	Erica Woodley
1982	Brian Cocks
1983 and 1984	Marina Arnold
1985 to 1987	Tina Cocks
1988 and 1989	Sue Walton
1990 to 1992	Ruth Hibberd
1993 to 1997	Emma Marshman
2000	Mark Lowrie
2001 to 2003	Philip Parfitt
2004 to 2008	Martin Atack
2009 to 2016	Alan Jones

Club patrons (2016)

Patron-in-chief
Sir Stirling Moss OBE

Sir Stirling remained Britain's most famous racing driver more than 50 years after his professional racing career ended. He was renowned as a racer of the old school, he took 16 Grand Prix wins from 66 starts between 1951 and 1961. Sadly, his Grand Prix career was cut short by a serious accident at Goodwood early in 1962. He later returned to touring cars and then historic racing and was still racing well into his 80s.

Patron
Derek Bell MBE

Derek is Britain's most successful sports-car racer with five wins at Le Mans between 1975 and 1987. He first came to prominence in 1-litre Formula 3 and later raced in Formula 2 and Formula 1, making nine Grand Prix starts between 1968 and 1974. His later role as a brand ambassador for Bentley kept him closely involved with the sport.

Patron
Richard Budge (died 2016)

Richard, boss of the RJB Mining business, sponsored the club's Group 6 Sports Car Championship through the 1990s and his vital financial backing helped the club through a very difficult period. He remained a valued Club Patron until his death in the summer of 2016. He was also an accomplished racer with a particular passion for Chevrons and raced with great success in B8s and B19s.

The office team

During the 50th anniversary season the team in the Club office was Alan Jones, Donna Skipworth-Mitchell, Carrie Bedford and Emma Jemmett.

The HSCC board

During 2016, the HSCC board members were:

Chairman:	Frank Lyons
Vice-Chairman:	Charles Barter
Executive Director:	Grahame White
Company Secretary:	Crispin Schlaefli
Chief Registrar:	Marcus Pye
Historic FF2000:	Alan Morgan
Historic Road Sports:	Kevin Kivlochan
Historic Touring Cars:	Peter Hore
Historic F2:	Roger Bevan
Classic F3:	Hugh Price
Classic Racing Cars:	David Pullen
Formula Junior:	Duncan Rabagliati
Guards Trophy:	Stuart Tizzard
Historic FF1600:	Andrew Mansell
Historic F3:	Keith Messer
Pre '80 Endurance:	Mark Richardson
General board member:	Bob Birrell
General board member:	Chris Alford

Chief Scrutineer
Dallas Smith

For a major portion of the HSCC's first 50 years, Dallas Smith has been a leading scrutineer for the club, using his vast experience to bring fairness, common sense and good humour to eligibility scrutineering.

Speaking in 2016, he said: "I'm now 86 and have done 58 years as a scrutineer and I've no plans to retire. I started with the HSCC in the 1970s as a scrutineer and I still enjoy it and do all the HSCC meetings. I've been the eligibility scrutineer for the club for the last 30 years. I used to do all the championships myself but I've given some of them to my son Matthew now.

"Over the last 20 years I've brought on nearly 30 new scrutineers. I did the Formula 2 cars in period and did Historic F1 for the first six years under the HSCC. John Foulston once offered me a full time job to be chief scrutineer for all of his circuits. He wanted continuity across his circuits."

Appendix 4
The marshals

The HSCC is very fortunate to have a dedicated band of marshals who support the club's race meetings up and down the country. In addition, many more attend their local events to help ensure safe and efficient race meetings.

Our marshals carry out a wide range of duties with professionalism, commitment and good humour and without them, there would be no racing.

As a small gesture of appreciation, the Club presents a 'marshal of the year' award at the end of each season. Of course, this only rewards one of the team, but it is a way of saying thank you to all of the crew.

HSCC Marshal of the Year

2004	David Morgan	Howden, East Yorkshire
2006	Mike Mayfield	Radcliffe-on-Trent, Notts
2007	Alan Couper	Scotland
2008	Nick Allison	London
2009	David Morgan	Howden, East Yorkshire
2010	David Morgan	Howden, East Yorkshire
2011	David Morgan	Howden, East Yorkshire
2012	Mike Mayfield	Radcliffe-on-Trent, Notts
2013	Ian Chalmers	Newbury
	and Peter Talling	Plymouth
2014	Peter Talling	Plymouth
2015	Ian Chalmers	Newbury